ORDER OF BATTLE
GERMAN
INFANTRY
IN
WWII

ORDER OF BATTLE
GERMAN INFANTRY
IN
WWII

CHRIS BISHOP

ZENITH PRESS

This edition published in 2008 by Zenith Press, an imprint of MBI Publishing Company, Galtier Plaza, Suite 200, 380 Jackson Street, St. Paul, MN 55101-3885 USA.

MBI Publishing Company titles are also available at discounts in bulk quantity for industrial or sales-promotional use. For details write to Special Sales Manager at MBI Publishing Company, Galtier Plaza, Suite 200, 380 Jackson Street, St. Paul, MN 55101-3885 USA.

ISBN: 978-0-7603-3187-3

Produced by:
Amber Books Ltd
Bradley's Close
74–77 White Lion Street
London N1 9PF
United Kingdom
www.amberbooks.co.uk

Project Editor: Michael Spilling
Design: Hawes Design
Picture Research: Terry Forshaw

Printed in Dubai

CONTENTS

German Infantry before World War II

Despite the well-known image of the panzer division or the Stuka *Geschwader* as the spearhead of German military power during World War II, the traditional *Landser*, or infantryman, remained the most important part of Hitler's armies until 1945.

Crowds greet German soldiers as they march into Vienna, 1938. Highly respected by the German people, the Army was one of the key unifying factors in German society.

The *Landser* may not have represented the cutting edge of military technology, but he was the muscle and sinew that provided the strength and exceptional staying power of the German war machine. Even at the height of the mechanized *Blitzkrieg* style of combat, most battles were eventually decided by a struggle of man against man, the fighting taking place in foxholes, ruined buildings and shattered woods in a desperate struggle to take or to defend contested ground.

German infantry fought with impressive tenacity all through World War II, remaining effective even after their units had suffered heavy losses. Statistical analyses have concluded that German troops inflicted at least 50 per cent greater casualties than they received, regardless of whether they were attacking or defending. It was the overwhelming Allied numerical advantage, together with total Allied air superiority in the later years of the war that eventually overcame the stubborn German infantrymen.

Fighting spirit

One of the fundamental elements of this phenomenal fighting power was unit cohesion. German soldiers continued to operate as an effective team despite devastating losses, long after the point where units of other armies would have, and often did, dissolve into a mass of individuals whose only aim was self-preservation. German soldiers also showed a remarkable ability to form *kampfgruppen*, or improvised battle groups, which were militarily effective even though they were often composed of stragglers, survivors and non-combatant support troops.

The German infantry came from diverse social, economic and professional backgrounds. Whereas most other armies tended to allocate manpower primarily according to class, education or aptitude, the Germans emphasized psychological traits. Personnel officers sought to evaluate each recruit's entire personality, including spiritual qualities and emotional attitudes, not just objective abilities. Particularly sought-after was *Einstazbereitschaft* (a sense of resolution and presence of mind, or a readiness to apply one's entire will to a certain act). Thus, the typical *Landser* by no means represented the dregs of German manpower, although by the war's latter stages the Germans were indeed scraping the bottom of the barrel.

Train hard, fight easy

Personal qualities would have counted for little, however, if not for the rigorous and relentless training imposed by the *Wehrmacht*. For the infantry recruit, the process began with 16 weeks of basic training (later reduced to eight, as Germany's situation became increasingly desperate). One of the German Army's most familiar mottoes was 'Sweat saves blood'. Recruits endured countless drills and exercises designed to inflict exhaustion – so-called 'hardness training'.

HIGH COMMAND

FÜHRER
Adolf Hitler

C-IN-C WEHRMACHT
Gen FM Werner von Blomberg;
Adolf Hitler (from 1938)

OKW	OKH	OKL	OKM
Adolf Hitler	**Gen FM Walther von Brauchitsch: Adolf Hitler (from 1941)**	**Gen FM – later Reichsmarschall – Hermann Göring**	**Gr Adm Erich Raeder; Gr Adm Karl Dönitz (from 1943)**

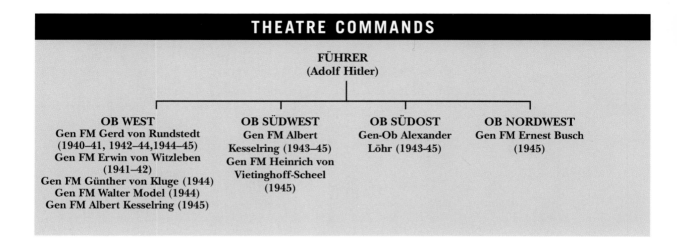

THEATRE COMMANDS

FÜHRER
(Adolf Hitler)

OB WEST
Gen FM Gerd von Rundstedt
(1940–41, 1942–44,1944–45)
Gen FM Erwin von Witzleben
(1941–42)
Gen FM Günther von Kluge (1944)
Gen FM Walter Model (1944)
Gen FM Albert Kesselring (1945)

OB SÜDWEST
Gen FM Albert
Kesselring (1943–45)
Gen FM Heinrich von
Vietinghoff-Scheel
(1945)

OB SÜDOST
Gen-Ob Alexander
Löhr (1943-45)

OB NORDWEST
Gen FM Ernest Busch
(1945)

Brutal in many ways, the training nevertheless had a higher purpose that distinguished such a regimen from mere petty sadism. Drill sergeants made their recruits understand that if they could not stand a little cold and some vague danger, they would never be able to survive at the front.

Nor did such hardships cease at the end of basic training. Officers continued to impose arduous exercises on their men in the field.

Sometimes the training was lethal. One company of 150 men, undergoing three weeks of live-fire training with Panzerfaust anti-tank rockets later in the war, lost four dead and 20 wounded.

Such ferocious training later saved lives in actual combat. After enduring such trials, it is little wonder that *Landsers* developed such strong bonds of comradeship. Indeed, German companies often took on the character of an extended family. The commanding officer became a father figure. The unit's senior NCO or warrant officer, traditionally called the *Spiess*, was often also known as 'Mother'. In the German Army, his role had more to do with morale than discipline, and he routinely acted as an intermediary to convey grievances up the chain of command and generally promote the men's welfare.

Ultimately, of course, discipline also played a critical role in holding the infantry together. Disciplinary problems, however, remained relatively uncommon, at least until 1945. Soviet commissars might have driven their troops like cattle, but German officers knew that combat effectiveness required willing soldiers.

The Army expected officers to lead by example, and generally they lived up to the ideal. Hans Werner Woltersdorf described this 'special leadership principle' as follows: 'The necessary qualification for an officer's career was not the high school diploma but exemplary ability, the true authority. Everyone who led a unit had to be the best man in his unit as well; not the uniform, not being in command, but example made the leader.'

Questionable quality

The German infantry was not perfect, however. The massive expansion of the army after 1933 considerably diluted the quality of the *Reichsheer* on which it was based: an elite, all volunteer force, the 100,000-man army of the *Reichswehr* just did not have enough men to lead the newly formed *Wehrmacht,* and there was a considerable shortage of officers and NCOs.

Transport remained distinctly old-fashioned. German industry could never build enough motor vehicles to meet the needs of the Army, with the heavy equipment and supplies of each infantry division needing some 2000 or more horses to keep them moving forwards.

Equipment shortages also plagued many infantry units, which were often equipped with older and obsolete weapons, such as the World War I vintage MG08 machine gun, used until they could be replaced by captured foreign equipment.

ORGANIZATION OF INFANTRY ARMIES: 1939-45

OKW

FIRST ARMY
(Western Front
1939–1945)

SECOND ARMY
(Western Front
1939–1941;
Eastern Front
1941–1945)

THIRD ARMY
(Poland 1939)

FOURTH ARMY
(Poland 1939;
France 1940;
Eastern Front
1940–1945)

FIFTH ARMY
(Western Front 1939)

SIXTH ARMY
(Western Front
1939–1941;
Eastern Front
1941–1945)

SEVENTH ARMY
(Western Front
1939–1945;
Eastern Front 1945)

EIGHTH ARMY
(Poland 1939;
Eastern Front
1943–1945)

NINTH ARMY
(Western Front
1940–1941;
Eastern Front
1941–1945)

TENTH ARMY
(Poland 1939;
Italy 1943–1945)

ELEVENTH ARMY
(Germany 1940–1941;
Eastern Front
1941–1945;
Western Front 1945)

TWELFTH ARMY
(Western Front
1939–1940;
Eastern Front
1940–1941;
Balkans 1941–1945;
Eastern Front 1945)

**FOURTEENTH
ARMY**
(Poland 1939;
Italy 1943–1945)

FIFTEENTH ARMY
(Western Front
1941–1945)

SIXTEENTH ARMY
(Western Front
1939–1941;
Eastern Front
1941–1945)

**SEVENTEENTH
ARMY**
(Eastern Front
1941–1945)

**EIGHTEENTH
ARMY**
(Western Front
1939–1940;
Eastern Front
1940–1945)

**NINETEENTH
ARMY**
(Western Front
1943–1945)

**TWENTY-FIRST
ARMY**
(Eastern Front 1945)

**TWENTY-FOURTH
ARMY**
(German Alps
1944–1945)

**TWENTY-FIFTH
ARMY**
(Western Front 1945)

**TWENTIETH
MOUNTAIN ARMY**
(Arctic 1942–1945)

ARMY OF NORWAY
(Norway/Finland
1940–1944)

**FIRST PARATROOP
ARMY**
(Western Front
1944–1945)

The *Reichswehr*

The Versailles Treaty of 1919 was designed by the Great Powers to emasculate Germany. War reparations insisted on by France were crippling. The treaty so limited German power that her armed forces could not guarantee the integrity of her borders.

As Germany was not allowed to participate in the negotiations, the treaty was rejected at home as a 'dictated peace'. The onerous terms ensured a foothold for antidemocratic forces, among which was the small right-wing group that would become the National Socialist German Workers Party.

For a proud nation with a strong military tradition, the treaty was an insult. Germany was limited to a 100,000-man army. The navy was allowed to retain a few obsolete warships, manning them with no more than 15,000 sailors. The Air Force and Naval Air Force were disbanded. The production and acquisition of heavy weapons such as tanks and aeroplanes was prohibited.

From the outset, the Weimar government attempted to lessen the harshest terms. This revisionist policy had some little success, although an attempt to reduce the reparations in 1923 led to a brutal French occupation of the Ruhr, Germany's industrial heartland.

Although avowedly socialist, the Weimar Government embarked upon a policy of secretly expanding its forces. Even limited to 100,000 men, the postwar *Reichswehr* was a significant military weapon. All of its men were superbly trained career professionals, and they would form the nucleus of a later field Army.

National Defence Force

On 6 March 1919, a decree established the *Vorläufige Reichswehr* (Provisional National Defence Force). On 30 September 1919, the Army was reorganized as the *Übergangsheer* (Transitional Army). This lasted until 1 January 1921, when the *Reichswehr* was officially established according to the limitations imposed by the Treaty of Versailles.

The *Reichswehr* was composed of former members of the imperial army and navy, and as such was highly anti-republican in nature. Adolf Hitler openly courted this significant power base.

In February 1933, three days after taking office as Chancellor of the German Reich, the *Führer* addressed a huge gathering of Nazi Party officials and senior officers of the German armed services upon the necessity of 'unqualified Germanization' in the east at least as far as the Urals. He announced plans to the *Reichswehr* generals for the rearming of Germany – plans he would not reveal to the rest of the world for another two years.

Hitler proclaimed himself Chancellor and *Führer* of the German Reich in August 1934, upon the death of President von Hindenburg. He ordered not just the creation of a German air force (forbidden to Germany under the terms of the 1919 Versailles Treaty) but also the rapid expansion of the German Army and Navy – the tools with which he intended to achieve his ends. In October 1933, Germany left the League of Nations and the Disarmament Conference. Early in 1934, the Army was instructed to treble its strength to 300,000 men, but in secret.

Secret expansion

In 1934, as the *Reichswehr* was secretly expanded to become the *Wehrmacht,* the seven original *Wehrkreiskommandos* became the nuclei of new Corps formations. The original seven divisions ceased to exist, while their units were used as the basis for the formation of a series of 21 completely new divisions.

Each *Wehrgauleitung* was named after the city in which it had its headquarters. These 21 *Wehrgauleitungen* were the true foundation for the first divisions of the new German Army. In March 1935, Hitler came out into the open. He had Göring announce the repudiation of the Treaty of Versailles and the reintroduction of conscription. The peacetime German Army would consist of 36 divisions organized into XII Corps: a strength of around half a million men.

ORGANIZATION OF THE REICHSWEHR: 1933

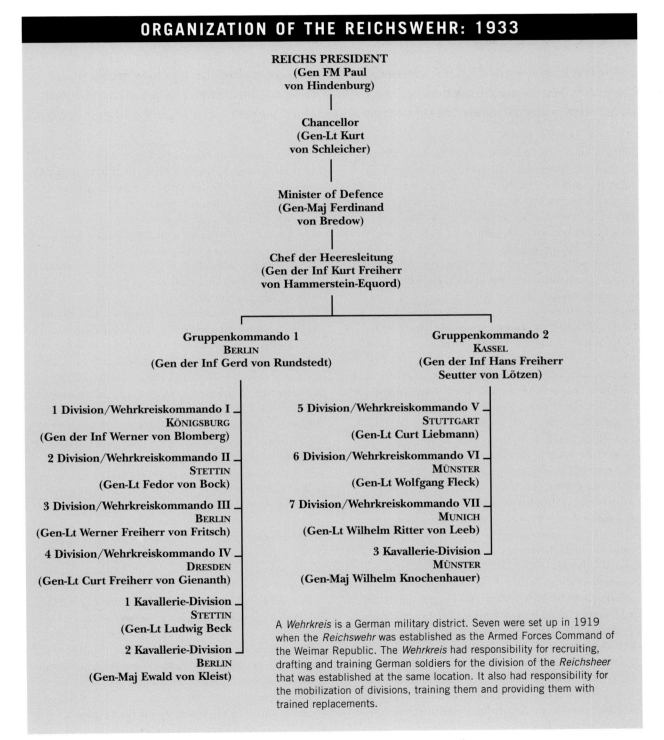

REICHS PRESIDENT
(Gen FM Paul
von Hindenburg)

Chancellor
(Gen-Lt Kurt
von Schleicher)

Minister of Defence
(Gen-Maj Ferdinand
von Bredow)

Chef der Heeresleitung
(Gen der Inf Kurt Freiherr
von Hammerstein-Equord)

Gruppenkommando 1
BERLIN
(Gen der Inf Gerd von Rundstedt)

Gruppenkommando 2
KASSEL
(Gen der Inf Hans Freiherr
Seutter von Lötzen)

1 Division/Wehrkreiskommando I
KÖNIGSBURG
(Gen der Inf Werner von Blomberg)

2 Division/Wehrkreiskommando II
STETTIN
(Gen-Lt Fedor von Bock)

3 Division/Wehrkreiskommando III
BERLIN
(Gen-Lt Werner Freiherr von Fritsch)

4 Division/Wehrkreiskommando IV
DRESDEN
(Gen-Lt Curt Freiherr von Gienanth)

1 Kavallerie-Division
STETTIN
(Gen-Lt Ludwig Beck

2 Kavallerie-Division
BERLIN
(Gen-Maj Ewald von Kleist)

5 Division/Wehrkreiskommando V
STUTTGART
(Gen-Lt Curt Liebmann)

6 Division/Wehrkreiskommando VI
MÜNSTER
(Gen-Lt Wolfgang Fleck)

7 Division/Wehrkreiskommando VII
MUNICH
(Gen-Lt Wilhelm Ritter von Leeb)

3 Kavallerie-Division
MÜNSTER
(Gen-Maj Wilhelm Knochenhauer)

A *Wehrkreis* is a German military district. Seven were set up in 1919 when the *Reichswehr* was established as the Armed Forces Command of the Weimar Republic. The *Wehrkreis* had responsibility for recruiting, drafting and training German soldiers for the division of the *Reichsheer* that was established at the same location. It also had responsibility for the mobilization of divisions, training them and providing them with trained replacements.

Prewar German Expansion

From the start, Adolf Hitler intended to rebuild German military power, using plans originally formulated under the Weimar Government. The *Führer* needed a powerful military in order to make his territorial ambitions possible.

Hitler knew that the fleets, divisions and squadrons he planned to create would all need the best weaponry. These would have to come from the industrial heartlands of the Saar and the Rhineland – the areas until recently occupied by troops of the Allied powers of 1918, which were still 'demilitarized' and still denied by treaty to German control.

He regained the Saar region in January 1935 by the simple expedient of holding a plebiscite, which naturally he won, enabling him to present the resumption of German control as a *fait accompli* to a generally uninterested and as yet unsuspecting world.

Rhineland re-militarized

Next, in March 1936, he sent his troops into the Rhineland – with some trepidation. The operation was codenamed Winter Exercise. Not long after dawn, 19 German infantry battalions and a handful of planes entered the Rhineland. They reached the Rhine by 11 a.m., then three battalions crossed to the west bank of the river. When German reconnaissance learned that thousands of French soldiers were congregating on the Franco-German border, General Blomberg, the Minister of Defence, begged Hitler to evacuate the German forces. Hitler inquired whether the French forces had actually crossed the border and when informed that they had not, he assured Blomberg that they would wait until this happened.

Hitler watched while Britain and France rationalized both his aggression and their own inaction with such evasions of responsibility as 'He is, after all, only walking into his own back yard.'

Two months after the reoccupation of the Rhineland, the Spanish Civil War broke out. Germany sent in aid the 6000 men of the Condor Legion, whose equipment included modern aircraft, tanks, transports and communications gear.

In the words of Hermann Göring, the Germans found Spain to be 'a place where we had the opportunity to test with live ammunition whether our military material was satisfactory for its purposes.'

Germany's rearmament and Hitler's aggressive speeches eventually began to get through to the governments in London and Paris.

France and Britain reluctantly began to stir themselves into action in 1937. An extension of France's main defences against possible German aggression – the Maginot Line – was agreed and construction actually began. Britain passed an Air Raid Precaution Bill through Parliament.

As in Germany, political life in Austria after World War I was polarized. Extremists like the Austrian Nazis had their fire stolen in the early 1930s, when Austria drifted from democracy to authoritarian government, first under Engelbert Dolfüss and then Schuschnigg. Nevertheless, on 25 July 1934, a group of Austrian Nazis, backed and armed by the SS, seized the Viennese Chancellery and attempted to proclaim a government. Dolfüss, whom they had taken prisoner, was murdered.

The rebels then appealed to Hitler for support, but the Führer could do nothing because the Fascist leader in Italy, Benito Mussolini, had sent heavy forces to the Brenner Pass to invade Austria in the event of a German intervention.

However, with Hitler growing ever more confident at home and abroad, it was only a matter of time before the aims of Austria's Nazis were realized.

Anschluss with Austria

On 12 March 1938, Hitler sent his troops across the Austrian border and into Vienna. The following day, he entered Vienna to declare the *Anschluss*. The German General Staff used the operation as an exercise in moving large numbers of troops by road.

HITLER'S ANNEXATIONS

Hitler's Annexations
1935–39

- Germany after 1919
- Troops into demilitarized Rhineland March 1936
- *Anschluss* (union with Austria), March 1938
- Occupation of Sudetenland October 1938
- Original Czechoslovakian border
- Former Czechoslovakia occupied March 1939
- Moravian territory to Poland October 1938
- Memel territory to Germany March 1939
- Protectorate of Slovakia territory to Hungary Nov. 1938
- Czechoslovakian territory to Hungary March 1939

1936–39

Hitler's first territorial acquisitions were Germany's traditional industrial heartlands of the Saar and the Rhineland – demilitarized areas until recently occupied by the Allied powers of 1918. The Saar he regained in January 1935 by plebiscite. In March 1936, he re-occupied the Rhineland.

On 12 March 1938, Hitler sent his troops across the Austrian border and into Vienna to a rapturous welcome. The following day, he himself travelled to Vienna to declare the *Anschluss* – the indissoluble reunion of Austria and Germany into the Greater German Reich. The German General Staff used the operation as an exercise in moving large numbers of troops by road.

In Czechoslovakia, the Sudetenland – the northern and western border areas facing Germany and Austria – had a German-speaking population of three million. The area had rich mineral resources, and it also housed major munitions factories at Pilsen. At Munich in September 1938, Britain, France, Italy and Germany agreed that the German-speaking Sudetenland should be transferred to the Reich – as the final stage of Hitler's territorial aggrandizement. Hitler had no intention of abiding by the agreement, however, and in March 1939 German troops moved forward from the Sudetenland, first to Prague and then on into the whole of Bohemia and Moravia.

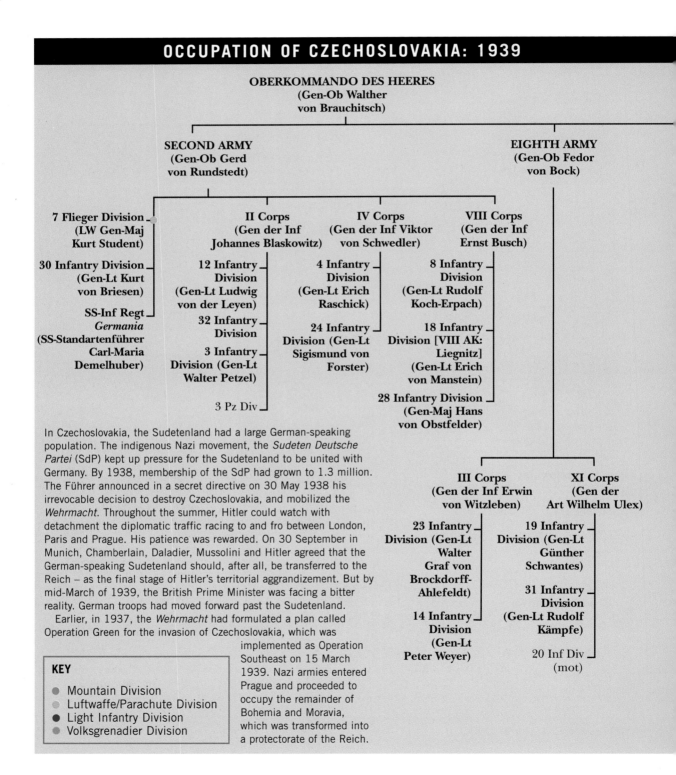

OCCUPATION OF CZECHOSLOVAKIA: 1939

OBERKOMMANDO DES HEERES
(Gen-Ob Walther
von Brauchitsch)

SECOND ARMY
(Gen-Ob Gerd
von Rundstedt)

EIGHTH ARMY
(Gen-Ob Fedor
von Bock)

7 Flieger Division
(LW Gen-Maj
Kurt Student)

30 Infantry Division
(Gen-Lt Kurt
von Briesen)

SS-Inf Regt
Germania
(SS-Standartenführer
Carl-Maria
Demelhuber)

II Corps
(Gen der Inf
Johannes Blaskowitz)

12 Infantry
Division
(Gen-Lt Ludwig
von der Leyen)

32 Infantry
Division

3 Infantry
Division (Gen-Lt
Walter Petzel)

3 Pz Div

IV Corps
(Gen der Inf Viktor
von Schwedler)

4 Infantry
Division
(Gen-Lt Erich
Raschick)

24 Infantry
Division (Gen-Lt
Sigismund von
Forster)

VIII Corps
(Gen der Inf
Ernst Busch)

8 Infantry
Division
(Gen-Lt Rudolf
Koch-Erpach)

18 Infantry
Division [VIII AK:
Liegnitz]
(Gen-Lt Erich
von Manstein)

28 Infantry Division
(Gen-Maj Hans
von Obstfelder)

III Corps
(Gen der Inf Erwin
von Witzleben)

23 Infantry
Division (Gen-Lt
Walter
Graf von
Brockdorff-
Ahlefeldt)

14 Infantry
Division
(Gen-Lt
Peter Weyer)

XI Corps
(Gen der
Art Wilhelm Ulex)

19 Infantry
Division (Gen-Lt
Günther
Schwantes)

31 Infantry
Division
(Gen-Lt Rudolf
Kämpfe)

20 Inf Div
(mot)

In Czechoslovakia, the Sudetenland had a large German-speaking population. The indigenous Nazi movement, the *Sudeten Deutsche Partei* (SdP) kept up pressure for the Sudetenland to be united with Germany. By 1938, membership of the SdP had grown to 1.3 million. The Führer announced in a secret directive on 30 May 1938 his irrevocable decision to destroy Czechoslovakia, and mobilized the *Wehrmacht*. Throughout the summer, Hitler could watch with detachment the diplomatic traffic racing to and fro between London, Paris and Prague. His patience was rewarded. On 30 September in Munich, Chamberlain, Daladier, Mussolini and Hitler agreed that the German-speaking Sudetenland should, after all, be transferred to the Reich – as the final stage of Hitler's territorial aggrandizement. But by mid-March of 1939, the British Prime Minister was facing a bitter reality. German troops had moved forward past the Sudetenland.

Earlier, in 1937, the *Wehrmacht* had formulated a plan called Operation Green for the invasion of Czechoslovakia, which was implemented as Operation Southeast on 15 March 1939. Nazi armies entered Prague and proceeded to occupy the remainder of Bohemia and Moravia, which was transformed into a protectorate of the Reich.

KEY

- Mountain Division
- Luftwaffe/Parachute Division
- Light Infantry Division
- Volksgrenadier Division

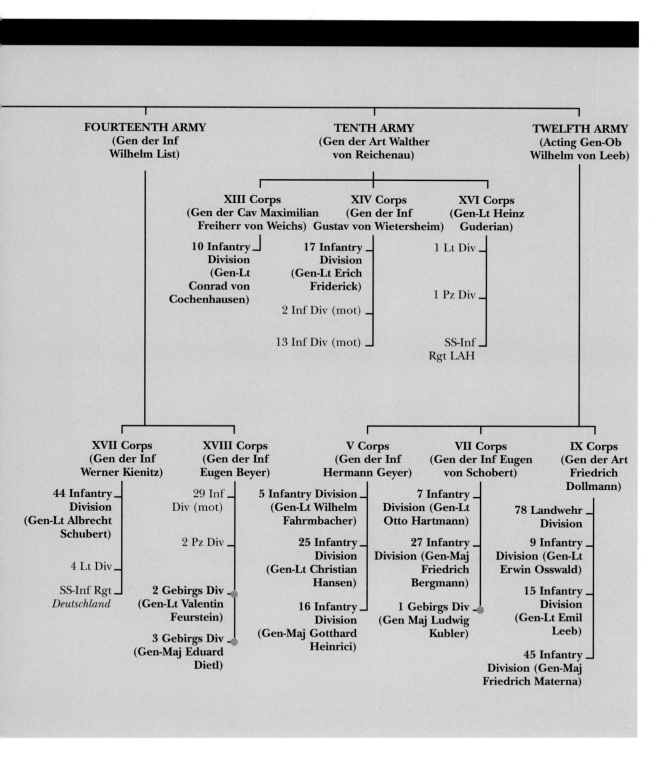

FOURTEENTH ARMY
(Gen der Inf
Wilhelm List)

TENTH ARMY
(Gen der Art Walther
von Reichenau)

TWELFTH ARMY
(Acting Gen-Ob
Wilhelm von Leeb)

XIII Corps
(Gen der Cav Maximilian
Freiherr von Weichs)

XIV Corps
(Gen der Inf
Gustav von Wietersheim)

XVI Corps
(Gen-Lt Heinz
Guderian)

**10 Infantry
Division**
(Gen-Lt
Conrad von
Cochenhausen)

**17 Infantry
Division**
(Gen-Lt Erich
Friderick)

1 Lt Div

2 Inf Div (mot)

1 Pz Div

13 Inf Div (mot)

SS-Inf
Rgt LAH

XVII Corps
(Gen der Inf
Werner Kienitz)

XVIII Corps
(Gen der Inf
Eugen Beyer)

V Corps
(Gen der Inf
Hermann Geyer)

VII Corps
(Gen der Inf Eugen
von Schobert)

IX Corps
(Gen der Art
Friedrich
Dollmann)

**44 Infantry
Division**
(Gen-Lt Albrecht
Schubert)

29 Inf
Div (mot)

5 Infantry Division
(Gen-Lt Wilhelm
Fahrmbacher)

**7 Infantry
Division** (Gen-Lt
Otto Hartmann)

**78 Landwehr
Division**

4 Lt Div

2 Pz Div

**25 Infantry
Division**
(Gen-Lt Christian
Hansen)

**27 Infantry
Division** (Gen-Maj
Friedrich
Bergmann)

**9 Infantry
Division** (Gen-Lt
Erwin Osswald)

SS-Inf Rgt
Deutschland

2 Gebirgs Div
(Gen-Lt Valentin
Feurstein)

**16 Infantry
Division**
(Gen-Maj Gotthard
Heinrici)

1 Gebirgs Div
(Gen Maj Ludwig
Kubler)

**15 Infantry
Division**
(Gen-Lt Emil
Leeb)

3 Gebirgs Div
(Gen-Maj Eduard
Dietl)

**45 Infantry
Division** (Gen-Maj
Friedrich Materna)

15

Poland: 1939

At 4.45 on the morning of the first of September 1939, aircraft of the *Luftwaffe* – Germany's air force – crossed the Polish frontier. The mission of almost 1400 fighters, bombers and dive-bombers was to begin the systematic destruction of Poland.

German infantry enter Poland as part of the invasion force, September 1939. Although the invasion of Poland is often characterized as a success for the Panzer arm's *blitzkrieg* tactics, the infantry played a key role in overwhelming the Polish Army in less than a month.

The attack on Poland was a natural development of Hitler's hunger for conquest. He had already absorbed Austria and Czechoslovakia: Poland was his next target. Rivalry between the two countries had already soured relations, and armies on both sides of the German-Polish border were preparing for war.

Hitler's early foreign policy worked to manoeuvre Poland into the Anti-Comintern Pact, forming a cooperative front against the Soviet Union. However, the Nazis' desire to redraw the border with Poland (because the German exclave of East Prussia was separated from the rest of the Reich by the 'Polish Corridor') was a major sticking point.

Many Germans also wanted to incorporate the Free City of Danzig into Germany. While Danzig had a predominantly German population, the Corridor constituted land that had long been disputed between Poland and Germany.

In 1938, Germany began pressuring the Poles to allow a roadway to be built to connect East Prussia with Germany proper, running through the Polish Corridor. German aggressiveness was beginning to worry the other European powers, and on 30 March 1930 Poland was backed by a guarantee from Britain and France, though neither country was willing to pledge military support in Poland's defence.

Preparation for invasion

In early 1939, Hitler had already issued orders to prepare for a possible 'solution to the Polish problem by military means'.

Planning for the invasion of Poland had begun in April 1939, when Hitler ordered the German General Staff to launch the operation, known as *Fall Weiss* ('Case White'), five months later.

In many ways, Poland was an ideal theatre for the new kind of combined arms operations being developed by the *Wehrmacht*. It was fairly flat, and therefore suitable for mechanized operations, while its long borders meant that the Polish Army was overstretched.

Another crucial step towards war was the surprise signing of the Molotov-Ribbentrop Pact on August 23, the product of secret Nazi-Soviet talks held in Moscow. With the agreement, Germany neutralized the possibility of Soviet opposition in a campaign against Poland.

In a secret protocol of this pact, the two sides agreed to divide Eastern Europe, including Poland, into two spheres of influence. The effect on Poland meant that in the event of its conquest, the western third of the country was to go to Germany and the eastern two-thirds to the Soviet Union.

Troops across the border

One hour after the initial *Luftwaffe* strikes, it was the turn of German ground forces to swing into action.

Over 40 German combat divisions were committed to the Polish campaign. Providing the spearhead of the German invasion force were six panzer divisions and eight motorized infantry divisions. These were supported by 27 foot-slogging infantry divisions.

The main role of the non-motorized infantry was to engage the bulk of the Polish army while the German mobile forces raced around the flanks, cutting through supply lines and striking at command and control centres to the rear. Fortunately, the bulk of the Polish forces were concentrated along the border with Germany, protecting the key industrialized area of Silesia, so the infantry did not have to march too far.

The role of the *Luftwaffe* was to provide close air support for the German ground forces. However, German aircraft also played a more strategic role, striking at Polish airfields and aircraft, road and rail centres, concentrations of troop reserves, and military headquarters.

GERMAN ARMY DIVISIONS: 1939		
	Sept 1939	**Oct 1939**
GERMAN ARMY DIVISIONS BY TYPE		
Panzer	10	10
Infantry (mot)	5	7
Infantry	94	96
Mountain	3	3
GERMAN ARMY DIVISIONS BY THEATRE: POLAND		
Germany	3	41
East	60	8
West	49	67

War of Manoeuvre

Fall Weiss was launched on 1 September 1939, opening World War II in Europe. Two powerful German assaults were to converge on Warsaw, while the main Polish army was to be encircled and destroyed west of the Vistula.

Rundstedt's Army Group South was made up of three armies. Eighth Army on the left drove for Lodz, while Fourteenth Army on the right aimed for Krakow. In the centre, von Reichenau's Tenth Army had the bulk of the group's armour. Its mission was first to pierce the gap between the Polish Lodz and Krakow armies, then link with Eighth Army mobile units and, finally, push on to Warsaw.

Attacking simultaneously was von Bock's Army Group North. Georg von Küchler's Third Army drove south from East Prussia while von Kluge's Fourth Army struck from the west, across the Polish Corridor. This attack was spearheaded by the panzers of Guderian's XIX Corps. A third, diversionary attack would be made from the south by Slovakian units under the control of Army Group South.

The world was stunned by the pace of the attack. While German panzers crossed the river Warta, Britain and France demanded the immediate withdrawal of all German forces. In the face of the contemptuous silence with which this was greeted in Berlin, the Allies consulted on how best to implement their promises to Poland.

A final ultimatum was sent to Berlin – and ignored.

At 11 a.m. on Sunday, 3 September, British Prime Minister Neville Chamberlain broadcast the news that Britain was now at war with Germany. The world would understand, he felt sure, how bitter a personal disappointment this was. After all, Hitler had given his word not to attack.

War of manoeuvre

The campaign was planned as a massive double pincer movement. The inner pincer was designed to close on the Vistula river, surrounding the bulk of the Polish field army, while the outer, faster-moving forces were targeted on the Bug, cutting off any possibility of escape.

The plan worked brilliantly. Never before had so much territory been gained in such a short space of time. After just three days of fighting, leading elements of the German army had pushed 80km (50 miles) into Poland. Whole Polish armies were in danger of being isolated. By the end of the first week, the Polish government had fled from Warsaw.

Von Kluge's Fourth Army had reached the Vistula by 3 September. The Third Army was approaching the Narew River at the same time.

In the South, the panzers of Walther von Reichenau's Tenth Army had already crossed the Warta river; two days later, his left wing was well to the rear of Lodz and his right wing had reached the town of Kielce.

Approaching Warsaw

By 8 September, one of his armoured corps was on the outskirts of Warsaw, having advanced 225km (140 miles) in the first week of war. The German 4 Panzer Division had advanced nearly 241km (150 miles), an average of more than 29km (18 miles) per day. The infantry, meanwhile, was engaging Polish forces that had been left behind by the headlong advance.

Light divisions on Reichenau's right were on the Vistula between Warsaw and the town of Sandomierz by September 9, while List, in the south, was on the river San above and below the town of Przemysl. At the same time, to the north, Guderian led his 3rd Army tanks across the Narew, attacking the line of the Bug River, and was already encircling Warsaw.

Ineffective resistance

All the German armies had made progress in fulfilling their parts of the *Fall Weiss* plan. The Polish armies were splitting up into uncoordinated fragments, some of which were retreating while others were delivering disjointed attacks on the nearest German columns.

In spite of some successful counterattacks early in the campaign, the Polish Air Force had been all but wiped out. With the elimination of any aerial threat, German Stuka dive-bombers were free to probe ahead of advancing panzer columns.

The momentum of the German advance continued virtually unchecked. In the same period, the Poles began to prepare Warsaw's defences.

On 9 September, initial German attempts to storm Warsaw were rebuffed. This was followed by a spirited Polish counterattack in the Bzura region, marking the start of the biggest battle of the campaign.

But by now, the entire Polish Army was becoming trapped inside an ever-decreasing circle of German forces. On 10 September, the *Luftwaffe* began to launch heavy raids on Warsaw, and the Polish government ordered a general military withdrawal to the southeast.

The initial Polish plans to stop a German attack on the border had failed. The industrial region of Silesia, the protection of which had been the incentive for the Polish forward defence strategy, had been abandoned.

Bzura Pocket

On 10 September, the Polish commander in chief, Marshal Edward Smygly-Rydz, ordered a general retreat to the southeast, towards the Romanian border. While they retreated, German troops were tightening their encirclement of the Polish forces west of the Vistula and were pushing forwards deep into eastern Poland.

The Battle of Bzura took place near the Bzura River west of Warsaw and lasted from 9–19 September. The Polish Poznan and Pomorze armies, which had been driven from the Polish Corridor, made a flank attack on Johannes Blaskowitz's Eighth Army, but were beaten off. Constant *Luftwaffe* attacks broke what remained of Polish resistance. Stukas destroyed the bridges across the Bzura River, trapping the Poles with nowhere to go. It was left to the German infantry divisions to mop up the Polish units, and resistance in the Bzura Pocket had ceased by 19 September. More than 100,000 men were taken prisoner.

Warsaw ultimatum

On 15 September, the Germans issued an ultimatum to Warsaw – surrender or be destroyed. The garrison,

WALTHER VON REICHENAU (1884–1942)

Born into a Prussian military family, von Reichenau was an artilleryman who was awarded the Iron Cross during World War I. A fervent supporter of the Nazis, he was one of Hitler's favourite generals. The *Führer* tried to make him Army Chief of Staff in 1938, but was thwarted by opposition from other senior generals.

• He commanded Tenth Army during the invasion of Poland in 1939, and led Sixth Army during the invasions of France (1940) and the USSR (1941).

• He was promoted to Field Marshal in August 1940.

• Notoriously anti-semitic, he supported the work of the *SS-Einsatzgruppen* in massacring Jews in the USSR. He died in January 1942 after suffering a cerebral haemorrhage followed by a heart attack.

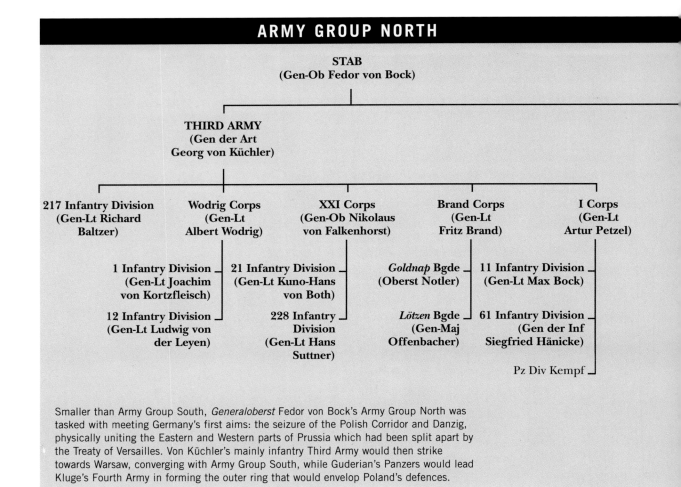

ARMY GROUP NORTH

STAB
(Gen-Ob Fedor von Bock)

THIRD ARMY
(Gen der Art
Georg von Küchler)

217 Infantry Division (Gen-Lt Richard Baltzer)	Wodrig Corps (Gen-Lt Albert Wodrig)	XXI Corps (Gen-Ob Nikolaus von Falkenhorst)	Brand Corps (Gen-Lt Fritz Brand)	I Corps (Gen-Lt Artur Petzel)
	1 Infantry Division (Gen-Lt Joachim von Kortzfleisch)	21 Infantry Division (Gen-Lt Kuno-Hans von Both)	*Goldnap* Bgde (Oberst Notler)	11 Infantry Division (Gen-Lt Max Bock)
	12 Infantry Division (Gen-Lt Ludwig von der Leyen)	228 Infantry Division (Gen-Lt Hans Suttner)	*Lötzen* Bgde (Gen-Maj Offenbacher)	61 Infantry Division (Gen der Inf Siegfried Hänicke)
				Pz Div Kempf

Smaller than Army Group South, *Generaloberst* Fedor von Bock's Army Group North was tasked with meeting Germany's first aims: the seizure of the Polish Corridor and Danzig, physically uniting the Eastern and Western parts of Prussia which had been split apart by the Treaty of Versailles. Von Küchler's mainly infantry Third Army would then strike towards Warsaw, converging with Army Group South, while Guderian's Panzers would lead Kluge's Fourth Army in forming the outer ring that would envelop Poland's defences.

supported by as many as 100,000 civilians determined to defend their city, chose to fight on.

Army Groups North and South met at Wlodawa on 17 September, completing the outer ring of the German double pincer. From this double encirclement, only a small fraction of the Polish Army could hope to escape, and on the same day even this hope was dashed.

Surrounded and besieged, the Poles received yet another crushing blow with the news that Soviet forces had also invaded from the east.

Signed the previous month, the secret Soviet–German Pact called for the division of Poland. While the Germans crushed any remaining Polish resistance in

the east, the Red Army advanced on two fronts north and south of the impassable Pripet marshes, meeting negligible opposition. The Polish government, which by now had been forced to change its location five times, fled into Romania.

Schnell Truppen
Throughout the Polish Campaign, the employment of panzers and motorized infantry was conventional, the *Schnell Truppen* being used primarily to ease the advance and to support the activities of the infantry.

It was the infantry that took and held ground, and it was the infantry, supported by the *Luftwaffe*, which faced

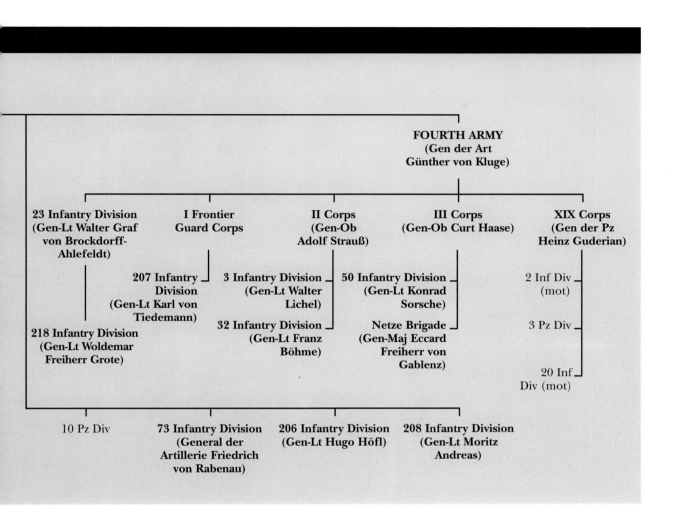

FOURTH ARMY
(Gen der Art
Günther von Kluge)

23 Infantry Division
(Gen-Lt Walter Graf
von Brockdorff-
Ahlefeldt)

**I Frontier
Guard Corps**

II Corps
(Gen-Ob
Adolf Strauß)

III Corps
(Gen-Ob Curt Haase)

XIX Corps
(Gen der Pz
Heinz Guderian)

**207 Infantry
Division**
(Gen-Lt Karl von
Tiedemann)

3 Infantry Division
(Gen-Lt Walter
Lichel)

50 Infantry Division
(Gen-Lt Konrad
Sorsche)

2 Inf Div
(mot)

218 Infantry Division
(Gen-Lt Woldemar
Freiherr Grote)

32 Infantry Division
(Gen-Lt Franz
Böhme)

Netze Brigade
(Gen-Maj Eccard
Freiherr von
Gablenz)

3 Pz Div

20 Inf
Div (mot)

10 Pz Div

73 Infantry Division
(General der
Artillerie Friedrich
von Rabenau)

206 Infantry Division
(Gen-Lt Hugo Höfl)

208 Infantry Division
(Gen-Lt Moritz
Andreas)

the bulk of the Polish Army. One of the key, if unsung, factors in the German success was the efficiency of German artillery, which had a devastating effect on many Polish units.

Tactical shortcomings

In spite of the successes in the Polish campaign, the Germans were not slow in recognizing a number of shortcomings even while the fighting continued. The majority of the tanks in use were lightweight Panzer Is and IIs, eked out by a number of Czech tanks. This proved to be excellent – except for the fact that they lacked heavy armament.

While artillery support was usually provided to the armoured forces when requested, often to great effect, the vast bulk of the equipment was still horse-drawn and too slow to follow up the rapid advances of the panzers. As a result, most of the artillery attached to the German armies was used to support infantry attacks.

The infantry itself found it difficult to keep up with the fast-moving motorized forces, and would have been unable to play a major role had the Germans been fighting a true *Blitzkrieg* campaign rather than a conventional envelopment. However, they carried out their primary mission, which was to engage and hold the main bulk of the Polish forces, west of the Vistula.

INVASION OF POLAND

Invasion of Poland
1–28 September 1939

- → German advance
- → Russian advance
- → Polish retreat
- German field work
- Polish defensive lines
- Polish positions
- German–Russian demarcation line

Poland Dismembered

The defeat of the Polish forces in the field, the flight of the Polish government into exile, the attack by the Red Army and the imminent fall of the Polish capital, Warsaw, signalled not only the conquest of Poland, but the destruction of the country.

Polish hopes of retreating to the Romanian bridgehead, where their forces would be able to reorganize, were dashed when more than 800,000 Red Army troops invaded the eastern regions of Poland. This was in violation of international agreements, including the Soviet–Polish Non-Aggression Pact. The Soviets, however, claimed that they were 'protecting' the Ukrainian and Belarusian minorities of eastern Poland in view of the imminent Polish collapse.

Two days after the defeat of the Polish armies in the Bzura Pocket, the Germans launched a massive bombardment of Warsaw. The next day, the Soviets occupied Lvov, and with the Germans, mounted a joint victory parade in Brest-Litovsk.

A further ultimatum was issued on 25 September to the citizens and defenders of Warsaw, emphasized by attacks by more than 400 bombers. Polish resistance began to weaken, and on 26 September the *Wehrmacht* launched an infantry assault on the city.

Fall of Warsaw

Within a day, the Germans had taken control of the outer suburbs, and the Polish commander, recognizing a lost cause, offered to surrender. A ceasefire came into effect the next day, 28 September.

To the victors went the spoils of war. The Soviet-German partition of Poland came into force immediately with the signing of a 'treaty of frontier regulation and friendship' on the 29th. Poland as a nation ceased to exist.

To seal his triumph, Hitler flew into Warsaw on 5 October and took the salute at a victory parade. Organized Polish resistance ceased the next day with the surrender of 8000 troops southeast of Warsaw. For the Poles, defeat was now complete.

Polish Army outclassed

Despite the desperate gallantry of its soldiers, the Polish Army had been outclassed by a vastly more efficient military force. The fatal weakness in Poland's defences lay in her lack of armour and mobile forces. At the start of the war, 30 Polish infantry divisions had been supported by 13 cavalry brigades, just two of which were motorized: the remaining 11 still used horses.

The whirlwind German campaign introduced a new type of warfare, making use of classic principles of fire and manoeuvre allied to the utilization of the latest weapons in both the air and the ground. Speed was a major contribution to the *Wehrmacht's* success, as was good intelligence. German troops unerringly found the weak spots in the Polish defences, which were exploited by fast-moving armour and mechanized infantry, driving towards their objectives while ignoring flank security.

1–28 September 1939

The invasion of Poland saw five German armies, amassing a total of more than 40 divisions, cross the border on 1 September 1939.

The Panzer divisions of the newly created *Panzerwaffe*, supported by light armoured divisions and motorized infantry divisions, formed the spearhead of the German drive on Warsaw, reaching the outskirts of the city within a week.

The campaign was not a true *Blitzkrieg* operation as envisaged by Guderian and others: rather, it was a massive double pincer movement, the inner pincer designed to close on the Vistula river, while the outer pincer – comprising faster-moving forces – was targeted on the Bug. Poland's fate was sealed when the Soviets invaded on 17 September 1939.

ARMY GROUP SOUTH

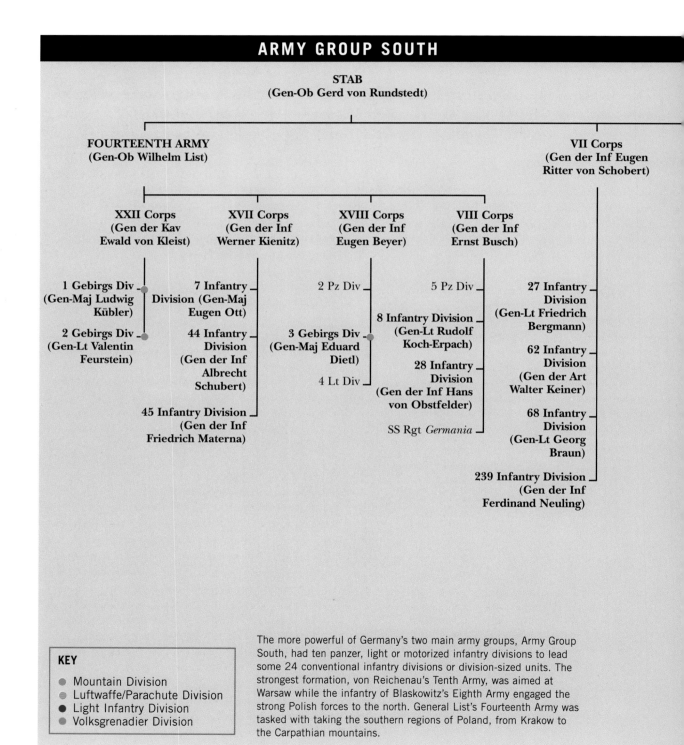

STAB
(Gen-Ob Gerd von Rundstedt)

FOURTEENTH ARMY
(Gen-Ob Wilhelm List)

VII Corps
(Gen der Inf Eugen
Ritter von Schobert)

XXII Corps
(Gen der Kav
Ewald von Kleist)

XVII Corps
(Gen der Inf
Werner Kienitz)

XVIII Corps
(Gen der Inf
Eugen Beyer)

VIII Corps
(Gen der Inf
Ernst Busch)

1 Gebirgs Div
(Gen-Maj Ludwig
Kübler)

7 Infantry
Division (Gen-Maj
Eugen Ott)

2 Pz Div

5 Pz Div

27 Infantry
Division
(Gen-Lt Friedrich
Bergmann)

2 Gebirgs Div
(Gen-Lt Valentin
Feurstein)

44 Infantry
Division
(Gen der Inf
Albrecht
Schubert)

3 Gebirgs Div
(Gen-Maj Eduard
Dietl)

8 Infantry Division
(Gen-Lt Rudolf
Koch-Erpach)

62 Infantry
Division
(Gen der Art
Walter Keiner)

4 Lt Div

28 Infantry
Division
(Gen der Inf Hans
von Obstfelder)

45 Infantry Division
(Gen der Inf
Friedrich Materna)

SS Rgt *Germania*

68 Infantry
Division
(Gen-Lt Georg
Braun)

239 Infantry Division
(Gen der Inf
Ferdinand Neuling)

The more powerful of Germany's two main army groups, Army Group South, had ten panzer, light or motorized infantry divisions to lead some 24 conventional infantry divisions or division-sized units. The strongest formation, von Reichenau's Tenth Army, was aimed at Warsaw while the infantry of Blaskowitz's Eighth Army engaged the strong Polish forces to the north. General List's Fourteenth Army was tasked with taking the southern regions of Poland, from Krakow to the Carpathian mountains.

KEY

- Mountain Division
- Luftwaffe/Parachute Division
- Light Infantry Division
- Volksgrenadier Division

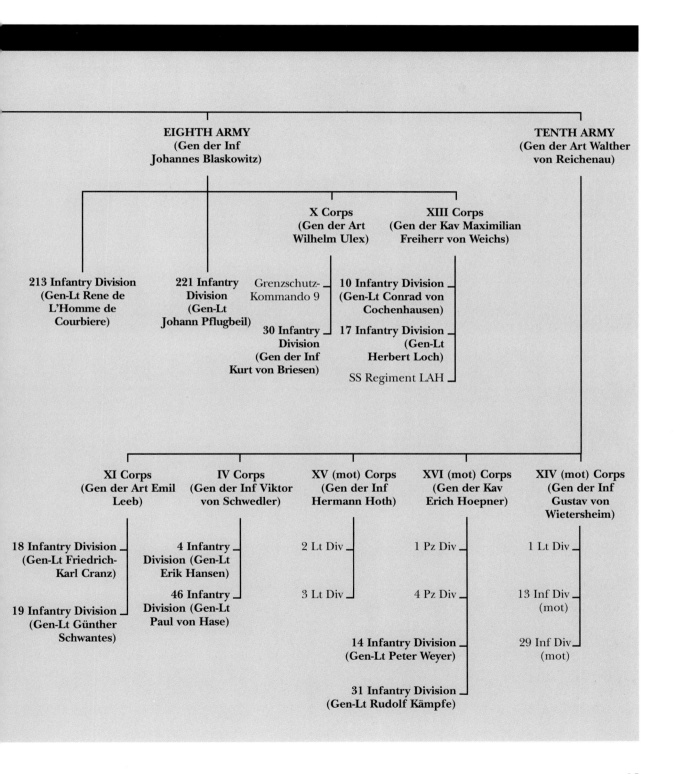

EIGHTH ARMY
(Gen der Inf
Johannes Blaskowitz)

TENTH ARMY
(Gen der Art Walther
von Reichenau)

X Corps
(Gen der Art
Wilhelm Ulex)

XIII Corps
(Gen der Kav Maximilian
Freiherr von Weichs)

213 Infantry Division
(Gen-Lt Rene de
L'Homme de
Courbiere)

221 Infantry
Division
(Gen-Lt
Johann Pflugbeil)

Grenzschutz-
Kommando 9

10 Infantry Division
(Gen-Lt Conrad von
Cochenhausen)

30 Infantry
Division
(Gen der Inf
Kurt von Briesen)

17 Infantry Division
(Gen-Lt
Herbert Loch)

SS Regiment LAH

XI Corps
(Gen der Art Emil
Leeb)

IV Corps
(Gen der Inf Viktor
von Schwedler)

XV (mot) Corps
(Gen der Inf
Hermann Hoth)

XVI (mot) Corps
(Gen der Kav
Erich Hoepner)

XIV (mot) Corps
(Gen der Inf
Gustav von
Wietersheim)

18 Infantry Division
(Gen-Lt Friedrich-
Karl Cranz)

4 Infantry
Division (Gen-Lt
Erik Hansen)

2 Lt Div

1 Pz Div

1 Lt Div

19 Infantry Division
(Gen-Lt Günther
Schwantes)

46 Infantry
Division (Gen-Lt
Paul von Hase)

3 Lt Div

4 Pz Div

13 Inf Div
(mot)

14 Infantry Division
(Gen-Lt Peter Weyer)

29 Inf Div
(mot)

31 Infantry Division
(Gen-Lt Rudolf Kämpfe)

INFANTRY RIFLE COMPANY: 1939

Although German infantry battalions were nominally reorganised several times during the war, the overall structure of the battalion and company remained largely unaltered from the beginning of the war to the end. The officer and three messengers of the platoon HQ carried a pistol and rifles respectively. The three men of the light mortar section carried rifles and served a single 5cm (2in) mortar. The three rifle squads were each 13 strong. Each squad included a machine gun group of four men, armed with three pistols and one rifle and serving a single MG34. In Poland the 13 man squad proved too large in action, and from 1940 a 10 man squad was introduced.

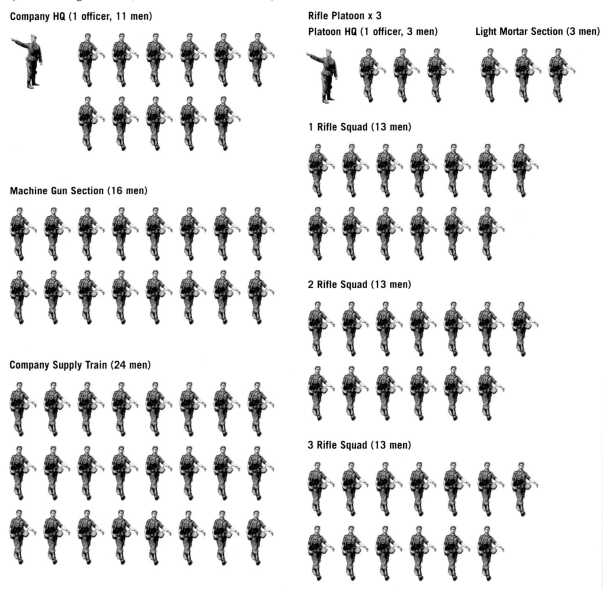

Company HQ (1 officer, 11 men)

Machine Gun Section (16 men)

Company Supply Train (24 men)

Rifle Platoon x 3

Platoon HQ (1 officer, 3 men)   **Light Mortar Section (3 men)**

1 Rifle Squad (13 men)

2 Rifle Squad (13 men)

3 Rifle Squad (13 men)

However, the panzers were generally subordinate to the infantry formations, and they did not push too far in front of the foot soldiers.

The *Wehrmacht's* triumph was recorded by scores of Propaganda Company cameramen, whose work was soon being shown in cinemas all over the world. This contributed greatly to the myth of *Blitzkrieg*, which would soon be terrifying Germany's enemies. Curiously, many western military professionals did not give the new tactics much attention, wrongly assuming the magnitude of the *Wehrmacht's* victory to be due to the incompetence of the Poles.

For Hitler, the Polish campaign had been a gamble that he had taken and won. The *Wehrmacht* had committed most of its forces to operations in Poland. No more than a token covering force in the west was left to face an overwhelming French Army of 70 divisions and a small British Expeditionary Force.

Allies do nothing
Although dangerously overexposed, Hitler had calculated correctly that the Allies would do nothing if he invaded Poland. Once the subjugation of Poland was completed in early October, Hitler was free to turn his attention to further campaigns in the west. However, fighting in Eastern Europe was far from over, and while there was no direct German involvement, the Winter War of 1939–40 was a direct result of the success of the *Wehrmacht* in Poland.

To the peoples of Western Europe, it seemed that military operations had ceased. The 'fighting war' was apparently over, and what United States Senator Boragh dubbed the 'Phoney War' began; Chamberlain called it the 'Twilight War', while the Germans called it the *'Sitzkrieg'*. Chamberlain refused to consider any deal with Hitler. He believed that in the spring of 1940 the German people 'would realize that they can't possibly win this war' and would therefore rid themselves of their *Führer*. The Allies would then be able to deal with some other German statesman, such as Marshal Göring.

Fixed defences
Similarly the French, and especially the French high command, believed they were arguing from a position of strength. Following the end of World War I, France had spent billions of francs on the construction of border fortifications known as the Maginot Line.

Stretching from the Swiss border to the Belgian border, the Maginot Line consisted of a series of immense concrete fortresses. These were designed to be impregnable to conventional attack. However, for political reasons, the Line did not extend along the Belgian border.

As the Allies geared for war, French troops occupied the Maginot Line, while the British Expeditionary Force proceeded smoothly to their positions along the Franco-Belgian border. There they built pill-boxes and dug trenches.

Preparations for war in the west
Both Britain and France still believed that war with Hitler could be avoided. There was no attempt to take pressure off the Poles during their ordeal by an Allied military action across the Rhine. This was much to the relief of senior *Wehrmacht* officers, who knew that a thrust into the Saar could not have been opposed by the Germans. Further, it could even have sparked the anti-Nazi popular revolt of which Chamberlain dreamed.

But nothing happened. Once the Poles had been beaten, the German divisions, tested in battle and with valuable experience to apply to future campaigns, redeployed swiftly across Germany to the French border.

GERMAN ARMY DIVISIONS: PHONEY WAR, 1939–40		
	Dec 1939	**Mar 1940**
GERMAN ARMY DIVISIONS BY TYPE		
Panzer	10	10
Infantry (mot)	7	7
Cavalry	0	1
Infantry	119	140
Mountain	3	3
Security	0	1
GERMAN ARMY DIVISIONS BY THEATRE		
Germany	31	46
East	10	17
West	98	99

Denmark and Norway: 1940

The opening of the war in the west came, not as most of the world expected, on the European mainland. Instead, German troops invaded Denmark and Norway.

German infantry manning an MG34 overlook a fjord on the Norwegian coast, following the occupation of the country.

The 'Phoney War' lasted through the winter and into the spring of 1940, until German forces invaded Denmark and Norway, forestalling an Allied landing by a matter of days. It was not until 10 May, eight months after the outbreak of war, that Hitler sent his armies west.

The Scandinavian attack had not been intended to happen, though planning had started at the beginning of the year, just in case it was necessary. It became necessary in April 1940.

On 8 April, the First Lord of the Admiralty, Winston Churchill, announced that the Royal Navy were laying mines in Norwegian waters in order to stop the iron ore traffic between Narvik and Germany – a flagrant violation of Norway's neutrality, which was justified on the curious ground that Germany's reaction was likely to be even more flagrant. As Norway was a distinctly friendly neutral, this struck many British people as odd. But not so odd as the news next morning.

Threat to iron ore supplies

It had been the Winter War beween Russia and Finland, and the possibility that British and French reinforcements and supplies might cross from Narvik to Lulea in Sweden, and thus interrupt Germany's supplies of iron ore, that first brought Hitler's attention to the possibility of occupying Norway.

Before that, his attention in the west had been concentrated on the Low Countries, but once he had seen the dangers that Allied exploitation of Norway might hold for Germany, and the advantages which would accrue to his *Kriegsmarine* by possession of Norwegian ports and control of her coastline, he ordered planning for what became known as *Weserübung* – Exercise Weser.

The *Altmark*

On 16 February 1940, British intelligence discovered that the *Altmark*, one of the *Graf Spee's* supply ships, was steaming down the Norwegian coast. The converted tanker had a large number of British seamen aboard, taken prisoner during the *Graf Spee's* raiding cruise. When threatened by the British 4th Destroyer Flotilla under Captain Vian, the *Altmark* took refuge in Norwegian territorial waters, putting in to Josenfiord.

With typically Churchillian panache, the orders went out from Whitehall to take the *Altmark*. Vian disregarded Norwegian neutrality, entered the fjord, forced the *Altmark* aground and rescued the prisoners, his boarding party making minor popular history with the call, 'The Navy's here!'

The British public were delighted, while the United States and other Western powers applauded discreetly – but Hitler's reaction was to order a speeding-up and consolidation of the planning for Operation *Weserübung*.

Two days later, *General der Infanterie* Nikolaus von Falkenhorst and his staff were given control of the operation – and it was one of the ironies of fate that, at the end of March, Hitler had decreed that it would be launched at dawn on 9 April – just one day after Churchill's announcement.

The result was that, to the watching world, Germany's reaction to the Royal Navy's mining of the Norwegian Leads, flagrant violation or not, appeared unbelievably rapid. OKW, the high command of the German armed forces, released a message to the world's press as operations against Denmark and Norway were launched: 'In order to counter British preparations to take away the neutrality of Denmark and Norway, the *Wehrmacht* is taking over the armed defence of both nations.'

Joint operation

Unlike the invasion of Poland, which had been planned and controlled by OKH, the High Command of the German Army, the Scandinavian operation was planned and controlled by the *Oberkommando der Wehrmacht*, with major input by both the *Kriegsmarine* and the *Luftwaffe*. In the interests of surprise, the invasion force would be transported in warships, which were much faster than transport vessels.

Operation *Weserübung* would be under the command of the XXI Army Group and include the 3rd Mountain Division and five as yet unblooded infantry divisions. Three companies of paratroopers were assigned by the *Luftwaffe* to seize key airfields.

On 1 March, Hitler issued a directive ordering the occupation of Denmark as well as Norway. Two infantry divisions and a motorized brigade were assigned to XXXI Corps for the operation, which would be supported by 1000 aircraft of various types.

Operation 'Spring Awakening'

Planning for the occupation of Denmark and Norway began at the beginning of 1940, with the *Kriegsmarine* having completed initial preparations by February. The key to success lay in surprise, and the initial attacks were made at great speed.

The first step was to occupy Denmark, which would provide a springboard into Norway. As of April 1940, the Danish army had fewer than 14,000 men under arms, including 8000 men conscripted in February and March. The men were poorly trained and equipped with little or no armour. On 9 April, German *fallschirmjäger* were dropped at the unused fortress of Madneso and at Aalborg airport. A battalion of infantry seized the Danish King and his government. Two divisions of the German XXI Infantry Corps crossed the border into Jutland. Totally outmatched, the Danish Army put up little resistance, although there was a brief firefight for possession of the Royal Palace in Copenhagen.

Denmark submits

At 9.20 a.m., after Germany threatened to use the *Luftwaffe* to bombard Copenhagen, the Danish government ordered a ceasefire. By the end of the day,

GERMAN ARMY DIVISIONS: APRIL 1940	
	NUMBER
GERMAN ARMY DIVISIONS BY TYPE	
Panzer	10
Infantry (mot)	7
Cavalry	1
Infantry	141
Mountain	3
Security	1
GERMAN ARMY DIVISIONS BY THEATRE	
Germany	40
East	18
West	100
Norway	6

Germany controlled all of Denmark. In addition to providing a platform for operations in Norway, the occupation of Denmark provided the *Kriegsmarine* with bases for operations in the North Sea and Atlantic. The *Luftwaffe* needed Danish territory for fighter bases and radar stations. Denmark also provided flank security for the vital supplies of Swedish steel coming to Germany across the Baltic.

The same day, German troops moved ashore at Oslo, Bergen, Trondheim and Narvik, over 1610km (1000 miles) from the German homeland. German paratroops seized Sola airport near Stavanger, while the *Kriegsmarine* ferried the army formations across the Skagerrak and Kattegat, though not without loss. Both the heavy cruiser *Blücher* and the light cruiser *Karlsruhe* were sunk, the first by Norwegian coastal guns and the second by the submarine *Truant*.

The heavy cruiser *Admiral Hipper* had 36.5m (120ft) torn out of her starboard bow when she was rammed by the British destroyer *Glowworm* in a self-sacrificial attack, an action that won her commander, Lieutenant-Commander G.B. Roope, the first posthumous Victoria Cross of the war.

Forces assigned to the attack on Oslo included a combat group of 2000 men from the 163 Infantry Division. After daybreak, following air attacks to suppress any defences, it was also planned to drop a *Fallschirm-Kompanie* to help secure Fornebu airfield just outside city, to be followed later by airlanding an additional 3000 men of 163rd Division.

Norwegians fight back

Oslo was defended by only three Guards companies, a total of less than 500 men. By 8.00 a.m., the Norwegian Army had decided to evacuate the capital declaring Oslo an open city. The troops from the 163 Division air-landed at Fornebu marched in to take control.

Elsewhere the Norwegian forces, reacting with admirable determination after the first shock, offered more resistance, but the Royal Navy could at least help at Narvik. Five destroyers led by Captain Warburton-Lee created chaos among the German warships in the harbour, sinking two German destroyers but losing two in the process.

On 12 April, the old battleship *Warspite,* accompanied by nine destroyers, raced up the Ototfjord and completed the destruction; but to the south the preponderance of German artillery and trained battalions – and the complete domination of the air by the *Luftwaffe* – ensured the *Wehrmacht's* ultimate success in Norway.

In eight days, brigades of the German 163rd and 196th Divisions had advanced 290km (180 miles) and now controlled the vital southern region; when hastily landed British reinforcements arrived, they were incorporated piecemeal into the ragged defences, and beaten, as were the Norwegians, by better trained, better armed and much better coordinated and commanded troops. The survivors of two British brigades landed at Andalsnes in the middle of April were re-embarked and evacuated by 1 May, and central and southern Norway was virtually abandoned to the Germans.

Trouble at Narvik

However, in the far north at Narvik, the situation for the German General Dietl and his 2000 mountain troops was not at first so favourable. Their naval transport and supply had been destroyed and they were chased out of Narvik itself by a combined force of British Guardsmen, French Chasseurs Alpins and Polish Chasseurs du Nord.

By 28 May, Narvik was at last firmly in Allied hands. Thus it was somewhat ironic that orders had already been issued for the return home of all Allied forces, as they and their weapons were urgently needed elsewhere.

On 15 May, the Germans dropped a *Fallschirmjäger* parachute battalion to reinforce Narvik. Several days later, the 137th Regiment of the German 3rd Mountain Division was also dropped, after a hasty parachute training course. The troops were widely dispersed and many soldiers were injured, but most of the men eventually joined the main German force at Narvik.

Perhaps the most illuminating comment upon the

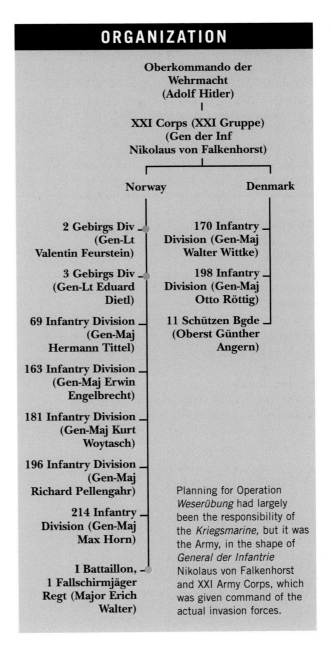

ORGANIZATION

Oberkommando der Wehrmacht (Adolf Hitler)

XXI Corps (XXI Gruppe) (Gen der Inf Nikolaus von Falkenhorst)

Norway | **Denmark**

2 Gebirgs Div (Gen-Lt Valentin Feurstein)

3 Gebirgs Div (Gen-Lt Eduard Dietl)

69 Infantry Division (Gen-Maj Hermann Tittel)

163 Infantry Division (Gen-Maj Erwin Engelbrecht)

181 Infantry Division (Gen-Maj Kurt Woytasch)

196 Infantry Division (Gen-Maj Richard Pellengahr)

214 Infantry Division (Gen-Maj Max Horn)

I Battaillon, 1 Fallschirmjäger Regt (Major Erich Walter)

170 Infantry Division (Gen-Maj Walter Wittke)

198 Infantry Division (Gen-Maj Otto Röttig)

11 Schützen Bgde (Oberst Günther Angern)

Planning for Operation *Weserübung* had largely been the responsibility of the *Kriegsmarine,* but it was the Army, in the shape of *General der Infantrie* Nikolaus von Falkenhorst and XXI Army Corps, which was given command of the actual invasion forces.

Allied conduct of the Norwegian Campaign was written years after the war by the man appointed to command the British reinforcements in central Norway. As Major-General Carton de Wiart, VC walked along Whitehall to answer an urgent summons to the War Office in early

April, 'It dawned on me that it might be Norway, as I had never been there and knew nothing about it!'

If the Norwegian Campaign was a setback for the British arms, it was a disaster for the British Prime Minister, Neville Chamberlain.

The House of Commons was packed, the mood of the members frustrated and angry – the anger concentrated on the figure of Chamberlain sitting in his usual place on the front bench, so pale with fury and humiliation that Churchill, despite the bitter arguments of the past few years, was filled with sympathy for his leader.

Nor was the attack delivered entirely by members of the Opposition, for it reached its zenith with a speech from one of Chamberlain's oldest friends and political colleagues, Leo Amery. Quoting Cromwell's scathing indictment of the leaders of Hampden's army as 'old decaying service men,' he turned directly on the Prime Minister and quoted Cromwell for the second time: 'You have sat here too long for any good you have been doing,' he proclaimed. 'Depart, I say, and let us have done with you! In the name of God, go!'

Later that day, Chamberlain admitted to Churchill that he felt that he could not continue to lead a one-party government in the prosecution of the war, and that a national government embracing members of all parties should be formed. However, he doubted if the Labour leaders would serve under his own direction.

Churchill takes over

So, in fact, it proved during the somewhat involved talks and negotiations of the next 48 hours. By 11 a.m. on 10 May, Chamberlain had accepted that he must give way to another leader, and sent for the two men between whom he felt the choice must be made: Lord Halifax and Winston Churchill.

'I have had many important interviews in my public life,' Churchill later wrote, 'and this was certainly the most important. Usually I talk a great deal, but on this occasion I was silent.'

It must have been a remarkable scene: Chamberlain, still icily certain of the rightness of his every action since taking office but prepared to yield in the face of such uncomprehending and incomprehensible hostility, now sure that his preference for Lord Halifax was justifiable; Churchill silent, feeling no doubt the weight of history

already pressing about him; Halifax uncertain, his sense of duty unsustained by any driving ambition. It was, as Churchill wrote, 'a very long pause.... It certainly seemed longer than the two minutes which one observes in the commemoration of Armistice Day.'

It was broken, at last, by Halifax. It would be, he said, very difficult for him to direct the War Cabinet from outside the House of Commons where all the major decisions must be debated, and where, as a member of the House of Lords, he was barred from speaking. It should be remembered that these were the days before a peer could disclaim his title. When he had finished, it was evident that Churchill's would be the name recommended to His Majesty, and after a little more desultory talk the three men parted.

The call to Churchill came late in the afternoon, and he was shown into the presence of the King, whom he was to serve so devotedly through such crucial years.

So began the premiership of one of the most remarkable men in British history and it is hard to believe that, for most of the rest of the world, the appointment itself and the events surrounding it passed for the moment almost unnoticed.

Hitler and Churchill

One of the few who might have taken heed of the new appointment was Adolf Hitler, who had been well aware of Churchill's opposition to the Nazis in the 1930s. Hitler had even invited Churchill to Germany for talks, but the Englishman refused. At the time, the *Führer* considered Churchill to be too much of an outsider to be a threat, but now the biggest foe of appeasement was in charge in London. However, the Germans thought that Churchill would only be a minor irritant, who would be swept aside as the full might of the *Wehrmacht* was unleashed.

Early on the morning of Churchill's appointment, the *Wehrmacht* had launched a massive offensive into Belgium and Holland, both of which had been neutral up to that time. As army and SS spearheads crossed the border into the Low Countries, the *Luftwaffe* bombarded Rotterdam and German *fallschirmjäger* were dropped onto key points along an obviously carefully planned attack route.

The days of the 'Phoney War' were gone for ever.

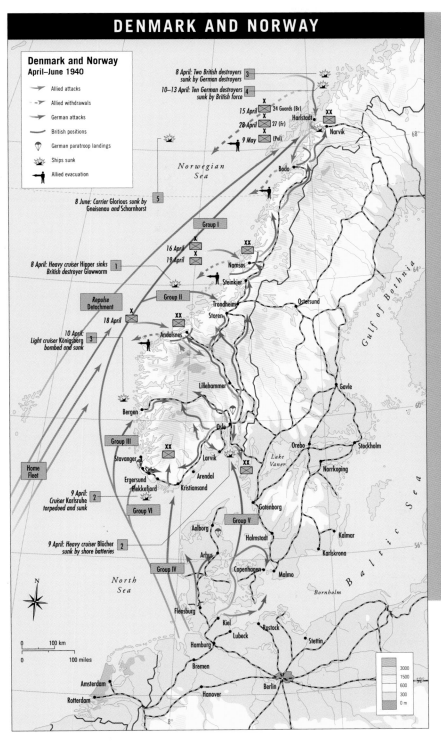

DENMARK AND NORWAY

Denmark and Norway
April–June 1940

→ Allied attacks

- -‣ Allied withdrawals

→ German attacks

⌐ British positions

⊽ German paratroop landings

⚓ Ships sunk

👤 Allied evacuation

8 April: Two British destroyers sunk by German destroyers [3]

10–13 April: Ten German destroyers sunk by British force [4]

X
15 April X ⊠ 24 Guards (Br)
X
28 April ⊠ 27 (Fr)   Harlstadt   ⊠ XX
X
9 May ⊠ (Pol)   Narvik

68°

Norwegian Sea   Bodo

8 June: Carrier Glorious sunk by Gneisenau and Scharnhorst [5]

Group I

16 April ⊠ XX
19 April X   Namsos
8 April: Heavy cruiser Hipper sinks British destroyer Glowworm [1]   Steinkjer

64°

Group II   Trondheim   Ostersund

Repulse Detachment   X   Storen
18 April   ⊠ XX

10 April: Light cruiser Königsberg bombed and sunk [3]   Andalsnes

Lillehammer   Gavle

60°
Bergen   Oslo
Group III   ⊠ XX   Orebo   Stockholm

Home Fleet   Stavanger   Larvik   *Lake Vaner*   ⊠ XX   Norrkoping
Sola
Ergersund   Arendal
9 April: Cruiser Karlsruhe torpedoed and sunk [2]   Flekkefjord   Kristiansand

Group VI   Gotenborg

Aalborg   Group V   Kalmar
Halmstadt   56°
9 April: Heavy cruiser Blücher sunk by shore batteries [2]   Arhus   Karlskrona
Copenhagen   Malmo
Group IV
North Sea   Bornholm

Gulf of Bothnia

Baltic Sea

N

| 0 | 100 km |

| 0 | 100 miles |

Flensburg

Kiel   Rostock
Lubeck   Stettin
Hamburg
Bremen   58°

	3000
	1500
	600
	300
	0 m

Amsterdam   Berlin
Hanover
Rotterdam   8°

April–June 1940

At 5.00 a.m. on 9 April, German *fallschirmjäger* were dropped at the unused fortress of Madneso in Denmark and then at Aalborg airport. At 6.00 a.m., a battalion of infantry, which had been hidden in a merchant ship in Copenhagen harbour, emerged to seize the Danish King and his government.

Two divisions of the German XXI Infantry Corps crossed the border and moved into Jutland. Totally outmatched, the Danish Army put up little resistance except in North Schleswig, and there was a brief firefight for possession of the Royal Palace in Copenhagen. At dawn on the same day, German troops were swarming ashore at Oslo, Bergen, Trondheim and even at Narvik, over 1610km (1000 miles) from Germany. German paratroops seized Sola airport near Stavanger and dropped later on to Fornebu airport near Oslo, while the *Kriegsmarine* ferried the army formations across the Skagerrak and Kattegat.

Allied landings and naval actions in the north around Narvik briefly reversed the tide of German success, but the British and French troops were withdrawn at the end of May after reverses in France meant that they were more urgently needed there.

France and the Low Countries: 1940

The real war in the west started in May 1940 when the *Wehrmacht* was unleashed against the Low Countries and France. The Allies were expecting and had prepared for a repeat of the German attack in 1914: they were to be unpleasantly surprised.

A section of German infantry march through a town in France badly damaged in recent fighting, June 1940.

The last time German soldiers had poured into France, in 1914, their initial drive had taken them close to Paris. But they were driven back, and had to endure four bloody years of trench warfare.

This time they would break the back of enemy resistance in a single week. After a little more than a fortnight, the British would be evacuating their soldiers, and France would be at Hitler's mercy. The humiliation of 1918 would be avenged – and it would be the *Führer's* master strategy that did it, not the General Staff.

Repeat of 1914

The original army plan for the invasion of western Europe was based on Germany's opening attack in World War I, but was actually less ambitious than the Schlieffen Plan of 1914. The generals intended to occupy Belgium and France's northern industrial regions but no further. They had no intention of repeating the ill-fated march on Paris tried in 1914. The Army high command believed that the ratio of forces and the power of modern defence admitted no other strategy; new objectives would require a further campaign in 1941.

Had the attack been delivered when first ordered in autumn 1939, the generals would have had the war they planned. But Hitler had other ideas. He had fought in Belgium, among the shattered villages around Ypres, where a million British and German soldiers were killed in 1917. He knew the ground and how artillery bombardments reduced the ground to a quagmire. Countless small rivers and streams offered endless obstruction to an invader. Surely it would be better to attack further south, perhaps through the forested hills of the Ardennes? The generals looked down their noses at the idea.

By the time the postponed offensive was ready to roll in the spring, Hitler discovered that at least some officers shared his vision. General Erich von Manstein was chief of staff to General von Rundstedt, commander in chief of Army Group A in the West. Manstein had studied the Ardennes region and come to the same conclusion as the *Führer*. He discussed the idea with the Germany's most influential tank expert, General Heinz Guderian. They argued for a radical strategy: to rush German panzer divisions along the narrow forest tracks

and out onto the gently rolling hills of northern France. Bursting into open country, they would punch through the enemy before the defences were ready for them.

Blitzkrieg

It would be difficult to bring enough artillery with these fast-moving formations, and other German commanders envisaged a pause while the guns were brought forward; a World War I-style battle would then take place along the river Meuse. Guderian and his tank men were far more sanguine, confident they could storm the French defences. The *Luftwaffe's* bombers, especially its fearsome Ju-87 'Stuka' dive-bombers, would provide close support in place of artillery. Hitler adopted the Manstein plan and changed the orders to his commanders. Manstein would receive due credit in time, but the orthodox generals resented having a junior officer's plan thrust upon them, and posted von Manstein to command an infantry corps in the rear.

One thing Hitler could not change was the odds. Although Germany enjoyed superiority in the air, with 4000 aircraft against 3000 Allied, the *Wehrmacht* had only 141 divisions with which to attack 144 Allied divisions. The Allies had some 3383 tanks compared to the German total of 2335 – many of these being light tanks of limited fighting capacity.

INVASION OF FRANCE AND THE LOW COUNTRIES	
	May 1940
GERMAN ARMY DIVISIONS BY TYPE	
Panzer	10
Infantry (mot)	8
Cavalry	1
Infantry	142
Mountain	3
Security	1
GERMAN ARMY DIVISIONS BY THEATRE	
Germany	29
East	15
West	114
Norway	7

Army Group A

The infantry units that made up the bulk of General Gerd von Rundstedt's Army Group A were left far behind as Guderian's panzers raced through northern France. However, they had an important task in mopping up pockets of French reistance.

Once the attack was launched in the West, German forces stormed across Holland and Belgium just as the Allies expected, the imposing concrete and steel fortress at Eban Emael falling to a crack unit of paratroops who landed by glider right on the roof. However, the forces under General von Bock – 30 infantry divisions of Army Group B – were actually a feint. Their intention was designed to convince the Allies that the Germans were following the same old plan which had not been successful in earlier wars.

Ardennes attack

The real punch came through the Ardennes, where the 44 divisions of von Runstedt's Army Group A, including 7 Panzer divisions under von Kleist, planned to catch the Allies by surprise. The bulk of the French troops were contained in the massive defences of the Maginot line, guarding against an attack across the German border. But the huge works did not cover the Belgian border, French planners having considered that a major attack through the Ardennes was impossible.

This was to be the first classic application of *Blizkrieg*. The panzer divisions would smash through a weak point in the French defences, fanning out to cause chaos in the French rear areas and across the Allied lines of communication.

Immediate support to the panzers was provided by motorized infantry, but the bulk of the force, following on behind, was standard infantry. Marching on foot, they were to engage by-passed French positions, securing the terrain behind the armoured spearheads and preventing any French counterattacks.

The German plan quickly became a reality. Encountering little resistance from Belgian troops in the Ardennes, the panzer divisions headed down the dirt roads in alarmingly dense columns. Crashing through the 'impassable' forests and hills as though on a peacetime exercise, brushing aside the French light cavalry unit which had been sent out to 'delay' them, the three divisions of General Guderian's Panzer Corps were across the French frontier and had reached the Meuse on each side of Sedan by the afternoon of 12 May.

Across the Meuse

On 13 May, Guderian's infantry paddled across the Meuse in rubber dinghies. At the same time, a *Luftwaffe* force of 300 twin-engine bombers and 200 Stukas pulverized the French defences. The dive-bombers attacked with particular accuracy, knocking out key French gun positions. The foot soldiers were across by 3.00 p.m. Combat engineers had a ferry operational in an hour, and by 4.30 p.m. a bridge was in place and the tanks could cross to the far bank.

Phoney War: 1939–40

The Phoney War over the winter of 1939 and 1940 saw the Allies waiting confidently for any German attack. The French felt safe behind the massive fortifications of the Maginot Line, while the British expected the Germans to attack through the Low Countries and made plans to advance into Belgium to counter a German offensive. Although Belgian neutrality complicated Allied planning, it was hoped that Belgian resistance would hold up the Germans long enough for the the Allies to move forward and into their new defensive positions along the River Dyle.

What they did not realize was that the Germans planned to strike through the supposedly 'impassable' Ardennes and cut the Allied forces in half, isolating British and Belgian forces along the North Sea and Channel coasts. 'Plan Yellow', as the German offensive was known, would be spearheaded by von Kleist's panzer divisions.

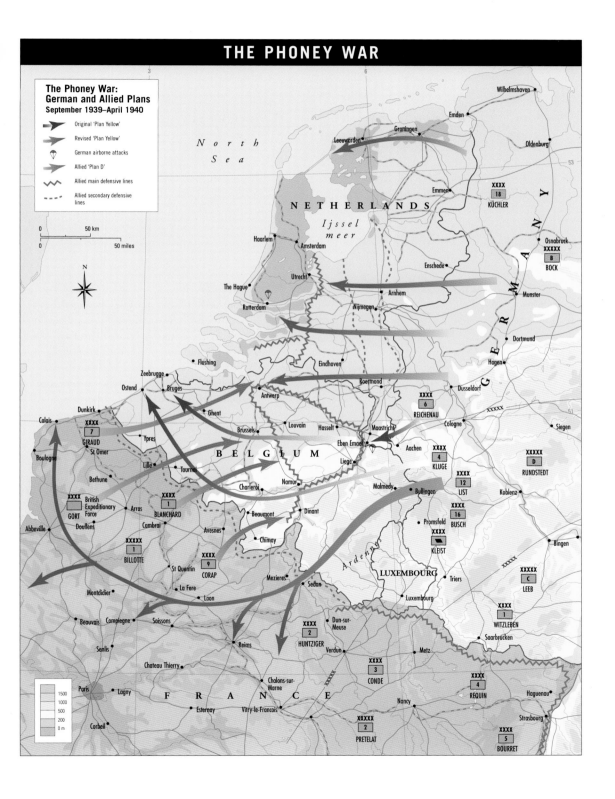

THE PHONEY WAR

**The Phoney War:
German and Allied Plans**
September 1939–April 1940

- Original 'Plan Yellow'
- Revised 'Plan Yellow'
- German airborne attacks
- Allied 'Plan D'
- Allied main defensive lines
- Allied secondary defensive lines

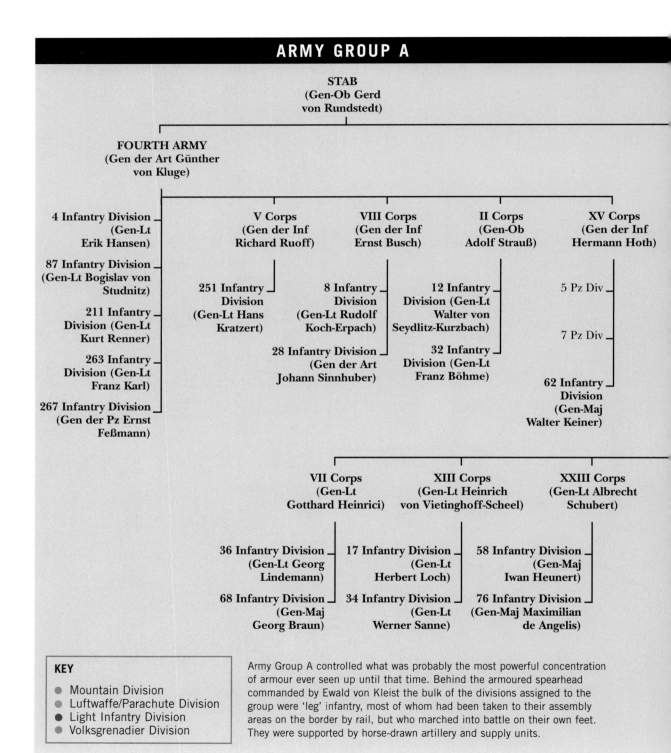

ARMY GROUP A

STAB
(Gen-Ob Gerd
von Rundstedt)

FOURTH ARMY
(Gen der Art Günther
von Kluge)

4 Infantry Division
(Gen-Lt
Erik Hansen)

87 Infantry Division
(Gen-Lt Bogislav von
Studnitz)

211 Infantry
Division (Gen-Lt
Kurt Renner)

263 Infantry
Division (Gen-Lt
Franz Karl)

267 Infantry Division
(Gen der Pz Ernst
Feßmann)

V Corps
(Gen der Inf
Richard Ruoff)

251 Infantry
Division
(Gen-Lt Hans
Kratzert)

VIII Corps
(Gen der Inf
Ernst Busch)

8 Infantry
Division
(Gen-Lt Rudolf
Koch-Erpach)

28 Infantry Division
(Gen der Art
Johann Sinnhuber)

II Corps
(Gen-Ob
Adolf Strauß)

12 Infantry
Division (Gen-Lt
Walter von
Seydlitz-Kurzbach)

32 Infantry
Division (Gen-Lt
Franz Böhme)

XV Corps
(Gen der Inf
Hermann Hoth)

5 Pz Div

7 Pz Div

62 Infantry
Division
(Gen-Maj
Walter Keiner)

VII Corps
(Gen-Lt
Gotthard Heinrici)

36 Infantry Division
(Gen-Lt Georg
Lindemann)

68 Infantry Division
(Gen-Maj
Georg Braun)

XIII Corps
(Gen-Lt Heinrich
von Vietinghoff-Scheel)

17 Infantry Division
(Gen-Lt
Herbert Loch)

34 Infantry Division
(Gen-Lt
Werner Sanne)

XXIII Corps
(Gen-Lt Albrecht
Schubert)

58 Infantry Division
(Gen-Maj
Iwan Heunert)

76 Infantry Division
(Gen-Maj Maximilian
de Angelis)

KEY

● Mountain Division
● Luftwaffe/Parachute Division
● Light Infantry Division
● Volksgrenadier Division

Army Group A controlled what was probably the most powerful concentration of armour ever seen up until that time. Behind the armoured spearhead commanded by Ewald von Kleist the bulk of the divisions assigned to the group were 'leg' infantry, most of whom had been taken to their assembly areas on the border by rail, but who marched into battle on their own feet. They were supported by horse-drawn artillery and supply units.

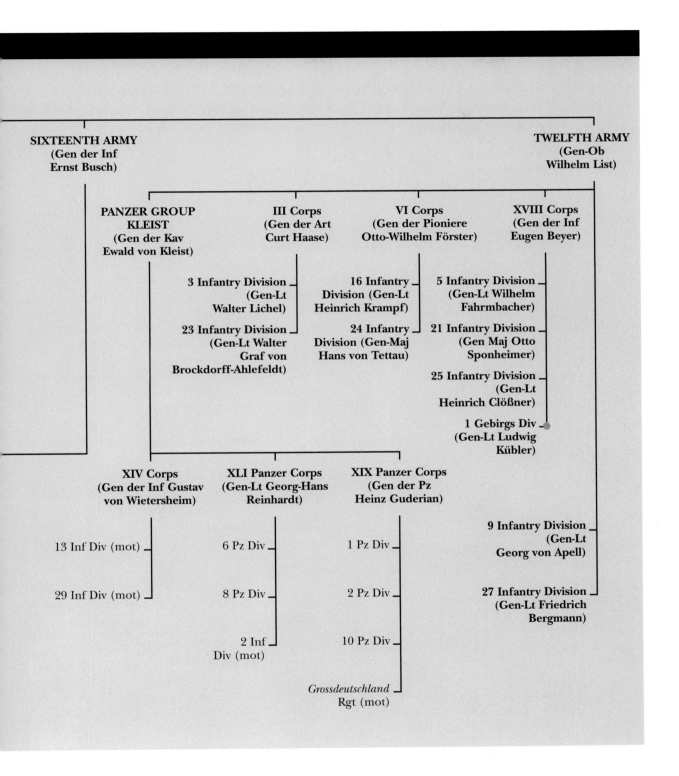

SIXTEENTH ARMY
(Gen der Inf
Ernst Busch)

TWELFTH ARMY
(Gen-Ob
Wilhelm List)

PANZER GROUP
KLEIST
(Gen der Kav
Ewald von Kleist)

III Corps
(Gen der Art
Curt Haase)

VI Corps
(Gen der Pioniere
Otto-Wilhelm Förster)

XVIII Corps
(Gen der Inf
Eugen Beyer)

3 Infantry Division
(Gen-Lt
Walter Lichel)

16 Infantry
Division (Gen-Lt
Heinrich Krampf)

5 Infantry Division
(Gen-Lt Wilhelm
Fahrmbacher)

23 Infantry Division
(Gen-Lt Walter
Graf von
Brockdorff-Ahlefeldt)

24 Infantry
Division (Gen-Maj
Hans von Tettau)

21 Infantry Division
(Gen Maj Otto
Sponheimer)

25 Infantry Division
(Gen-Lt
Heinrich Clößner)

1 Gebirgs Div
(Gen-Lt Ludwig
Kübler)

XIV Corps
(Gen der Inf Gustav
von Wietersheim)

XLI Panzer Corps
(Gen-Lt Georg-Hans
Reinhardt)

XIX Panzer Corps
(Gen der Pz
Heinz Guderian)

9 Infantry Division
(Gen-Lt
Georg von Apell)

13 Inf Div (mot)

6 Pz Div

1 Pz Div

29 Inf Div (mot)

8 Pz Div

2 Pz Div

27 Infantry Division
(Gen-Lt Friedrich
Bergmann)

2 Inf
Div (mot)

10 Pz Div

Grossdeutschland
Rgt (mot)

Army Group B

Shortly after 2.30 on the morning of 10 May 1940, 64 men of the German Army crossed the Dutch frontier. This was the very spearhead of the *Wehrmacht's* advance into France and the Low Countries.

In the Netherlands, paratroopers were dropped onto key bridges near Rotterdam, the Hague, Dordrecht and Moerdijk, paralyzing any effective Dutch response to the flood coming across the border. More troops crossed the Albert canal into Flanders. They should have been held back by the huge Belgian fort at Eben Emael, but at 5.30 a.m., glider-borne troops had dropped over the border to capture and demolish the strongpoint.

Five minutes later, the 30 divisions of Army Group B under General Fedor von Bock flooded forward across the frontiers from Maastricht up to the coast at the Ems estuary, while to the south General von Rundstedt's Army Group A of 44 divisions, including the main striking force of seven panzer divisions under General Kleist, moved forward into the Belgian Ardennes – the wooded country that French military commanders had been proclaiming impassable by tanks since 1919.

Allies take the bait

With an almost suicidal alacrity, the Allied armies in the north did exactly what the Germans wanted them to do. Five divisions of the British Expeditionary Force, eight divisions of the French First Army on their right and seven divisions of the French Seventh Army up on the coast around Dunkirk left the defensive positions they had spent the bitterly cold winter so arduously preparing, and now moved forward to join the Belgian army in accordance with the Dyle Plan. This envisaged a defensive line running along the Dyle and Meuse rivers.

There were obviously some difficulties to be overcome on the way, for the *Luftwaffe* was busy overhead all the time, and this was the occasion for the baptism of Allied troops by dive-bombing. It took time for them to become accustomed to the nerve-wraking howl that accompanied it. Moreover, the violence and speed of the German advance and the seemingly continuous *Luftwaffe* attacks had spread panic among the civilian population, and the roads over which the Allied troops were travelling were soon choked with refugees fleeing ahead of Bock's advancing infantry.

Poor Allied defences

Many of the Allied battalion and brigade commanders were dismayed by the fragmentary nature of the defences they now occupied, and their troops were equally unhappy. They had spent the winter preparing extensive field fortifications along the French border, and now they were expected to hold back the advancing *Wehrmacht* from defensive positions that, at best, were rudimentary and, in many cases, non-existent.

At the same time, the divisional and higher commanders were alarmed by news of events further to the south. But, as yet, none of them were aware of the fact that Bock's slowly advancing Army Group was, in fact, 'the matador's cloak' tempting the mass of the

FRANCE AND THE LOW COUNTRIES	
	June 1940
GERMAN ARMY DIVISIONS BY TYPE	
Panzer	10
Infantry (mot)	8
Cavalry	1
Infantry	143
Mountain	4
Security	1
GERMAN ARMY DIVISIONS BY THEATRE	
Germany	11
East	7
West	142
Norway	7

INFANTRY BATTALION: 1939–1940

Each infantry battalion consisted of a battalion HQ, a machine gun company (illustrated below) and three rifle companies. Each of the machine gun platoons was equipped with six MGs on sustained fire mounts and a mortar platoon of 30 men with six 81mm (3.2in) mortars. Each of the rifle companies was comprised of an HQ section of 12 men and three rifle platoons (see table on page 26). Support elements within each company consisted of a heavy weapons platoon with an HQ section of four men, a mortar section of nine men equipped with three 50mm (2in) mortars, and an MG section with 12 men, equipped with three MGs on mounts.

Battalion Headquarters (5 officers, 15 men)

Communications Platoon (19 men)

Battalion Supply Train (2 officers, 32 men)

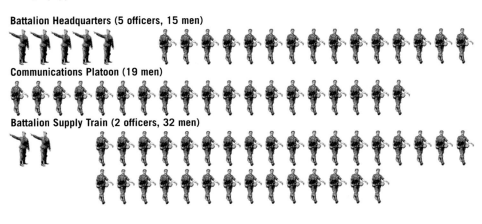

Machine Gun Company, Company HQ (1 officer, 20 men)

Company Train (14 men)

Mortar Platoon (1 officer, 30 men)

Machine Gun Platoon (1 officer, 36 men)

Machine Gun Platoon (1 officer, 36 men)

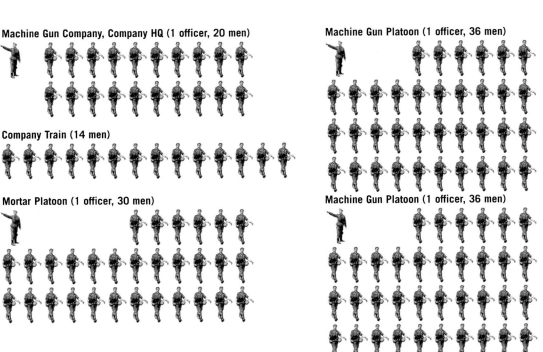

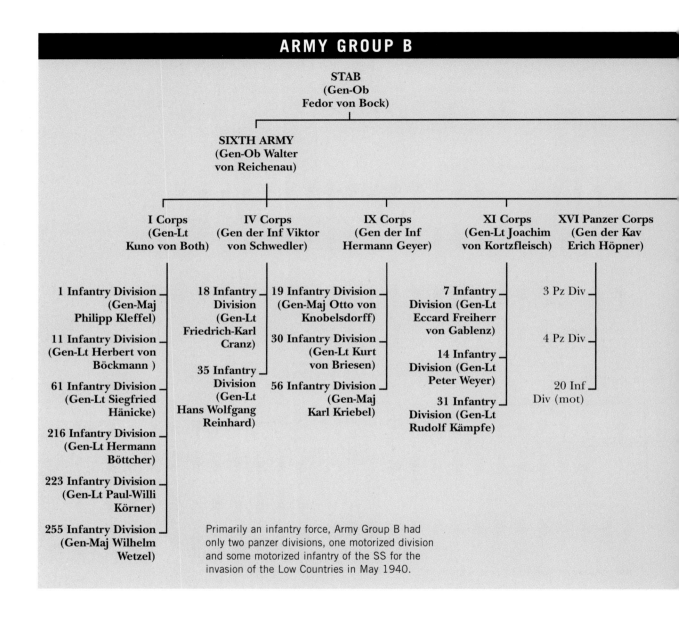

ARMY GROUP B

STAB
(Gen-Ob
Fedor von Bock)

SIXTH ARMY
(Gen-Ob Walter
von Reichenau)

I Corps (Gen-Lt Kuno von Both)	IV Corps (Gen der Inf Viktor von Schwedler)	IX Corps (Gen der Inf Hermann Geyer)	XI Corps (Gen-Lt Joachim von Kortzfleisch)	XVI Panzer Corps (Gen der Kav Erich Höpner)
1 Infantry Division (Gen-Maj Philipp Kleffel)	18 Infantry Division (Gen-Lt Friedrich-Karl Cranz)	19 Infantry Division (Gen-Maj Otto von Knobelsdorff)	7 Infantry Division (Gen-Lt Eccard Freiherr von Gablenz)	3 Pz Div
11 Infantry Division (Gen-Lt Herbert von Böckmann)	35 Infantry Division (Gen-Lt Hans Wolfgang Reinhard)	30 Infantry Division (Gen-Lt Kurt von Briesen)	14 Infantry Division (Gen-Lt Peter Weyer)	4 Pz Div
61 Infantry Division (Gen-Lt Siegfried Hänicke)		56 Infantry Division (Gen-Maj Karl Kriebel)	31 Infantry Division (Gen-Lt Rudolf Kämpfe)	20 Inf Div (mot)
216 Infantry Division (Gen-Lt Hermann Böttcher)				
223 Infantry Division (Gen-Lt Paul-Willi Körner)				
255 Infantry Division (Gen-Maj Wilhelm Wetzel)				

Primarily an infantry force, Army Group B had only two panzer divisions, one motorized division and some motorized infantry of the SS for the invasion of the Low Countries in May 1940.

Allied armies forward into the trap that would release Kleist's Panzer Group for the killing thrust.

After sucking the Allied mobile forces northwards, Bock was tasked with securing Holland before moving southwards into Belgium and France. The first task for the Germans was to take key fortifications around which the Dutch and Belgian defences were based. The imposing concrete and steel fortress at Eben Emael had already fallen to a glider assault. Other paratroopers were needed to secure the bridges that made it possible to operate across Holland's vast canal network, before driving for the major Dutch cities near the coast.

By 13 May, the German Eighteenth Army under General Georg von Küchler was pushing into 'Fortress Holland', crossing bridges seized by paratroopers in the previous days. Near Breda, they encountered the French

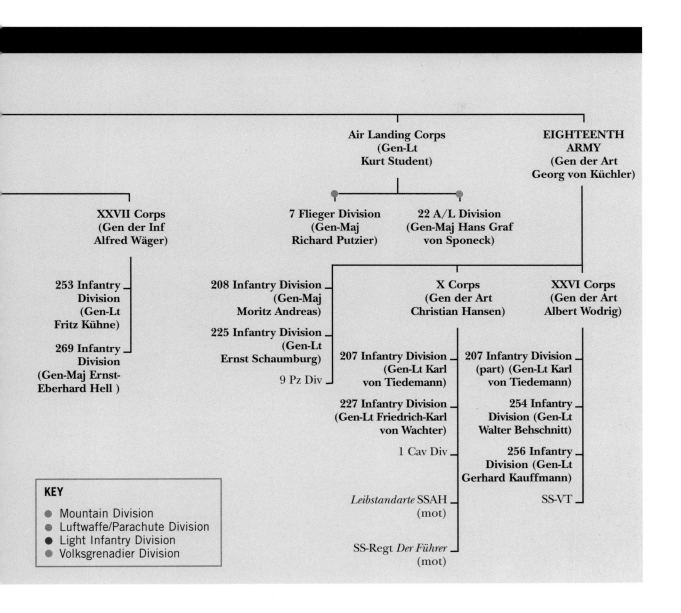

Air Landing Corps
(Gen-Lt
Kurt Student)

EIGHTEENTH
ARMY
(Gen der Art
Georg von Küchler)

XXVII Corps
(Gen der Inf
Alfred Wäger)

7 Flieger Division
(Gen-Maj
Richard Putzier)

22 A/L Division
(Gen-Maj Hans Graf
von Sponeck)

253 Infantry
Division
(Gen-Lt
Fritz Kühne)

269 Infantry
Division
(Gen-Maj Ernst-
Eberhard Hell)

208 Infantry Division
(Gen-Maj
Moritz Andreas)

225 Infantry Division
(Gen-Lt
Ernst Schaumburg)

9 Pz Div

X Corps
(Gen der Art
Christian Hansen)

XXVI Corps
(Gen der Art
Albert Wodrig)

207 Infantry Division
(Gen-Lt Karl
von Tiedemann)

207 Infantry Division
(part) (Gen-Lt Karl
von Tiedemann)

227 Infantry Division
(Gen-Lt Friedrich-Karl
von Wachter)

254 Infantry
Division (Gen-Lt
Walter Behschnitt)

1 Cav Div

256 Infantry
Division (Gen-Lt
Gerhard Kauffmann)

Leibstandarte SSAH
(mot)

SS-VT

SS-Regt *Der Führer*
(mot)

KEY
- Mountain Division
- Luftwaffe/Parachute Division
- Light Infantry Division
- Volksgrenadier Division

Seventh Army under Henri Giraud, which had moved along the coast through Belgium and into Holland.

The Dutch destruction of the key bridges across the Ijssel and the flooding of much of the countryside meant that the German push towards Amsterdam, which was spearheaded by the *Leibstandarte SS,* was slowed considerably. Since Hitler did not want his 'show troops' to get bogged down in an infantry slogging match, they

were moved south on 13 May to join with the SS-VT regiments and the 9th Panzer Division in the drive on Rotterdam. German *Fallschirmjäger* had already captured the key Moerdijk bridges intact, and the way into the city was open. On the morning of the 14th, the SS men accompanying the panzers relieved the lightly armed paratroopers holding the Moerdijk bridge. Dutch resistance, though patchy, was holding up the German

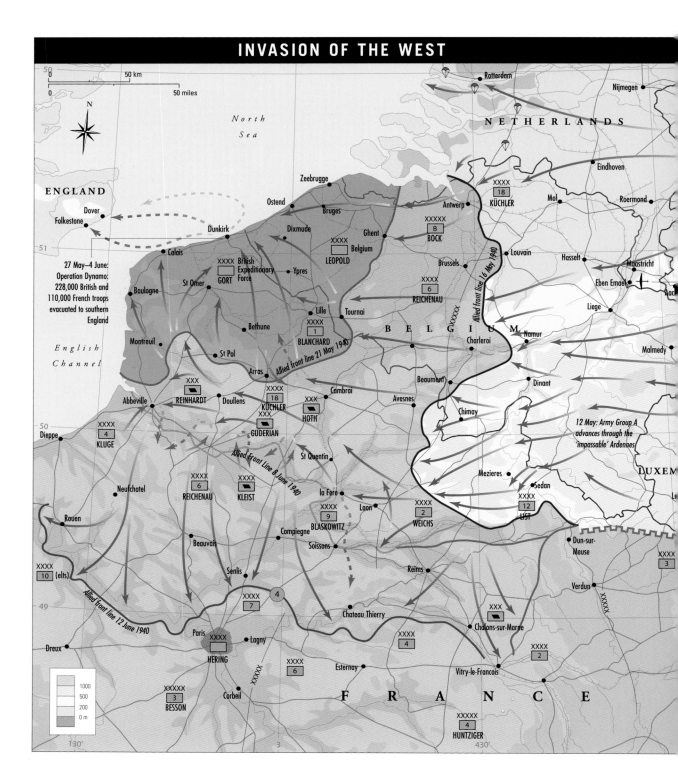

INVASION OF THE WEST

27 May–4 June:
Operation Dynamo:
228,000 British and
110,000 French troops
evacuated to southern
England

12 May: Army Group A
advances through the
'impassable' Ardennes

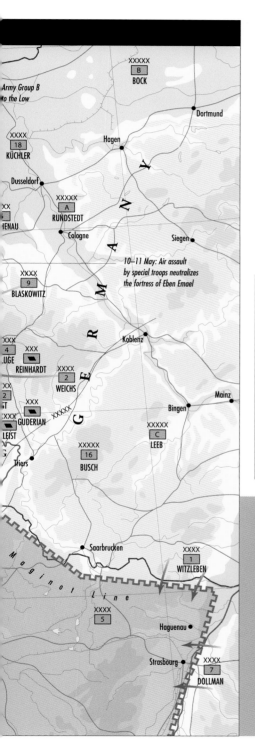

Invasion of the West
May–June 1940

→ German attacks

→ Allied counterattacks

▪ ▪ ▶ Allied retreats

⌣ Allied front lines

⊓⊔ Allied defensive lines

⊽ German paratroop drops

✛ German glider assault

timetable. The German high command issued an ultimatum, threatening to destroy Rotterdam by artillery and air bombardment unless Dutch resistance ceased. The Dutch, cut off from their British and French allies, had no choice but to comply.

Belgium under pressure

Further south, von Reichenau's Sixth Army poured across the Albert Canal into Belgium. The Belgian army fell back to the line of the River Dyle, where it was joined by elements of the British Expeditionary Force and by General Georges Blanchard's First French Army. By 15 May, some 35 Allied divisions were concentrated between Namur and Antwerp. The German Sixth Army was probing their hastily built defences, while the Eighteenth Army was pushing southwards out of Holland and threatening to take the Allied force in the flank. However, even as they prepared to take on Bock's armies, the Allies were hit by shocking news from the southeast. The French centre had been shattered by new German forces, and all of the Allied troops in Belgium were in danger of being cut off. The German plan was, with a few minor exceptions, working as predicted.

May–June 1940

After brushing aside the weak French resistance on the Meuse, Rundstedt's Army Group A, spearheaded by Guderian's panzer corps, broke out into the French countryside beyond. Instead of driving towards Paris, the panzers raced to the northwest, towards the Channel.

The French lacked the reserves to be able to react to the German challenge. A French tank counterattack on 17 May, led by Colonel Charles de Gaulle, was brushed aside without difficulty by the 1st Panzer Division. A British attack near Arras was much more threatening, and was held off only when General Erwin Rommel of the 7th Panzer Division used his 8.8cm Flak guns in the anti-tank role.

The attacks came too late: Guderian's panzers had already reached the Channel coast on the 20 May. The Allied armies were cut off.

Army Group C

The German invasion of 1940 was designed to bypass and isolate France's powerful Maginot Line. Army Group C, the smallest of the German Army Groups, was primarily a decoy force intended to divert the large French forces garrisoning the line.

During the advance to the English Channel, the Germans overran France's border defence with Belgium and captured several Maginot Forts in the Maubeuge area. A few of the weaker, unconnected forts known as *petits ouvrages,* which were little more than glorified blockhouses, were attacked and a number were taken. The story would be far different against the much more powerful *gros ouvrages,* or great fortifications, which formed the real strength of the Line.

On 19 May, the German Sixteenth Army successfully captured the *petit ouvrage* La Ferte, southeast of Sedan, after conducting a deliberate assault by combat engineers backed up by heavy artillery. The entire French crew of 107 soldiers were killed in the action.

Attacking the Line

On 14 June 1940, the day Paris fell, Army Group C went over to the offensive. Launching Operation Tiger, partly

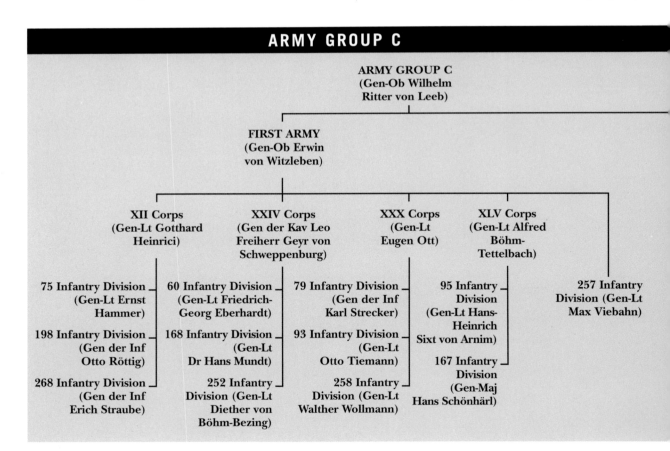

ARMY GROUP C

ARMY GROUP C
(Gen-Ob Wilhelm Ritter von Leeb)

FIRST ARMY
(Gen-Ob Erwin von Witzleben)

XII Corps
(Gen-Lt Gotthard Heinrici)

XXIV Corps
(Gen der Kav Leo Freiherr Geyr von Schweppenburg)

XXX Corps
(Gen-Lt Eugen Ott)

XLV Corps
(Gen-Lt Alfred Böhm-Tettelbach)

75 Infantry Division (Gen-Lt Ernst Hammer)

198 Infantry Division (Gen der Inf Otto Röttig)

268 Infantry Division (Gen der Inf Erich Straube)

60 Infantry Division (Gen-Lt Friedrich-Georg Eberhardt)

168 Infantry Division (Gen-Lt Dr Hans Mundt)

252 Infantry Division (Gen-Lt Diether von Böhm-Bezing)

79 Infantry Division (Gen der Inf Karl Strecker)

93 Infantry Division (Gen-Lt Otto Tiemann)

258 Infantry Division (Gen-Lt Walther Wollmann)

95 Infantry Division (Gen-Lt Hans-Heinrich Sixt von Arnim)

167 Infantry Division (Gen-Maj Hans Schönhärl)

257 Infantry Division (Gen-Lt Max Viebahn)

at the *Führer's* direct instigation, the German First Army attacked the Maginot Line between St. Avoid and Saarbrücken.

After hard fighting, the Germans broke through the fortification line as defending French forces retreated southward. In the following days, infantry divisions of the First Army attacked fortifications on each side of the penetration; successfully capturing four *petits ouvrages*.

The First Army also conducted two attacks against the Maginot Line further to the east in northern Alsace. One attack broke through a weak section of the Line in the Vosges Mountains, but a second attack was stopped by the French defenders near Wissembourg.

On 15 June, infantry divisions of the German Seventh Army attacked across the Rhine River in Operation Small Bear, penetrating the defences and capturing the cities of Colmar and Strasbourg.

By early June, the German forces had cut off the Line from the rest of France and the French government was making overtures for an armistice, which was signed on June 22 in Compiègne. As the Line was surrounded, the German Army attacked a few *ouvrages* from the rear, but were unsuccessful in capturing any significant fortifications.

Anti-fortification tactics

The *Wehrmacht* employed a three-prong strategy. Firstly, to weaken the forts' defensive capability through concentrated heavy artillery and bombing. Then to move in close and blind the defenders, mainly by destroying apertures with direct fire from high velocity 8.8-cm flak guns.

Finally, the fortification was to be taken by a direct combined arms assault. Every time they attacked one of

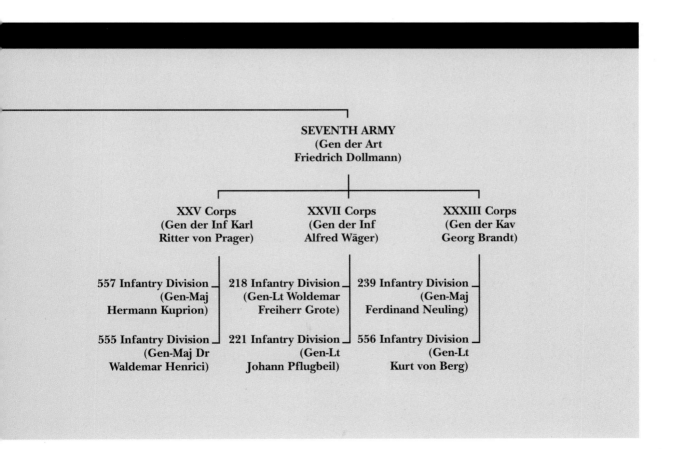

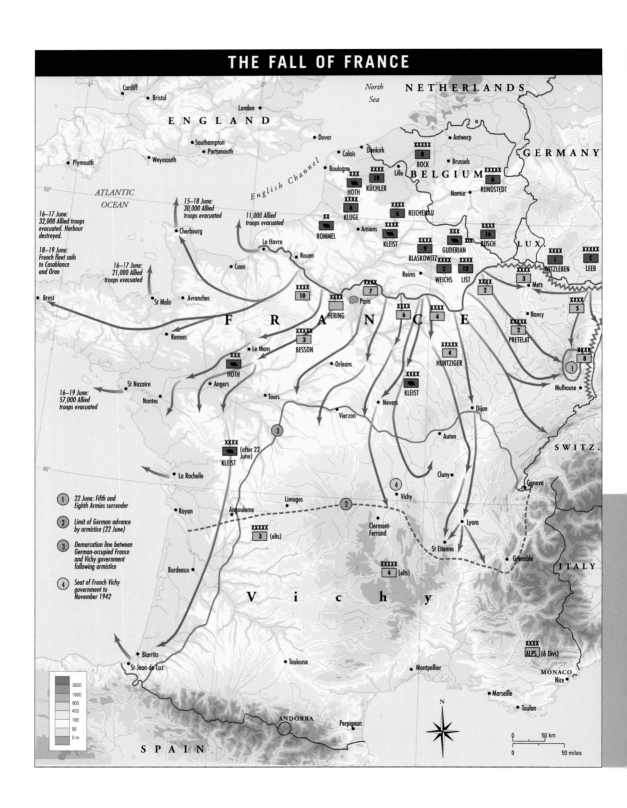

THE FALL OF FRANCE

ENGLAND

NETHERLANDS

GERMANY

Cardiff
Bristol
London
Dover
Southampton
Portsmouth
Weymouth
Plymouth

North Sea

Antwerp
Brussels
Calais
Dunkirk
Boulogne
Lille

BELGIUM

Namur

XXXXX
B
BOCK

XXXXX
A
RUNDSTEDT

English Channel

XXX
18
KÜCHLER

XXXX
HOTH

XXXX
4
KLUGE

XXXX
6
REICHENAU

LUX

XXXX
WITZLEBEN

XXXXX
C
LEEB

*ATLANTIC
OCEAN*

15–18 June:
30,000 Allied
troops evacuated

11,000 Allied
troops evacuated

16–17 June:
32,000 Allied troops
evacuated. Harbour
destroyed.

18–19 June:
French fleet sails
to Casablanca
and Oran

Cherbourg

Le Havre

Rouen

Amiens

Reims

Metz

Nancy

16–17 June:
21,000 Allied
troops evacuated

Brest

St Malo

Avranches

Caen

XX
ROMMEL

XXXX
KLEIST

XXXX
9
BLASKOWITZ

XXX
GUDERIAN

XIX

XXXX
16
BUSCH

XXXX
2
WEICHS

XXXX
12
LIST

XXXX
3

XXXX
2

XXXX
5

F R A N C E

XXXX
10

XXXX
HERING

XXXX
7

Paris

XXXX
6

XXXX
4

XXXX
2
PRETELAT

XXXX
8

1

Mulhouse

Rennes

XXXX
3
BESSON

Le Mans

XXXX
HOTH

Angers

Orleans

XXXX
4
HUNTZIGER

XXXX
4
KLEIST

Nancy

Nantes

16–19 June:
57,000 Allied
troops evacuated

St Nazaire

Tours

Nevers

Vierzon

Dijon

SWITZ.

Auton

XXXX (after 22 June)
KLEIST

3

La Rochelle

Cluny

Geneva

4
Vichy

Lyons

ITALY

① 22 June: Fifth and
Eighth Armies surrender

② Limit of German advance
by armistice (22 June)

③ Demarcation line between
German-occupied France
and Vichy government
following armistice

④ Seat of French Vichy
government to
November 1942

Royan

Angouleme

Limoges

2

Clermont-
Ferrand

St Etienne

Grenoble

XXXXX
3 (elts)

XXXXX
4 (elts)

Bordeaux

V i c h y

XXXX
ALPS (6 Divs)

Biarritz
St-Jean-de-Luz

Toulouse

Montpellier

MONACO
Nice

Marseille

Toulon

SPAIN

ANDORRA

Perpignan

N

3600
1800
900
450
180
90
0 m

0   50 km
0   50 miles

the *gros ouvages*, the German assaults failed. Despite the employment of large numbers of heavy weapons, the Maginot forts went unscathed.

Intense barrages by siege cannon did no damage – nor did Stukas accurately placing 907kg (2000lb) armour-piercing bombs. The German assault teams were unable to get close. The French pounded their every move with accurate deadly barrages.

Fruitless attacks

Even as France fell to the triumphant *Wehrmacht*, the main fortifications of the Maginot Line were still mostly intact and fully manned.

A number of the commanders on the spot wanted to continue the fight. At Simserhof, soldiers from the German 257th Division tried and failed to get close to the fort. Every German move was targetted by accurate artillery: the Division was struck by as many as 15,000 artillery shells in a matter of days. Any vehicle trying to get close to the fort was destroyed. Elsewhere, the complex of forts at the Ensemble de Bitche lay within supporting cannon fire of the other and all German attacks were beaten off.

Although undefeated, the rest of France had fallen, and the Maginot line eventually surrendered to Army Group C.

June 1940

After a pause for reorganization, the Germans launched their assault on the rest of France on 5 June. As the panzers cut deeper and deeper into the heart of France, French morale plummeted and the French army moved ever closer to disintegration.

Resistance was light, though on occasion diehard French troops put up a stiff fight. The Germany infantrymen had to clear towns and villages street by street. More often than not, however, the ordinary French soldiers surrendered.

By 20 June, German troops were in Lyons and Grenoble in the south, along the Swiss border to the east and controlling much of the Biscay coast to the west. In just three weeks, they had forced the French government to sue for an armistice.

FEDOR VON BOCK (1880–1945)

Born into a Prussian aristocratic family, Fedor von Bock joined the Imperial Foot Guards in 1898 and was awarded the *Pour le Merite* during World War I.

• Bock commanded the the troops who occupied Vienna in March 1938 during the *Anschluss* and commanded an army in the invasion of Czechoslovakia.

• He commanded Army Group North during the Invasion of Poland in 1939 and Army Group B during the Invasion of France in 1940.

• He was promoted to Field Marshal in July 1940.

• Commander of Army Group Centre during Operation *Barbarossa*, he was dismissed by Hitler from his final command, Army Group South, in 1942.

He died with his wife and daughter on 4 May 1945, when his car was strafed near Kiel by an RAF fighter.

The Balkans and Crete: 1941–45

The last thing that Hitler wanted in the spring of 1941 was war in the Balkans, with the invasion of the Soviet Union about to be launched. His fellow dictator Mussolini was in trouble, however, and German troops and aircraft were needed to prevent catastrophe.

German infantrymen march through a town in central Greece, April 1941. Although panzers featured largely in the initial attack, it was the infantry that had to take and hold the country in the face of an increasingly determined partisan campaign.

M uch of the blame for the Balkans war was Mussolini's. The Italian leader had originally been the dominant figure in European fascism. However, as the Nazis consolidated their grip on Germany, he was rapidly being surpassed by his German rival.

Jealous of Hitler's military triumphs, which confirmed Germany as the senior partner in the Axis alliance, Il Duce resolved to carve out his own place in the sun. Past military adventures had been restricted to targets unable to resist and with no friends to intervene. Libya, Abyssinia and Albania were incorporated into his latter-day Roman Empire. This was achieved at only the minor cost of international censure from the toothless League of Nations. Mussolini waited until the defeat of France was certain before declaring war, but unlike the triumphant *Wehrmacht,* the Italian Army suffered a humiliating setback as the French held the invaders back in the south of the country.

Italian blunder

On 28 October 1940, Italy invaded Greece. Unfortunately for Mussolini, the Greek army was a different prospect from the ill-equipped African tribesmen that his armies had defeated in the 1930s. Not only did the Italian invasion break down that winter; a Greek counteroffensive in December drove the invaders back into Albania and back another 80km (50 miles) for good measure. Mussolini's invasion of Greece infuriated Hitler.

The German dictator was annoyed with the blatant disregard of his stated opinions on the subject, and with its effect upon his own long-term plans. It soon became obvious that Hitler could not leave Mussolini's chestnuts merrily blazing in the fire. And pulling them out would necessarily be a military, not a political, matter.

Hitler had already laid plans for a drive down through Bulgaria to occupy the northeast coast of the Aegean. This was intended to secure the southern flank of his planned onslaught on the Soviet Union. The operation, codenamed 'Marita', also made provision for dealing with Greek resistance.

If the government in Athens could not be persuaded to accept German occupation of the north of the country, the operation also included plans for the conquest of the whole of mainland Greece, should such a move become necessary.

Hitler had already got the cooperation of Hungary, Romania and Bulgaria, which were to the north and east of Greece, but Yugoslavia lay in the path of German forces. Yugoslavia in the 1930s was governed by a royal dictatorship led by the regent Prince Paul. Yugoslavia had been created out of parts of the Ottoman and Austro-Hungarian empires after World War I, but early friendship with the Western powers gradually changed as the country began to drift into the Fascist camp. Following agreements with Hungary, Romania and Bulgaria that they would join the Axis, Hitler put pressure on Yugoslavia to join the Tripartite Pact.

The Regent, Prince Paul of Yugoslavia, succumbed to this pressure on 25 March 1941. However, this move, while popular in some parts of the country, was deeply unpopular amongst the dominant Serbian public and the military. A coup d'état was launched on 27 March, and King Peter II of Yugoslavia was placed on the throne to replace Prince Paul. Hitler was enraged at the Yugoslav action, and decided that they needed to be punished for their defiance. This took the form of a sudden invasion by German, Italian, Hungarian and Bulgarian forces in April.

GERMAN FORCES: THE BALKANS	
	April 1941
GERMAN ARMY DIVISIONS BY TYPE	
Panzer	21
Infantry (mot)	15
Cavalry	1
Infantry	147
Mountain	6
Security	8
GERMAN ARMY DIVISIONS BY THEATRE	
Germany	62
East	46
West	53
Norway	7
Finland	1
Balkans	28

Invasions of the Balkans

The *Wehrmacht* had been funnelling troops into Hungary and Romania – allied to Germany by treaty – since the autumn of 1940. By February 1941, more than 650,000 were in place, primarily to secure the southern flank of the invasion of the USSR.

On 6 April 1941, Axis armies invaded from all sides and the *Luftwaffe* bombed Belgrade. The German Second Army drove southwards from Austria and southwestern Hungary. The advance was coordinated with the other divisions attacking the Yugoslav capital.

A second force, detached from Twelfth Army, advanced towards Belgrade from western Bulgaria, taking the capital, and securing the Danube for river traffic. A third force thrust from southwestern Bulgaria in the direction of Skopje in an effort to cut off the Yugoslav Army from the Greek and British forces, while at the same time easing the Italian position in Albania.

Finally, other elements of Twelfth Army, ready to invade Greece from Bulgarian bases, passed through the southern tip of Yugoslavia, outflanking the main Greek fortified positions.

Fall of the Balkans

Yugoslav resistance quickly collapsed. The Greeks, reinforced by British, Australian and New Zealand forces, did not last much longer. German soldiers raised the swastika flag over the famous Acropolis in Athens on 27 April. Greek, British and British Commonwealth soldiers who escaped from Greece moved to the nearby island of Crete, where they were joined by fresh New Zealand, British and Australian forces.

Hitler's men hit them hard with a new form of German *blitzkrieg* warfare, the first major airborne assault ever attempted. General Kurt Student's parachutists landed on 20 May, followed by air-landing troops delivered by Ju 52 transports. Although the Germans suffered many losses, they had driven Allied forces out of Crete by the end of the month.

6–28 April 1941

When it became necessary to take action against the Greeks, who were putting up a stiff fight against the Italians, Hitler bullied the Bulgarians and Yugoslavs into signing the Tripartite Pact. After the lightning victory in Yugoslavia, the Germans moved on to Greece when *Generalfeldmarschall* List's Twelfth Army crossed the borders.

The Germans attacked the Metaxas line from Bulgaria, while mobile troops pressed southwards through Yugoslavia. The Greeks could do nothing to stop the Germans, and their British allies were forced to evacuate what forces they could to Crete.

A month later, the Germans mounted the world's first full-scale airborne assault and captured the island, suffering heavy casualties in the process.

INVASION OF CRETE (MAY 1941)

Fliegerkorps XI
(Gen der Flieger
Kurt Student)

7 Flieger Division	**5 Gerbirgs Division**	**22 Luftlande Division**
(Gen-Lt Willhelm Süssman)	**(Gen-Maj Julius Ringel)**	**(General Hans Graf von Sponeck)**

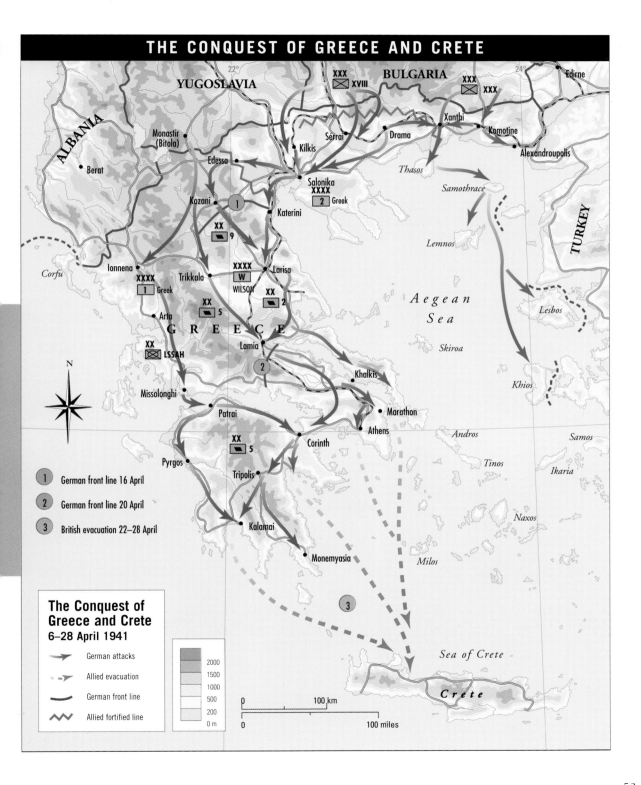

THE CONQUEST OF GREECE AND CRETE

YUGOSLAVIA

BULGARIA

ALBANIA

Berat

Monastir (Bitola)

Edessa

Kozani

Katerini

Salonika
XXXX
2 Greek

Kilkis

Serrai

Drama

Xanthi

Komotine

Alexandroupolis

Edirne

Thasos

Samothrace

TURKEY

Lemnos

Ionnena

Corfu

Trikkala

XXXX
1 Greek

Arta

XX
LSSAH

G R E E C E

Larisa

XXXX
W
WILSON

XX
2

XX
5

Lamia

XX
9

Khalkis

Marathon

Athens

Aegean Sea

Skiroa

Khios

Lesbos

Missolonghi

Patrai

Corinth

XX
5

Tripolis

Pyrgos

Kalamai

Monemvasia

Andros

Samos

Tinos

Ikaria

Naxos

Milos

Sea of Crete

C r e t e

(1) German front line 16 April

(2) German front line 20 April

(3) British evacuation 22–28 April

The Conquest of Greece and Crete
6–28 April 1941

➤ German attacks

- -▶ Allied evacuation

— German front line

⌃⌃⌃ Allied fortified line

N

0   100 km

0   100 miles

2000
1500
1000
500
200
0 m

BALKANS INVASION FORCE (APRIL 1941)

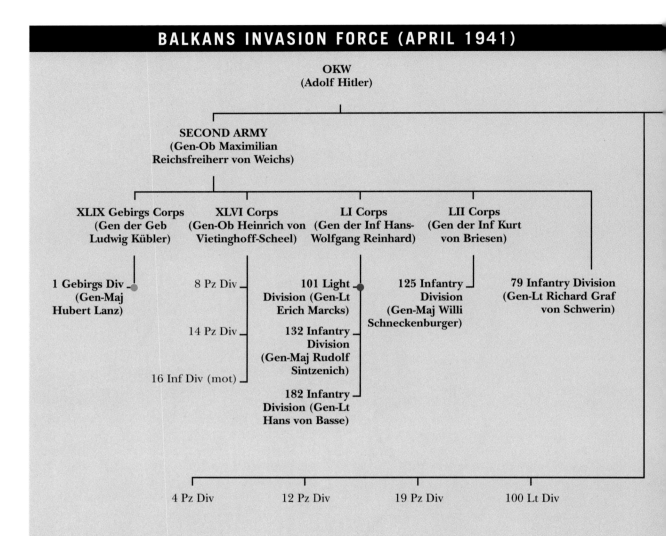

OKW
(Adolf Hitler)

SECOND ARMY
(Gen-Ob Maximilian
Reichsfreiherr von Weichs)

XLIX Gebirgs Corps
(Gen der Geb
Ludwig Kübler)

XLVI Corps
(Gen-Ob Heinrich von
Vietinghoff-Scheel)

LI Corps
(Gen der Inf Hans-
Wolfgang Reinhard)

LII Corps
(Gen der Inf Kurt
von Briesen)

1 Gebirgs Div
(Gen-Maj
Hubert Lanz)

8 Pz Div

101 Light
Division (Gen-Lt
Erich Marcks)

125 Infantry
Division
(Gen-Maj Willi
Schneckenburger)

79 Infantry Division
(Gen-Lt Richard Graf
von Schwerin)

14 Pz Div

132 Infantry
Division
(Gen-Maj Rudolf
Sintzenich)

16 Inf Div (mot)

182 Infantry
Division (Gen-Lt
Hans von Basse)

4 Pz Div

12 Pz Div

19 Pz Div

100 Lt Div

Two army commands were assigned to the conquest of the Balkans.
Twelfth Army was already poised to invade Greece from Bulgarian bases,
a campaign planned to secure the southern flank of the forthcoming
invasion of the Soviet Union. Second Army, which had returned from
France to the Reich to prepare for the attack on the Soviet Union, was
diverted to take part in the invasion of Yugoslavia. As a result, it did not
take part in the opening stages of Operation *Barbarossa*, but eventually
joined Army Group Centre in July.

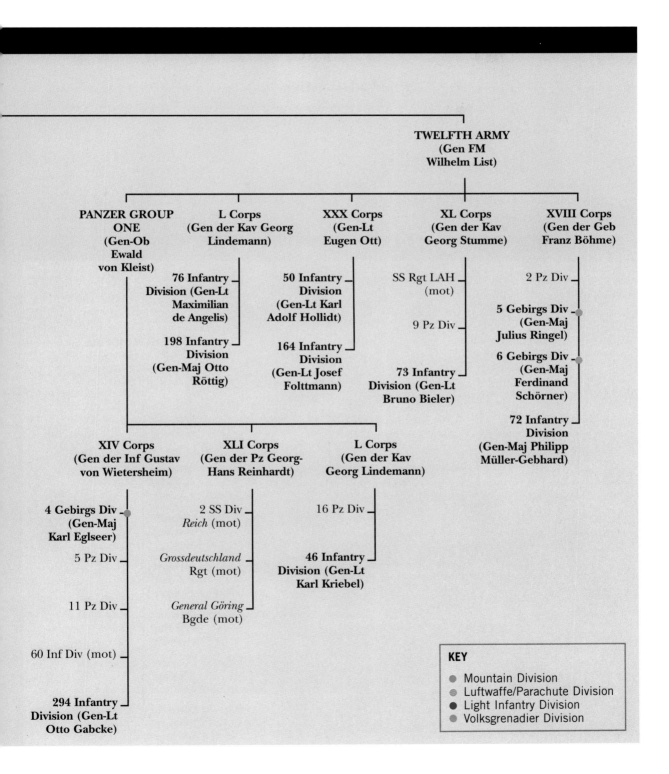

TWELFTH ARMY
(Gen FM
Wilhelm List)

PANZER GROUP
ONE
(Gen-Ob
Ewald
von Kleist)

L Corps
(Gen der Kav Georg
Lindemann)

XXX Corps
(Gen-Lt
Eugen Ott)

XL Corps
(Gen der Kav
Georg Stumme)

XVIII Corps
(Gen der Geb
Franz Böhme)

76 Infantry
Division (Gen-Lt
Maximilian
de Angelis)

50 Infantry
Division
(Gen-Lt Karl
Adolf Hollidt)

SS Rgt LAH
(mot)

2 Pz Div

9 Pz Div

5 Gebirgs Div
(Gen-Maj
Julius Ringel)

198 Infantry
Division
(Gen-Maj Otto
Röttig)

164 Infantry
Division
(Gen-Lt Josef
Folttmann)

73 Infantry
Division (Gen-Lt
Bruno Bieler)

6 Gebirgs Div
(Gen-Maj
Ferdinand
Schörner)

72 Infantry
Division
(Gen-Maj Philipp
Müller-Gebhard)

XIV Corps
(Gen der Inf Gustav
von Wietersheim)

XLI Corps
(Gen der Pz Georg-
Hans Reinhardt)

L Corps
(Gen der Kav
Georg Lindemann)

4 Gebirgs Div
(Gen-Maj
Karl Eglseer)

2 SS Div
Reich (mot)

16 Pz Div

5 Pz Div

Grossdeutschland
Rgt (mot)

46 Infantry
Division (Gen-Lt
Karl Kriebel)

11 Pz Div

General Göring
Bgde (mot)

60 Inf Div (mot)

294 Infantry
Division (Gen-Lt
Otto Gabcke)

KEY
- Mountain Division
- Luftwaffe/Parachute Division
- Light Infantry Division
- Volksgrenadier Division

Fighting the Partisans: 1941–43

If Spain was like a bleeding ulcer for Napoleon, the same was true of Yugoslavia for Hitler. Although the country was conquered very quickly, a fierce partisan war erupted and tied down, by some estimates, as many as 35 German divisions needed elsewhere.

The invasion of Yugoslavia began on 6 April 1941 and ended with the occupation and dismemberment of the country by the Axis powers. In Bosnia and Herzegovina, parts of Croatia and Syrmia, the puppet 'Independent State of Croatia' was set up by Germany and Italy; in Serbia and the Banat (the region of northen Yugoslavia

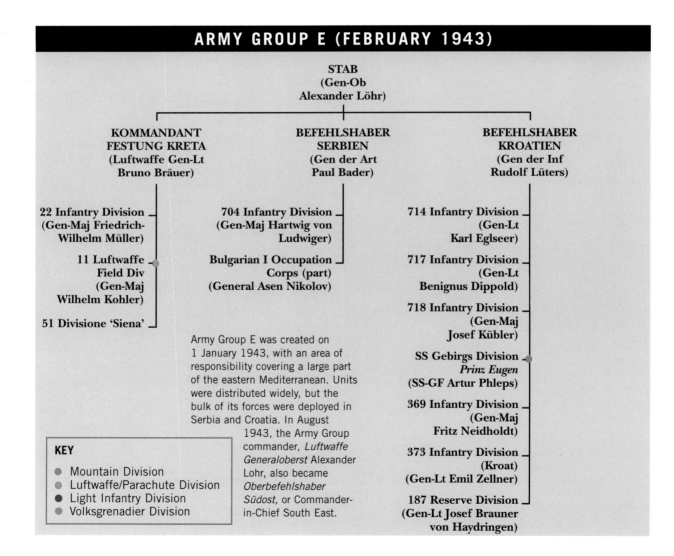

ARMY GROUP E (FEBRUARY 1943)

STAB
(Gen-Ob
Alexander Löhr)

KOMMANDANT FESTUNG KRETA
(Luftwaffe Gen-Lt
Bruno Bräuer)

BEFEHLSHABER SERBIEN
(Gen der Art
Paul Bader)

BEFEHLSHABER KROATIEN
(Gen der Inf
Rudolf Lüters)

22 Infantry Division
(Gen-Maj Friedrich-
Wilhelm Müller)

11 Luftwaffe Field Div
(Gen-Maj
Wilhelm Kohler)

51 Divisione 'Siena'

704 Infantry Division
(Gen-Maj Hartwig von
Ludwiger)

Bulgarian I Occupation Corps (part)
(General Asen Nikolov)

714 Infantry Division
(Gen-Lt
Karl Eglseer)

717 Infantry Division
(Gen-Lt
Benignus Dippold)

718 Infantry Division
(Gen-Maj
Josef Kübler)

SS Gebirgs Division Prinz Eugen
(SS-GF Artur Phleps)

369 Infantry Division
(Gen-Maj
Fritz Neidholdt)

373 Infantry Division (Kroat)
(Gen-Lt Emil Zellner)

187 Reserve Division
(Gen-Lt Josef Brauner
von Haydringen)

Army Group E was created on 1 January 1943, with an area of responsibility covering a large part of the eastern Mediterranean. Units were distributed widely, but the bulk of its forces were deployed in Serbia and Croatia. In August 1943, the Army Group commander, *Luftwaffe Generaloberst* Alexander Lohr, also became *Oberbefehlshaber Südost*, or Commander-in-Chief South East.

KEY
- Mountain Division
- Luftwaffe/Parachute Division
- Light Infantry Division
- Volksgrenadier Division

bordering on Hungary), a puppet Serbian state was also set up by Germany; in Montenegro, the Italians established the puppet Independent State of Montenegro.

Resistance groups form

After the Yugoslav government requested an armistice on 14 April, two separate groups of Serbs scattered into the rugged, mountainous terrain, refusing to accept the German conquest. Some, loyal to the monarchy, were led by former Yugoslav general Draza Mihailovich. The other main resistance force were the Communists, who were dominated by the Croat Josip Broz, the guerrilla leader known as 'Tito'. The stage was set for an internecine war that was to reverberate at the end of the twentieth century.

The German occupation of Yugoslavia opened a vicious can of worms. In general, the Croats supported the Germans. Indeed, Croatian Ustase fascists conducted a genocidal campaign against the Serbs in Croatia and Bosnia.

Some Serbs, led by local quisling General Nedic, also supported the Germans. The pro-royalist fragments of the army and gendarmerie led by Mihailovich adopted the Serbian name of Chetnik, from *ceta*, or regiment.

Internecine war

But the Chetniks were also deadly foes of the Partisans – the communist rebels led by Tito. The Chetniks offered to come over to the German side to fight the Communists – while continuing to fight the Croatian fascists, who were being supplied by the Germans. Internal rivalries were often more important than resisting the invaders. Serb fought Croat, Chetnik fought Partisan, and Muslims, Catholics and Orthodox killed each other with unbridled enthusiasm. Similar diverse partisan movements were also rising in Greece.

Throughout the remainder of the war, active Greek and Yugoslav resistance movements forced Germany and her allies to garrison hundreds of thousands of soldiers permanently in the two countries, denying them to the other fronts.

Especially after 1943, the threat of an Allied invasion and the activities of the partisans necessitated large-scale counterinsurgency operations, involving several divisions,

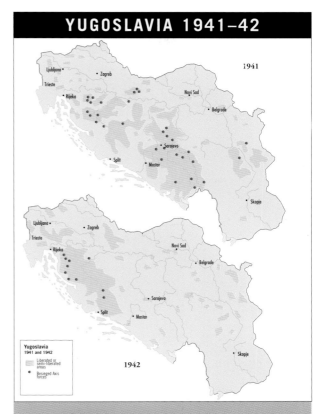

YUGOSLAVIA 1941–42

Yugoslavia 1941 and 1942
▨ Liberated or semi-liberated areas
● Besieged Axis forces

Partisan control

Axis power ran little beyond the towns and main roads. The remote mountain regions were held by the resistance forces, which soon emerged. Before the Germans could crush these movements in their earliest and most vulnerable days in 1941, their forces were redeployed from Yugoslavia to eastern Europe, in preparation for Operation *Barbarossa*.

Whenever the Partisans established control of an area within occupied Yugoslavia, they forged a disciplined Communist mini-state. Tito's first 'liberated base area' was known as the Uzice Republic. It was located in western Serbia, just 40km (25 miles) south of the Chetnik stronghold of Ravna Gora.

Early in 1942, the growing Partisan threat, and the inability of the *Wehrmacht* garrison to deal with it, led Himmler to raise a division specifically to help in the anti-partisan effort. The 7th SS Mountain Division *Prinz Eugen* was mobilized in Serbia in March 1942, recruited mainly from so-called ethnic Germans (*Volksdeutsche*) from southeastern Europe.

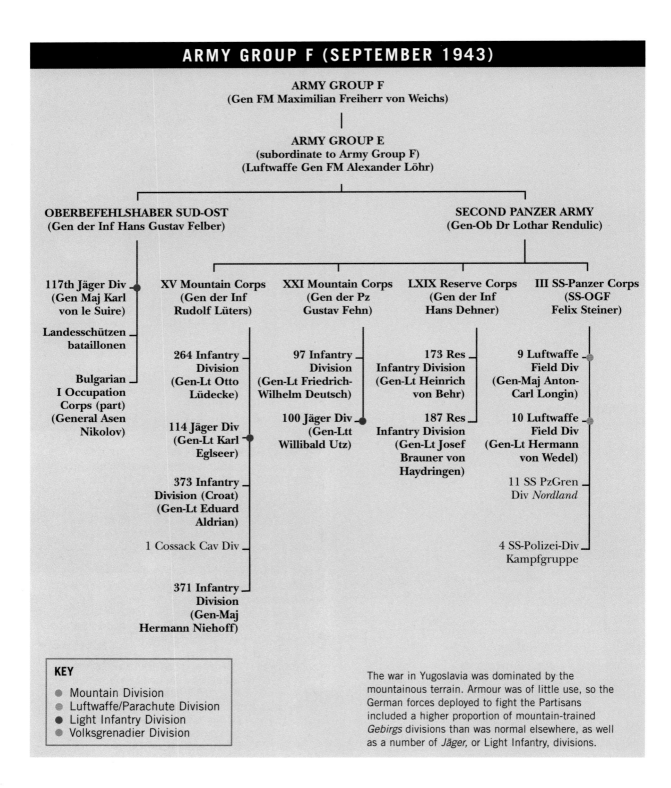

ARMY GROUP F (SEPTEMBER 1943)

ARMY GROUP F
(Gen FM Maximilian Freiherr von Weichs)

ARMY GROUP E
(subordinate to Army Group F)
(Luftwaffe Gen FM Alexander Löhr)

OBERBEFEHLSHABER SUD-OST
(Gen der Inf Hans Gustav Felber)

SECOND PANZER ARMY
(Gen-Ob Dr Lothar Rendulic)

117th Jäger Div
(Gen Maj Karl
von le Suire)

Landesschützen
bataillonen

Bulgarian
I Occupation
Corps (part)
(General Asen
Nikolov)

XV Mountain Corps
(Gen der Inf
Rudolf Lüters)

264 Infantry
Division
(Gen-Lt Otto
Lüdecke)

114 Jäger Div
(Gen-Lt Karl
Eglseer)

373 Infantry
Division (Croat)
(Gen-Lt Eduard
Aldrian)

1 Cossack Cav Div

371 Infantry
Division
(Gen-Maj
Hermann Niehoff)

XXI Mountain Corps
(Gen der Pz
Gustav Fehn)

97 Infantry
Division
(Gen-Lt Friedrich-
Wilhelm Deutsch)

100 Jäger Div
(Gen-Ltt
Willibald Utz)

LXIX Reserve Corps
(Gen der Inf
Hans Dehner)

173 Res
Infantry Division
(Gen-Lt Heinrich
von Behr)

187 Res
Infantry Division
(Gen-Lt Josef
Brauner von
Haydringen)

III SS-Panzer Corps
(SS-OGF
Felix Steiner)

9 Luftwaffe
Field Div
(Gen-Maj Anton-
Carl Longin)

10 Luftwaffe
Field Div
(Gen-Lt Hermann
von Wedel)

11 SS PzGren
Div *Nordland*

4 SS-Polizei-Div
Kampfgruppe

KEY
- Mountain Division
- Luftwaffe/Parachute Division
- Light Infantry Division
- Volksgrenadier Division

The war in Yugoslavia was dominated by the mountainous terrain. Armour was of little use, so the German forces deployed to fight the Partisans included a higher proportion of mountain-trained *Gebirgs* divisions than was normal elsewhere, as well as a number of *Jäger*, or Light Infantry, divisions.

YUGOSLAVIA 1943

Yugoslavia
1941–1943

Liberated or
semi-liberated
areas

Besieged Axis
forces

1943

By early 1943, the Germans were having to deploy an increasing number of *Wehrmacht*, *Waffen-SS*, Italian and locally recruited troops simply to establish effective cordons around Partisan bases. In response, the Partisans infiltrated networks of spies into the Italian and locally recruited forces. German commanders then set up special forces units to provide detailed intelligence of Partisan deployments to allow effective offensives to be launched. Even with these innovative tactics, the Germans were unable to contain Tito's Partisans.

including elite Panzer, SS and *Gebirgsjäger* units. Tito's Partisan army won the support of the Western allies in preference to the unreliable Serbian Chetniks since their

actions tied down no less than 35 German divisions. Occupying and quisling forces were quite aware of the Partisan problem, and tried to solve it in seven major anti-Partisan offensives. The biggest, including *Fall Weiss* ('Operation White') and the succeeding *Fall Schwarz*, or 'Operation Black', combined contributions from the *Wehrmacht,* the SS, Fascist Italy, the Croatian Ustase, Serbian Chetniks (fighting on the side of the Germans in this instance) and Bulgarian forces. *Fall Weiss* was supposed to seek out and destroy Tito's Partisans, but although large numbers of bodies were counted, Tito and his command escaped.

Partisan strategy

Partisan strategy often sought to attack the Axis forces in way that was calculated to provoke appalling reprisals – the Germans usually worked on the basis of 100 executions for every German soldier killed by the resistance. This in turn would set the local population against the Germans, thereby promoting the partisan cause. During 1943, the Partisans gained significant ground by spearheading the fight against Axis occupation, while simultaneously paving the way for socialist revolution by crushing the Chetniks.

The continuing failure to catch the Communist leader had become costly. Over the previous three years, the Yugoslav Army of National Liberation (JANL) had grown from a few scattered bands of guerrillas into a major military force that claimed more than 200,000 men and women under arms.

Yugoslavia: 1944–45

As the great Soviet summer offensive of 1944 wound down, another campaign was about to open, with perhaps more political than military motivation. The Balkans were as great an attraction to Stalin as they had been for centuries to the Russian Tsars.

The Yugoslav government-in-exile in London found itself at odds with the Partisans, who formed their own government in November 1943. The Allies were offering their support to Tito, for the pragmatic reason that his

Partisans were the most successful anti-German force in the region.

By the end of August 1944, Romania was in the process of being occupied by the Red Army, which then moved on to Hungary; and Bulgaria was about to be invaded by a Soviet army, which was driving down the Black Sea coast.

In the aftermath of the Red Army's drive, the situation for German forces in the Balkans became precarious. To avoid being cut off in Crete, Greece and Albania, German units began withdrawing northward in the early autumn of 1944. SS and other troops held open the Vardar Corridor, allowing 350,000 troops of Army Group Lohr to escape through Macedonia and Bulgaria.

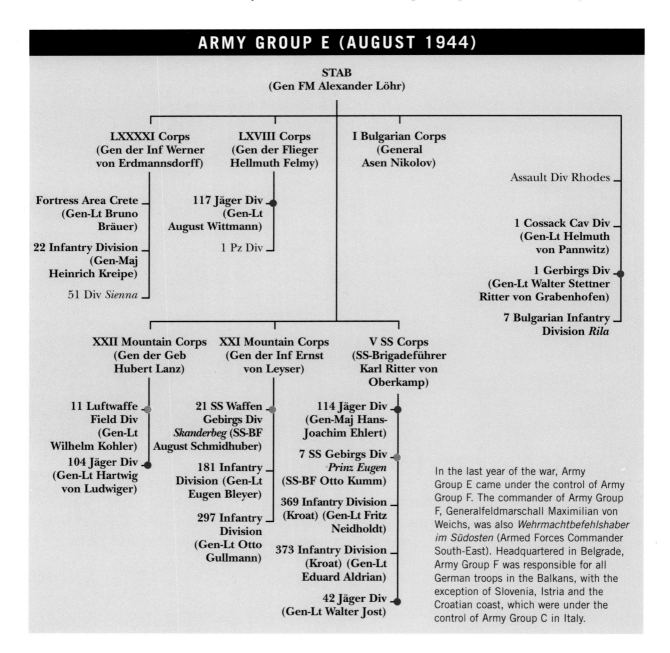

ARMY GROUP E (AUGUST 1944)

STAB
(Gen FM Alexander Löhr)

LXXXXI Corps
(Gen der Inf Werner von Erdmannsdorff)

LXVIII Corps
(Gen der Flieger Hellmuth Felmy)

I Bulgarian Corps
(General Asen Nikolov)

Assault Div Rhodes

Fortress Area Crete
(Gen-Lt Bruno Bräuer)

117 Jäger Div
(Gen-Lt August Wittmann)

1 Cossack Cav Div
(Gen-Lt Helmuth von Pannwitz)

22 Infantry Division
(Gen-Maj Heinrich Kreipe)

1 Pz Div

1 Gerbirgs Div
(Gen-Lt Walter Stettner Ritter von Grabenhofen)

51 Div *Sienna*

7 Bulgarian Infantry Division *Rila*

XXII Mountain Corps
(Gen der Geb Hubert Lanz)

XXI Mountain Corps
(Gen der Inf Ernst von Leyser)

V SS Corps
(SS-Brigadeführer Karl Ritter von Oberkamp)

11 Luftwaffe Field Div
(Gen-Lt Wilhelm Kohler)

21 SS Waffen Gebirgs Div *Skanderbeg* (SS-BF August Schmidhuber)

114 Jäger Div
(Gen-Maj Hans-Joachim Ehlert)

104 Jäger Div
(Gen-Lt Hartwig von Ludwiger)

181 Infantry Division (Gen-Lt Eugen Bleyer)

7 SS Gebirgs Div *Prinz Eugen* (SS-BF Otto Kumm)

297 Infantry Division (Gen-Lt Otto Gullmann)

369 Infantry Division (Kroat) (Gen-Lt Fritz Neidholdt)

373 Infantry Division (Kroat) (Gen-Lt Eduard Aldrian)

42 Jäger Div
(Gen-Lt Walter Jost)

In the last year of the war, Army Group E came under the control of Army Group F. The commander of Army Group F, Generalfeldmarschall Maximilian von Weichs, was also *Wehrmachtbefehlshaber im Südosten* (Armed Forces Commander South-East). Headquartered in Belgrade, Army Group F was responsible for all German troops in the Balkans, with the exception of Slovenia, Istria and the Croatian coast, which were under the control of Army Group C in Italy.

ARMY GROUP F (SEPTEMBER 1944)

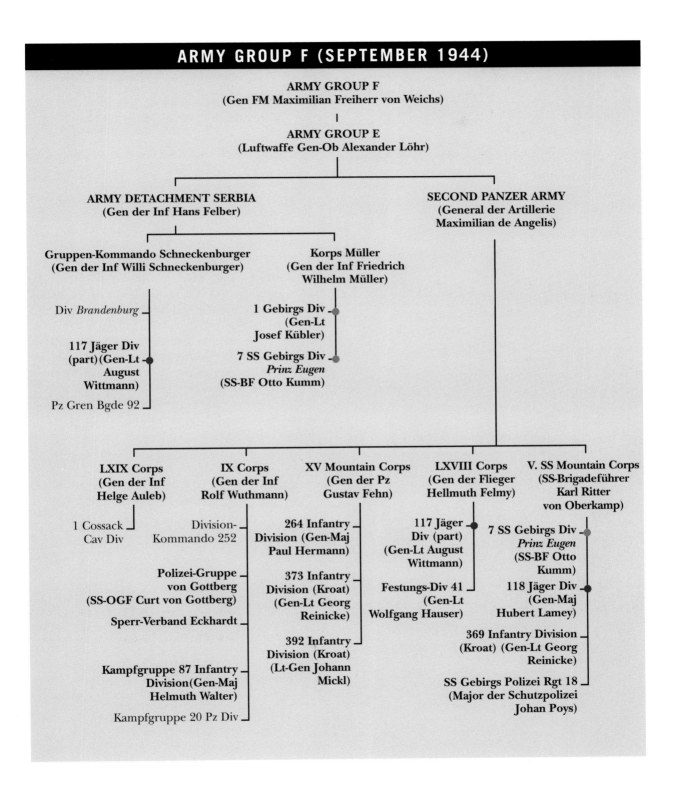

ARMY GROUP F
(Gen FM Maximilian Freiherr von Weichs)

ARMY GROUP E
(Luftwaffe Gen-Ob Alexander Löhr)

ARMY DETACHMENT SERBIA
(Gen der Inf Hans Felber)

SECOND PANZER ARMY
(General der Artillerie
Maximilian de Angelis)

Gruppen-Kommando Schneckenburger
(Gen der Inf Willi Schneckenburger)

Korps Müller
(Gen der Inf Friedrich
Wilhelm Müller)

Div *Brandenburg*

1 Gebirgs Div
(Gen-Lt
Josef Kübler)

117 Jäger Div
(part)(Gen-Lt
August
Wittmann)

7 SS Gebirgs Div
Prinz Eugen
(SS-BF Otto Kumm)

Pz Gren Bgde 92

LXIX Corps
(Gen der Inf
Helge Auleb)

IX Corps
(Gen der Inf
Rolf Wuthmann)

XV Mountain Corps
(Gen der Pz
Gustav Fehn)

LXVIII Corps
(Gen der Flieger
Hellmuth Felmy)

V. SS Mountain Corps
(SS-Brigadeführer
Karl Ritter
von Oberkamp)

1 Cossack
Cav Div

Division-
Kommando 252

**264 Infantry
Division** (Gen-Maj
Paul Hermann)

**117 Jäger
Div** (part)
(Gen-Lt August
Wittmann)

7 SS Gebirgs Div
Prinz Eugen
(SS-BF Otto
Kumm)

Polizei-Gruppe
von Gottberg
(SS-OGF Curt von Gottberg)

**373 Infantry
Division** (Kroat)
(Gen-Lt Georg
Reinicke)

Festungs-Div 41
(Gen-Lt
Wolfgang Hauser)

118 Jäger Div
(Gen-Maj
Hubert Lamey)

Sperr-Verband Eckhardt

**392 Infantry
Division** (Kroat)
(Lt-Gen Johann
Mickl)

369 Infantry Division
(Kroat) (Gen-Lt Georg
Reinicke)

**Kampfgruppe 87 Infantry
Division**(Gen-Maj
Helmuth Walter)

SS Gebirgs Polizei Rgt 18
(Major der Schutzpolizei
Johan Poys)

Kampfgruppe 20 Pz Div

Belgrade was jointly liberated in October 1944 jointly by the Partisans and the Soviets, after which the Red Army left the fighting to the Partisans. They were more interested in fighting Chetniks, Ustashe and others than against the retreating Germans.

German withdrawal

With the withdrawal of German forces from the region, the focus of the fighting in Greece switched to the struggle between communists and royalists. The royalists had the support of Britain – British troops landed in Greece on 12 October 1944 with the intention of assisting the government in exile to return to power.

Greek partisans had formed numerous anti-German groups during the years of occupation, but with the withdrawal of the Nazis the mutual antipathy between the groups spilled over into violence. The Communists had hoped for support from Stalin, but the Soviet dictator had his eyes on other parts of the Balkans, and was quite happy for Greece to fall within the British sphere of influence. As a result, the Communists were left to fend for themselves.

Although Greece had been officially declared liberated on 4 November 1944, the various partisan factions continued to fight each other. The civil conflict would continue well into the postwar years.

MAXIMILIAN VON WEICHS
(1881–1954)

Maximilian Maria Joseph Karl Gabriel Lamoral Reichsfreiherr von Weichs zu Glon was a Bavarian aristocrat who served with the Bavarian Cavalry during World War I.

• He commanded a Corps during the invasion of Poland (September 1939), and led the Second Army in France (May 1940) and the Balkans (April 1941) and as part of Army Group Centre during Operation *Barbarossa* (June 1941).

• He commanded Army Group B in 1942, but fell out of favour with Hitler after warning his Army Group was stretched too thin in the drive on Stalingrad.

• Promoted to Field Marshal in February 1943, von Weichs was appointed Commander of Army Group F in the Balkans in August 1943, fighting a bitter partisan war. Late in 1944, he managed the successful German retreat from Greece and Yugoslavia.

8 August–15 December 1944

As the Red Army drove through Romania and Bulgaria, Hitler's east European allies deserted him. On 20 August, Malinovsky's 2nd Ukrainian Front broke through powerful German defences, and the Red Army reached the Bulgarian border on 1 September. Within a week, the Soviets were at the Yugoslav frontier, and on 8 September Bulgaria and Romania declared war on Germany.

As Army Groups E and F, under Field Marshal von Weichs, were forced back through Yugoslavia, the ethnic volunteer 7th SS Freiwilligen-Gebirgs Division *Prinz Eugen* was destroyed south of Vukovar in January 1945, and the survivors withdrew into Austria.

In October 1944, the Red Army crossed the Hungarian border and raced for the Danube, reaching the river to the south of Budapest and establishing a bridgehead on the west bank, from where it could launch future operations.

SOVIET ADVANCE INTO ROMANIA AND HUNGARY

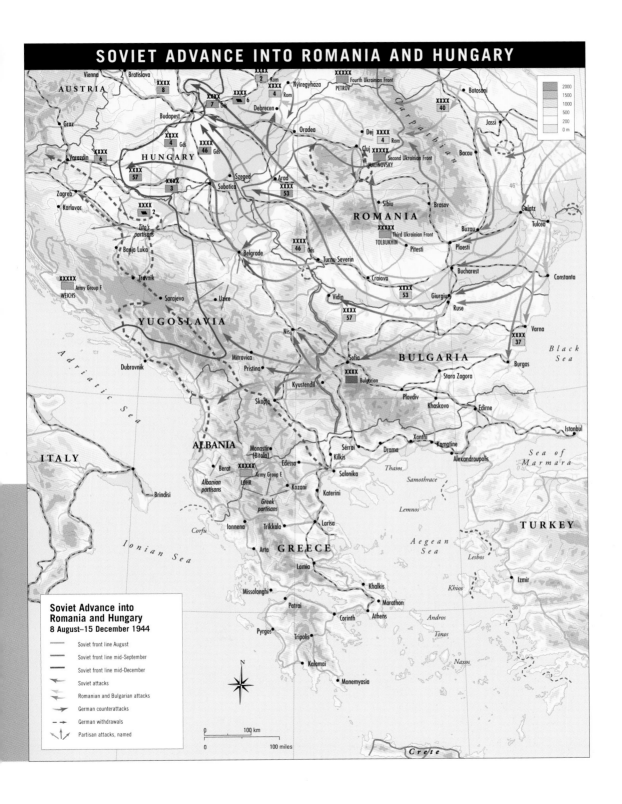

Soviet Advance into Romania and Hungary
8 August–15 December 1944

- Soviet front line August
- Soviet front line mid-September
- Soviet front line mid-December
- Soviet attacks
- Romanian and Bulgarian attacks
- German counterattacks
- German withdrawals
- Partisan attacks, named

0   100 km
0   100 miles

North Africa: 1941–43

The forces Germany sent to the aid of Benito Mussolini in North Africa in 1941 were exclusively armoured or mobile infantry formations. However, they were operating alongside much greater numbers of Italian units, including regular infantry.

A *Luftwaffe* crew manning one of the fearsome 8.8-cm Flak 18 anti-aircraft guns await a British armoured attack in Africa.

Rommel's first offensive in 1941 was a headlong advance that was to set the standard for two years of highly mobile war. He had recovered all the territory lost by the Italians in 1940, and he was soon talking to his staff about Egypt and the Suez canal. However, he would have to take into account the reactions of the Italians.

It is worth noting that the Axis forces in North Africa remained under Italian command until early 1943. At this time, Rommel was only a corps commander. The theatre commander in Africa was Italian, as were the majority of Rommel's troops.

In that lay part of the problem. Italian units had dash and élan, but no endurance. Importantly, in the mobile warfare for which Rommel was so suited, their infantry divisions were not mechanized and so could rarely exploit the successes of German armour. All of the Afrika Korps units were mobile, and therefore the German infantry could keep pace with the panzers and exploit the breaches made in the allied lines.

Italian units

Under Rommel's leadership, two Italian divisions – the Ariete armoured division and Trieste motorized division – fought extremely well. The rest of the forces were of varying levels of mediocrity and, when under pressure, could be counted upon to fold like a house of cards. They did, however, prove reasonably effective if they were 'corsetted' at key points by intermingling with German units.

The quality of Italian equipment was also suspect. In spite of the appearance given by triumphalist propaganda, Italy's economy was not geared to produce the quantity of equipment required of a modern war. The tanks that she did field were slow, undergunned and poorly armoured – indeed, they were christened 'mobile coffins' by their crews. The same prewar models were produced right up until the Italian surrender, no funds being made available for weapons development.

Desert warfare

The desert war was unusual in many respects. There were few cities, few obstacles to the rapid movement of mechanized forces. Armies required vast quantities of petrol and water. Supplies of fresh vegetables and fruit were scarce for both sides. Without enough water to drink, there was certainly none to be spared for washing. Occupation of oases was vital to both sides: any fight over a water source was guaranteed to be hard, and when won was enjoyed to the full by the troops.

Supply nightmares

Getting supplies to the advancing troops was a hell in its own right. This was a war won by logistics. The length of the supply lines dictated the yo-yo nature of the North African campaign. The further from the supply port, the more difficult it was to sustain the advance. Conditions were not helped by the poor state of the roads – deeply rutted dust tracks in the summer and quagmires in winter. Consequently, there were never enough supplies. Rommel insisted on eating the same rations as his men, and his health steadily deteriorated as a result. His officers fell by the wayside too.

Over the next 18 months, the tide of war would swing backwards and forwards across the desert. General Wavell responded to Rommel's first drive with Operation Brevity in May, followed by Operation Battleaxe in June. After beating off the British, Rommel planned to capture the port of Tobruk.

Attack and retreat

In November, the Axis forces were taken by surprise by Operation Crusader, a major British offensive. Rommel responded by outflanking the British and making a 'dash for the wire' on the Egyptian border. However, he had outrun his supplies and was forced to retreat to Gazala.

Rommel was not the man to allow either men or material to stay idle if he could see a worthwhile purpose for their employment. On 21 January 1942, the Axis forces caught the British by surprise, who were soon again in helter-skelter retreat.

Rommel pre-empted another British offensive at the Battle of Gazala in May 1942, driving the British back to the Egyptian border and beyond. He captured Tobruk on 21 June, but all forward progress was stopped by the strong British defensive line at the first battle of El Alamein.

The Germans did not know it, but the tide of war was about to turn against them.

Retreat from Alamein

Rommel's last offensive in Africa had ground to a halt at a small railway station called El Alamein. Now, some three months later, the British had been massively reinforced, and General Bernard Montgomery had taken command of Eighth Army.

By late October 1942, Montgomery's forces had built up enough men and matériel in Egypt to outnumber the Axis forces in North Africa by at least three to one.

Turn of the tide

After the battle, Churchill would say that El Alamein marked 'the end of the beginning', but this had not been obvious before it started. The British had known a summer of reverses, and the certainty of victory was far from their minds.

The progress of the battle went against the Germans, outnumbered and outgunned in every way. Rommel now realized that the African dream was over, and the only choice left open, if he wanted to save the remnants of his once proud formations, was to extricate them from the threatened envelopment by the British armour.

But even as he began to do so, Rommel received a command from the *Führer* not to retreat. Indeed, he was to throw everything into the battle. Rommel, infuriated but obedient, submitted to the *Führer's* command. The next day, he had a heated meeting with Field Marshal

Kesselring, the Mediterranean commander in chief, who took it upon himself to cancel the order. The withdrawal continued. By the time the British succeeded in punching through the German defences, at Tel El Aqqaqir on 4 November, they discovered that the Germans had abandoned their positions.

The Germans who did manage to reach Rommel's first makeshift defensive line at Fuka were worth little more than a battalion, and even when joined by the 90th and 164th Divisions constituted in battle-ready terms a brigade only. Ramcke's parachute formation

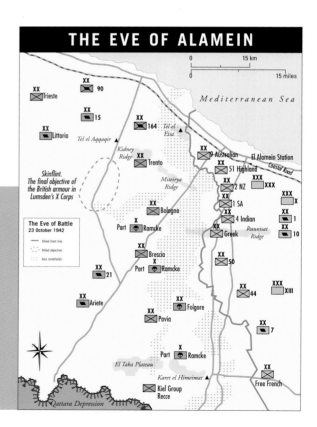

THE EVE OF ALAMEIN

23 October 1942

Prior to the attack on 24 October, the men of the Afrika Korps had to endure the greatest artillery barrage so far launched in North Africa. The British succeeded in softening up the Axis defences, but as their armour deployed on that first morning, it immediately came under fire from the surviving German and Italian artillery.

The next eight days saw an intensive series of actions taking place between the coast and Miteiya Ridge. Rommel, for once not calling the shots, had to release his reserves to contain the British attacks, and was further disadvantaged as the *Luftwaffe* had completely lost out in the air battle. As a result, German armour could not call on the close support usually provided by the Stukas.

made its own way back to the German lines virtually intact, but received only Rommel's scorn.

Montgomery failed to press home the advantage and finish off the remnants of the Afrika Korps. The British General's caution, always a feature of his command, was exacerbated by the poor weather, his innate respect for the enemy, and his own administrative problems. At that moment, Rommel's force consisted of just 4000 men, 11 tanks, 24 of the feared '88s', 25 other anti-tank guns and 40 assorted artillery pieces.

But now Rommel had more than just the Eighth Army to worry about. On 8 November 1942, British and American forces landed in Morocco and Algeria. It was the most ambitious amphibious operation up to that time: some 35,000 US troops were shipped straight across from America; another 49,000 from their bases in Britain, together with 23,000 British and Commonwealth soldiers.

Hitler, who had for so long starved Rommel of troops, now, in extremis, poured in men and materials to bolster the Tunisian bridgehead. The man chosen by the *Führer* to handle this developing crisis was Field Marshal Albert Kesselring. Kesselring was politically astute as well as being an able commander.

He soon appreciated that his brief in Africa, especially after Operation Torch, was to fight a series of delaying actions. His ultimate aim was to keep the Allies away from the southern borders of the Reich. Italy was now very much the sick partner of the axis.

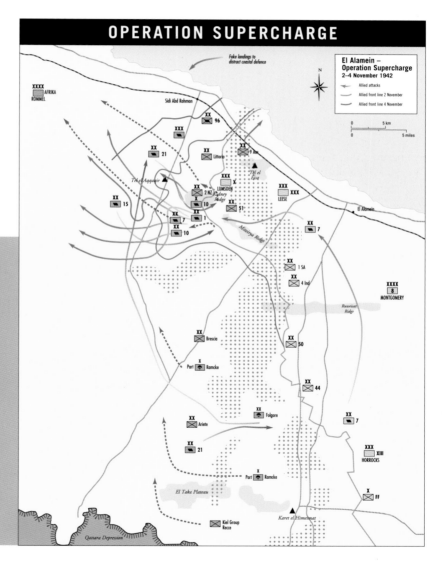

2–4 November 1942

As the initial fighting at Alamein continued, Montgomery, who enjoyed an immense logistical advantage, prepared his armour for a further thrust. This was launched on 2 November 1942.

Although the initial British tank force of 100 machines was virtually annihilated by the Axis infantry and anti-tank guns, Rommel impetuously launched his own massed armour counterattack in the hope of exploiting a weak position in the English line. But there was no weakness, and the Afrika Korps was that day broken in its repeated charges against Allied gunnery. By dusk, Rommel's panzer divisions had only 35 tanks between them.

Army Group Afrika

The German position looked fairly promising at the end of 1942, at any rate in comparison to the dire predictions made two months previously at the beginning of Torch. But the delicate balance was tipped at the beginning of 1943.

By early 1943, the Axis were being squeezed between the pincers of Eighth Army driving north and the Americans driving east. Germany needed a miracle to avoid being swept from Africa.

Rommel did not favour waiting to be driven into the sea. He opted for a bold plan to sweep the Allies from

Africa before their strength became too overwhelming. He chose for his target the inexperienced American formations whom he rightly assessed as being still frighteningly green.

However, his victory at Kasserine did little to stave off the eventual German defeat. Within days, the lost

April–May 1943

The final battle in North Africa began on 6 May. The Germans were pinned into a narrowing bridgehead around Bizerta, Tunis and the Cape Bon peninsula. On the left, the US II Corps, now commanded by Omar Bradley, pushed along the coast and up through Mateur towards Bizerta. The First Army held the centre of the line driving through Medjerda towards Tunis whilst Eighth Army kept the attentions of Arnim around Enfidaville, so distracting him from the armoured punch directed at Tunis.

Organized resistance collapsed that morning, Arnim's weak divisions having so little fuel that counterattacks were no longer possible. By the afternoon of the following day, British troops were on the outskirts of Tunis and the defence had fragmented into isolated pockets.

Within two days of the final assault, both Bizerta and Tunis had been captured. The *Führer* had refused to countenance any evacuation of the Tunisian bridgehead, and when the last German pocket surrendered at Cape Bon on 13 May only 800 troops out of 200,000 had made good their escape. This had been another Stalingrad – dubbed 'Tunisgrad' by the bitter survivors.

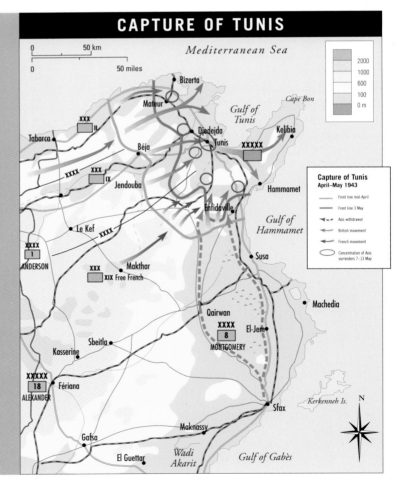

CAPTURE OF TUNIS

Mediterranean Sea

Capture of Tunis
April–May 1943

— Front line mid-April
— Front line 3 May
⟶ Axis withdrawal
⟶ British movement
⟶ French movement
◯ Concentration of Axis surrenders 7–13 May

ground was recovered by the British and Americans. From then on, and with ever growing certainty, the noose around the remaining Axis forces in Tunisia began to tighten.

On 15 April, Army Group Africa was established along a reduced 217km (135 mile) front. Arnim, who had replaced an ailing Rommel, still theoretically had 16 Divisions, but the nine German Divisions numbered only 60,000 men with 100 tanks. The end was inevitable,

and the last Axis forces surrendered on 13 May.

Hitler had clung too long to his African enclave. The only advantage to the *Wehrmacht* was that the campaign had kept the Allies away from Italy until the autumn, by which time the *Wehrmacht* had vastly increased its strength in the country and made its conquest much more difficult.

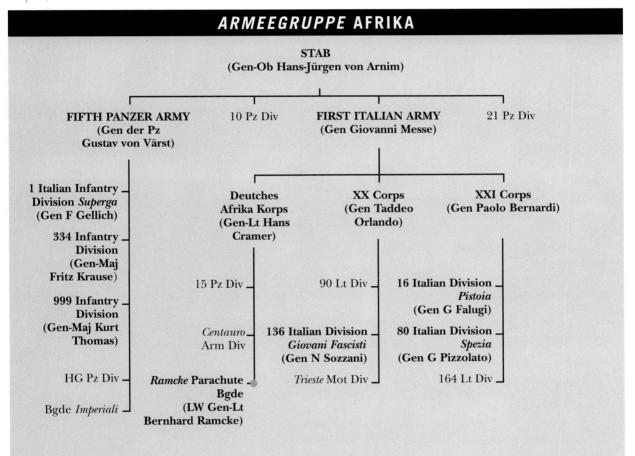

ARMEEGRUPPE AFRIKA

STAB
(Gen-Ob Hans-Jürgen von Arnim)

FIFTH PANZER ARMY
(Gen der Pz
Gustav von Värst)

10 Pz Div

FIRST ITALIAN ARMY
(Gen Giovanni Messe)

21 Pz Div

1 Italian Infantry Division *Superga* **(Gen F Gellich)**

334 Infantry Division (Gen-Maj Fritz Krause)

999 Infantry Division (Gen-Maj Kurt Thomas)

HG Pz Div

Bgde *Imperiali*

Deutches Afrika Korps (Gen-Lt Hans Cramer)

15 Pz Div

Centauro Arm Div

Ramcke **Parachute Bgde (LW Gen-Lt Bernhard Ramcke)**

XX Corps (Gen Taddeo Orlando)

90 Lt Div

136 Italian Division *Giovani Fascisti* **(Gen N Sozzani)**

Trieste Mot Div

XXI Corps (Gen Paolo Bernardi)

16 Italian Division *Pistoia* **(Gen G Falugi)**

80 Italian Division *Spezia* **(Gen G Pizzolato)**

164 Lt Div

By 1943, an *Armeegruppe* usually consisted of two or three adjacent armies, possibly but not always one German and one Axis-allied army (rather than a *Heeresgruppe*, which was usually all German), with one of the Army HQs (usually the German) temporarily placed in command over the others. *Armeegruppe Afrika* was established under Rommel's command in February 1943 to manage the defence of Tunisia. The combat units of *Deutsch-Italienischen Panzerarmee* were turned over to the Italian First Army. Command of the Army Group passed to Hans-Jürgen von Arnim in March.

The Eastern Front: 1941–45

Hitler did not regard the Nazi–Soviet pact of 1939 as a permanent feature of German strategic planning, a fact he never concealed from his generals.

German infantrymen march past their primary logistics resource in Russia—the horses that moved supplies and artillery.

The *Führer* advised his commanders in November 1939 that 'we can oppose Russia only when we are free in the West'. Russia 'is not dangerous' for the moment, he assured them. The victory in the West gave him the freedom of action he required to look eastwards. Britain was the only country unsubjugated, the military implications of which he chose to ignore or marginalize.

The decision to attack the Soviet Union was a monumental one, equalled only by its rapidity. The failure to knock Britain out in a single stroke, combined with the temptation, the power and the sense of occasion, gave this Herculean step a structure and reality all of its own.

Years of brooding and moments of intoxication thus fused fiercely into what General Warlimont, the Deputy Chief of the Operations Staff at the *Wehrmacht* High Command, subsequently called 'this ghastly development'. War with the Soviet Union is perhaps less baffling if viewed not as a strategic or military decision that was simply irrational in the normal sense; rather it is an example of Hitler's logic.

The invasion of the Soviet Union ordered

Führer Directive No 21 was given on 18 December 1940, setting out the objectives of the campaign, planned to be launched in May the following year. This Directive stated:

'The bulk of the Russian Army stationed in western Russia will be destroyed by daring operations led by deeply penetrating armoured spearheads. Russian forces still capable of giving battle will be prevented from withdrawing into the depths of Russia. The enemy will then be energetically pursued and a line will be reached from which the Russian Air Force can no longer attack German territory.

'The final objective of the operation is to erect a barrier against Asiatic Russia on the general line Volga-Archangel. The last surviving industrial areas of Russia in the Urals can then, if necessary, be eliminated by the *Luftwaffe*.'

Tukhachevsky purges

The Soviet armed forces had been decimated by Stalin's purges (named after the most prominent officer executed, Marshal Mikhail Tukhachevsky). Between 1937 and 1939, Stalin carried out the systematic destruction of the Soviet High Command, the primary motive being to secure his position as absolute ruler of the Soviet Union. It has been suggested that information detailing an alleged 'Military-Troskyist Conspiracy' had been fabricated by Reinhard Heydrich of the German *Sicherheitsdienst*, knowing that Stalin's paranoia would force him to take steps against a potential rival.

Few events had more effect on the Soviet Red Army of 1941: three out of five marshals of the Soviet Union, 11 deputy commissars of defence, 13 out of 15 army commanders, and all the military district commanders of May 1937, as well as the leading members of the naval and air force commands, were shot or disappeared without trace.

The same fate was suffered by the political apparatus that was supposed to advise the professional soldiers. During those two fearful years, some 35,000 officers were dismissed, imprisoned or executed. This purge damaged the ability of the Soviet Red Army to resist the German invasion when it came.

Opposing forces

The Soviet Red Army, totally paralyzed logistically and operationally by the loss of some of its most able men, had pitted against it 11 German armies, four of them armoured, and three air fleets. On paper, the odds appeared to be uneven, with the Red Army outnumbering the *Wehrmacht* in virtually every arm of service. Crucially, however, many of the Soviet formations were in the interior of Russia or in the Far East: the advance of the *Wehrmacht* was obstructed by only about 130 Soviet divisions.

The diversion of troops to the Balkans in the spring of 1941 meant that *Barbarossa* was postponed by a month, and was scheduled to start on 22 June 1941.

EASTERN FRONT, JUNE 1941: OPPOSING FORCES				
Force	Men	Divisions	Tanks	Aircraft
SOVIET	12 million	230	20,000	8000
GERMAN	3 million	134	3300	2770

Operation *Barbarossa*: 1941

By the time Operation *Barbarossa* was launched in June 1941, the *Wehrmacht* had amassed enough supplies, stores dumps, fuel and ammunition depots along the Soviet border from Prussia to Romania to sustain an advance of up to 645km (400 miles).

Army Group Centre under Field Marshal Fedor von Bock was the most powerful of the German forces, though Army Group South was numerically larger. Its mobile spearhead included nine panzer divisions and five motorized infantry divisions, which was the most powerful armoured strike force ever seen in warfare up to that time. It was supported by some 35 infantry divisions, including reserve formations, as well as three security divisions, a cavalry division and the elite *Grossdeutschland* reinforced infantry regiment.

Field Marshal Gerd von Rundstedt, commanding Army Group South, was allocated five panzer divisions supported by four motorized infantry divisions. The bulk of his forces was made up from 50 infantry divisions. However, these included three security divisions, 15 Romanian divisions, two Hungarian divisions and two Italian divisions. In spite of the lower quality of training, weapons and equipment in the Allied formations, it was an impressive force.

The weakest of the army groups, Army Group North, was commanded by Field Marshal Ritter von Leeb. Leeb's forces included only three panzer divisions, three motorized, and about 20 infantry divisions.

Logistics
Over half a million lorries waited in massed parks, ready to rush supplies forward when necessary. German industry had not been able to provide the necessary vehicles, and the lorry parks were made up from a quartermaster's nightmare of trucks drawn from all over occupied Europe.

Motor vehicles were not the only means of moving supplies forwards. Included in the German logistics plan was stabling and fodder for more than 300,000 horses: the bulk of the German infantry divisions still marched on foot, and horses were essential elements in their lines of communication.

The disposition of the Army Groups, and the directions in which they were to advance, was dictated to a large extent by one inescapable geographical reality. The Pripet Marshes were a heavily forested, swampy area some 160km (100 miles) from north to south and over 480km (300 miles) from east to west. Located between the Ukraine and Byelorussia, it was difficult enough terrain for infantry formations on foot, and virtually impassible to motorized and armoured units.

Because of this, there could be little contact between the two largest Army Groups, at least in the early stages of the operation.

Objectives
Army Group South was centred on the area around Lublin, and its drive was directed to Kiev and the area around the lower Dniepr River. Army Group Centre, to

OPERATION *BARBAROSSA*		
	June 1941	**October 1941**
GERMAN ARMY DIVISIONS BY TYPE		
Panzer	21	23
Infantry (mot)	15	15
Cavalry	1	1
Infantry	158	157
Mountain	6	8
Security	8	9
GERMAN ARMY DIVISIONS BY THEATRE		
Germany	38	0
East	93	149
West	51	50
Norway	8	7
Finland	3	6
Southeast	14	9

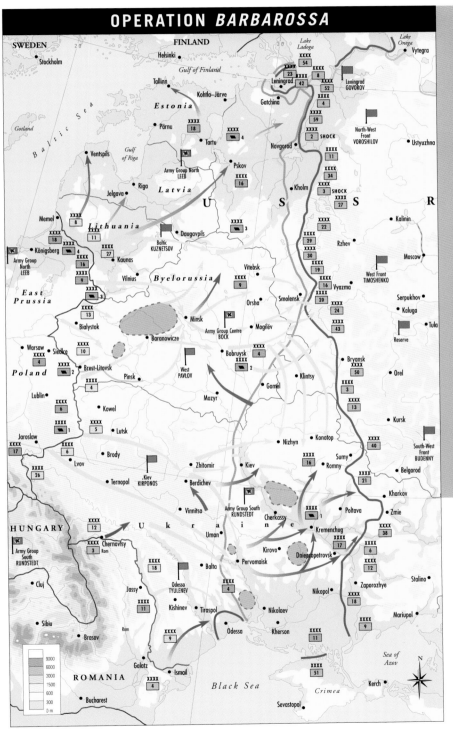

OPERATION *BARBAROSSA*

22 June–early October 1941

The German plan involved three Army Groups (North, South and Centre), with the bulk of the forces concentrated in Army Groups North and Centre. Army Group Centre, which contained around half the German armour, was to shatter Soviet forces in Byelorussia before turning to assist Army Group North in the drive on Leningrad. Army Group South, meanwhile, was to deal with Soviet forces in the Ukraine. At 3.05 a.m. on 22 June, Army Group North began the drive to Leningrad. By the evening of the first day, the leading panzers were 60km (37 miles) into Lithuania. By the end of the second day, only the wrecks of 140 Soviet tanks lay between the panzer divisions and Pskov. But the *Panzergruppe*'s infantry could not keep up. The terrain encountered on the Soviet side of the border was so marshy and impenetrable that even the motorized infantry was reduced to the pace of the marching columns.

Operation *Barbarossa*
22 June–early October 1941

- German attack
- **XXXX** 6 — Soviet positions 22 June
- Soviet units encircled
- Soviet counterattacks
- German front line, end of August
- German front line, early October
- **XXXX** 6 — Soviet positions early October

the north of the marshes, was expected to drive through Byelorussia to Smolensk and Minsk. From there, at least in the minds of the General Staff, they would drive on to the ultimate target – Moscow. Army Group North launched its attack out of East Prussia. Its mission was to clear the Baltic states, driving on towards Lake Peipus

and the former Russian capital now known as Leningrad.

The operational goal of Operation *Barbarossa* was the rapid conquest of the European part of the Soviet Union, west of a line that connected the cities of Arkhangelsk and Astrakhan – a line which was often

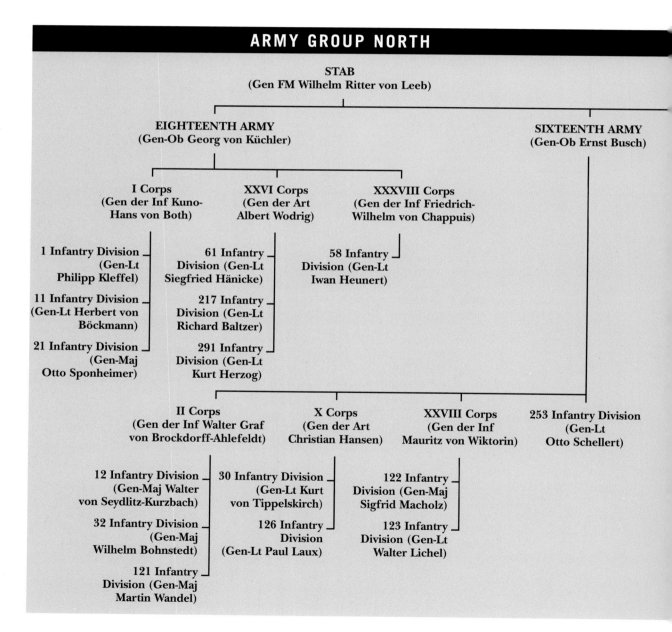

ARMY GROUP NORTH

STAB
(Gen FM Wilhelm Ritter von Leeb)

EIGHTEENTH ARMY
(Gen-Ob Georg von Küchler)

SIXTEENTH ARMY
(Gen-Ob Ernst Busch)

I Corps
(Gen der Inf Kuno-Hans von Both)

XXVI Corps
(Gen der Art Albert Wodrig)

XXXVIII Corps
(Gen der Inf Friedrich-Wilhelm von Chappuis)

1 Infantry Division (Gen-Lt Philipp Kleffel)

11 Infantry Division (Gen-Lt Herbert von Böckmann)

21 Infantry Division (Gen-Maj Otto Sponheimer)

61 Infantry Division (Gen-Lt Siegfried Hänicke)

217 Infantry Division (Gen-Lt Richard Baltzer)

291 Infantry Division (Gen-Lt Kurt Herzog)

58 Infantry Division (Gen-Lt Iwan Heunert)

II Corps
(Gen der Inf Walter Graf von Brockdorff-Ahlefeldt)

X Corps
(Gen der Art Christian Hansen)

XXVIII Corps
(Gen der Inf Mauritz von Wiktorin)

253 Infantry Division (Gen-Lt Otto Schellert)

12 Infantry Division (Gen-Maj Walter von Seydlitz-Kurzbach)

32 Infantry Division (Gen-Maj Wilhelm Bohnstedt)

121 Infantry Division (Gen-Maj Martin Wandel)

30 Infantry Division (Gen-Lt Kurt von Tippelskirch)

126 Infantry Division (Gen-Lt Paul Laux)

122 Infantry Division (Gen-Maj Sigfrid Macholz)

123 Infantry Division (Gen-Lt Walter Lichel)

referred to as the A-A line after its description in Hitler's initial directive.

The surprise was complete: *Stavka*, the Soviet High Command, was alarmed by reports of German units approaching the border in combat formations. It issued a general order just after midnight to warn the troops manning border defences that war was imminent. In the event, few front-line units were alerted in time.

The shock to the Soviets stemmed less from the timing of the attack than from the sheer number of Axis troops striking into Soviet territory at once. Aside from the three million German fighting men engaged in or

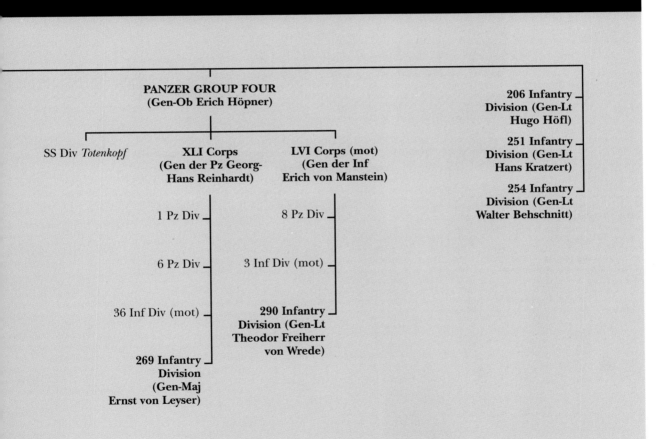

The infantry divisions of Army Group North attacked through the Baltic states, and were not expected to make the same kind of progress as the armoured attack by Panzer Group Four directed north through western Russia. However, the roads in Lithuania, Latvia and Estonia were so much better than those in Soviet Russia that Generaloberst Georg von Küchler's Eighteenth Army was moving almost as fast as the panzers.

WILHELM RITTER VON LEEB (1876–1956)

Wilhelm von Leeb (pictured above left) joined the Bavarian Army in 1895 and was commissioned in the artillery. Awarded a knighthood after service on both the western and eastern fronts in World War I, he became Wilhelm Ritter von Leeb in 1916.

• As a member of the *Reichswehr,* he assisted in putting down the Nazi Beer Hall Putsch in 1923. This action, together with his strong Catholic beliefs, led to some animosity from Hitler when he came to power in 1933, and he was pensioned off.

• Recalled to service on the outbreak of war, he commanded Army Group C in the Battle of France (May 1940).

• After promotion to Field Marshal he led Army Group North in Operation *Barbarossa* (June 1941).

• After his failure to capture Leningrad, von Leeb resigned in January 1942. He would never again command in the field.

earmarked for the Eastern campaign, about 500,000 Romanian, Hungarian, Slovakian and Italian troops eventually accompanied the German forces, while the Army of Finland made a major contribution to the campaign in the north.

The task of the *Luftwaffe* was to neutralize the Soviet Air Force. This was achieved in the first days of operations, because the Soviets had concentrated aircraft in huge groups, making them ideal targets. The *Luftwaffe* claimed to have destroyed 1489 aircraft on the first day of operations. Hermann Göring, Chief of the *Luftwaffe,* distrusted the reports and ordered the figure checked. Picking through the wreckages of Soviet airfields overrun by ground troops on the first day of the campaign, the *Luftwaffe's* figures proved conservative, as more than 2000 destroyed Soviet aircraft were found.

Soviet counterattacks

Moscow at first failed to grasp the dimensions of the catastrophe that had befallen the Soviet Union. Marshal Timoshenko ordered all Soviet forces to launch a general counteroffensive, but with supply and ammunition dumps destroyed, and a complete collapse of communication, the attacks failed.

Marshal Zhukov signed the infamous Directive of People's Commissariat of Defence No 3, which demanded that the Red Army start an offensive: this commanded the troops 'to encircle and destroy the enemy grouping near Suwalki and to seize the Suwalki region by the evening of June 26'. Although Soviet troops attempted to obey his orders, they were confused and disorganized, and the attack failed.

Rapid progress

The early stages of the attack were almost unbroken successes. Army Group North encircled and destroyed a Soviet armoured force near Dvinsk. Army Group Centre had encircled Minsk by 27 June, trapping eight Soviet tank divisions and 32 infantry divisions.

Only Army Group South encountered real organized resistance. On 26 June, five Soviet mechanized corps with over 1000 tanks mounted a massive counterattack near Brody, which took four days of hard fighting by Panzer Group One to defeat, at the cost of the heaviest casualties of the opening stages of the campaign.

Objective Moscow

On 3 July, Hitler finally gave the go-ahead for the panzers to resume their drive east once the infantry divisions had caught up. However, a rainstorm typical of Russian summers slowed their progress as Soviet defences stiffened.

The delay caused by the weather gave the Soviets time to organize for a massive counterattack against Army Group Centre. The ultimate objective of the current phase of the German offensive was the city of Smolensk, which commanded the road to Moscow. Facing the Germans was an old Soviet defensive line that was held by six armies.

On 6 July, the Soviets launched an attack with some 700 tanks against the Panzer Group Three. The Germans defeated this counterattack using their overwhelming air superiority. The Panzer Group Two crossed the River Dnieper and closed on Smolensk from the south while the 3rd Panzer Group, after defeating the Soviet counterattack, closed in Smolensk from the north. Trapped between their pincers were three Soviet armies. On 26 July, the panzers closed the gap. Although many Soviet troops escaped, they left behind much of their equipment, and about 300,000 Red Army troops were taken prisoner.

Diversion of force

Four weeks into the campaign, the Germans realized they had grossly underestimated the strength of the Soviets. The German troops had run out of their initial supplies but had still not progressed as far as the High Command had anticipated, and continuing Soviet resistance meant that the *Wehrmacht's* panzer forces could not operate as freely as expected. They had to wait for the following infantry divisions to protect them from Soviet counterattacks.

Operations were now slowed down to allow for a resupply; the delay was to be used to adapt the strategy to the new situation. Even though the Germans had captured huge numbers of Soviet prisoners, new Soviet troops kept on coming in a seemingly endless stream.

Hitler now had a change of heart. He believed he could defeat the Soviets by seizing their key industrial and agricultural areas, depriving the Soviet government of the industrial capacity to continue the war.

That meant the seizure of the industrial centre of Kharkov, the Donets Basin and the oil fields of the Caucasus in the south, and a speedy capture of Leningrad, a major centre of military production, in the north. Hitler then issued an order to send Army Group Centre's tanks to the north and south, halting the drive to Moscow. The German generals vehemently opposed the plan. Moscow was a key target: not only the capital of the USSR, but the crucial railroad hub for the entire European part of the Soviet Union. Additionally, they felt that the best way to destroy the Soviet means of waging war was to destroy its armed forces in battle. As a large proportion of the Red Army was deployed to

ARMY GROUP CENTRE: OCTOBER 1941		
	Army Group Centre	All Army Divs
ARMY DIVISIONS		
Panzer	14	23
Infantry (mot)	8	15
Cavalry	1	1
Infantry	49	157
Mountain	0	8
Security	4	9
GERMAN ARMY DIVISIONS BY THEATRE		
Germany	0	
East	149	
West	40	
Norway	7	
Finland	6	
Southeast	9	
North Africa	2	

ARMY GROUP CENTRE

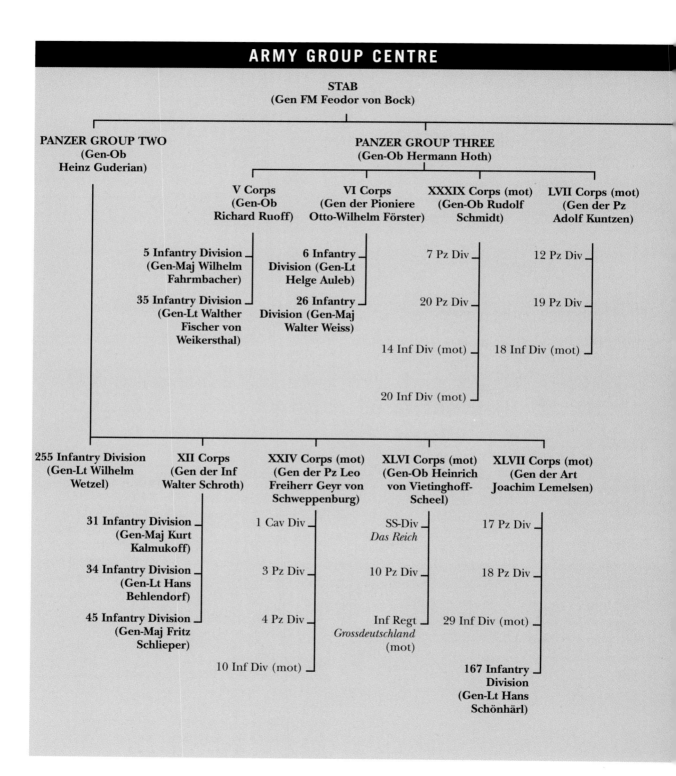

STAB
(Gen FM Feodor von Bock)

PANZER GROUP TWO
(Gen-Ob
Heinz Guderian)

PANZER GROUP THREE
(Gen-Ob Hermann Hoth)

V Corps
(Gen-Ob
Richard Ruoff)

VI Corps
(Gen der Pioniere
Otto-Wilhelm Förster)

XXXIX Corps (mot)
(Gen-Ob Rudolf
Schmidt)

LVII Corps (mot)
(Gen der Pz
Adolf Kuntzen)

5 Infantry Division
(Gen-Maj Wilhelm
Fahrmbacher)

6 Infantry
Division (Gen-Lt
Helge Auleb)

7 Pz Div

12 Pz Div

35 Infantry Division
(Gen-Lt Walther
Fischer von
Weikersthal)

26 Infantry
Division (Gen-Maj
Walter Weiss)

20 Pz Div

19 Pz Div

14 Inf Div (mot)

18 Inf Div (mot)

20 Inf Div (mot)

255 Infantry Division
(Gen-Lt Wilhelm
Wetzel)

XII Corps
(Gen der Inf
Walter Schroth)

XXIV Corps (mot)
(Gen der Pz Leo
Freiherr Geyr von
Schweppenburg)

XLVI Corps (mot)
(Gen-Ob Heinrich
von Vietinghoff-
Scheel)

XLVII Corps (mot)
(Gen der Art
Joachim Lemelsen)

31 Infantry Division
(Gen-Maj Kurt
Kalmukoff)

1 Cav Div

SS-Div
Das Reich

17 Pz Div

34 Infantry Division
(Gen-Lt Hans
Behlendorf)

3 Pz Div

10 Pz Div

18 Pz Div

45 Infantry Division
(Gen-Maj Fritz
Schlieper)

4 Pz Div

Inf Regt
Grossdeutschland
(mot)

29 Inf Div (mot)

10 Inf Div (mot)

167 Infantry
Division
(Gen-Lt Hans
Schönhärl)

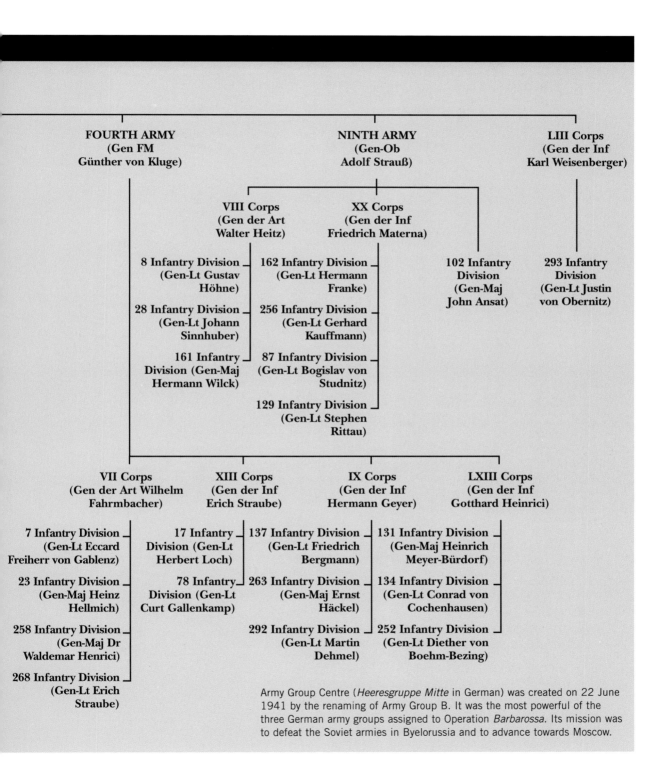

FOURTH ARMY
(Gen FM
Günther von Kluge)

NINTH ARMY
(Gen-Ob
Adolf Strauß)

LIII Corps
(Gen der Inf
Karl Weisenberger)

VIII Corps
(Gen der Art
Walter Heitz)

XX Corps
(Gen der Inf
Friedrich Materna)

8 Infantry Division
(Gen-Lt Gustav
Höhne)

162 Infantry Division
(Gen-Lt Hermann
Franke)

102 Infantry
Division
(Gen-Maj
John Ansat)

293 Infantry
Division
(Gen-Lt Justin
von Obernitz)

28 Infantry Division
(Gen-Lt Johann
Sinnhuber)

256 Infantry Division
(Gen-Lt Gerhard
Kauffmann)

161 Infantry
Division (Gen-Maj
Hermann Wilck)

87 Infantry Division
(Gen-Lt Bogislav von
Studnitz)

129 Infantry Division
(Gen-Lt Stephen
Rittau)

VII Corps
(Gen der Art Wilhelm
Fahrmbacher)

XIII Corps
(Gen der Inf
Erich Straube)

IX Corps
(Gen der Inf
Hermann Geyer)

LXIII Corps
(Gen der Inf
Gotthard Heinrici)

7 Infantry Division
(Gen-Lt Eccard
Freiherr von Gablenz)

17 Infantry
Division (Gen-Lt
Herbert Loch)

137 Infantry Division
(Gen-Lt Friedrich
Bergmann)

131 Infantry Division
(Gen-Maj Heinrich
Meyer-Bürdorf)

23 Infantry Division
(Gen-Maj Heinz
Hellmich)

78 Infantry
Division (Gen-Lt
Curt Gallenkamp)

263 Infantry Division
(Gen-Maj Ernst
Häckel)

134 Infantry Division
(Gen-Lt Conrad von
Cochenhausen)

258 Infantry Division
(Gen-Maj Dr
Waldemar Henrici)

292 Infantry Division
(Gen-Lt Martin
Dehmel)

252 Infantry Division
(Gen-Lt Diether von
Boehm-Bezing)

268 Infantry Division
(Gen-Lt Erich
Straube)

Army Group Centre (*Heeresgruppe Mitte* in German) was created on 22 June 1941 by the renaming of Army Group B. It was the most powerful of the three German army groups assigned to Operation *Barbarossa*. Its mission was to defeat the Soviet armies in Byelorussia and to advance towards Moscow.

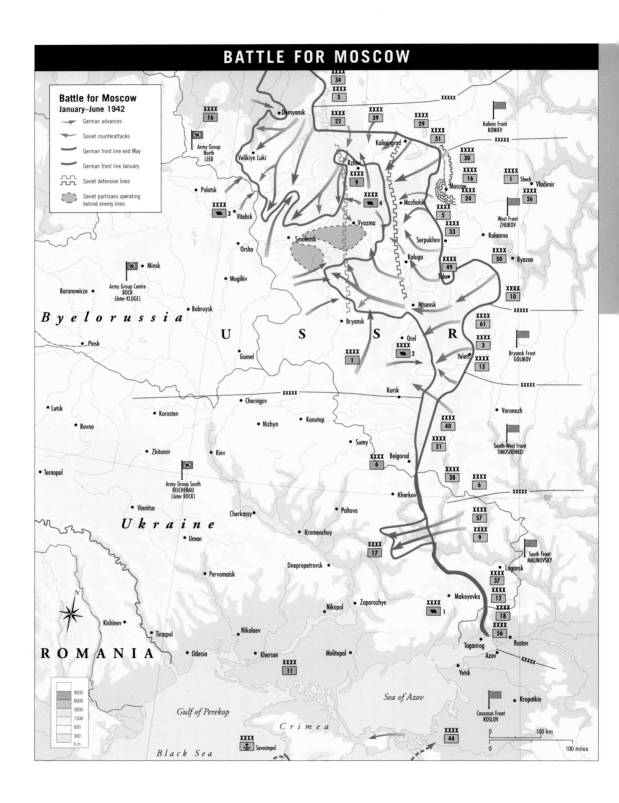

BATTLE FOR MOSCOW

Battle for Moscow
January–June 1942

→ German advances
← Soviet counterattacks
German front line end May
German front line January
Soviet defensive lines
Soviet partisans operating behind enemy lines

January–March 1942

In January 1942, 12 German armies were locked in combat with 22 Soviet armies. On a front stretching from the Crimea to the Gulf of Finland, 141 divisions, including 11 from Axis allies, faced more than 300 Soviet formations. The very size of the war zone was in the *Wehrmacht*'s favour. Stalin was trying not only to relieve Moscow and Leningrad but also to destroy Army Group Centre. His generals knew what happened to commanders who failed, and Red Army offensives were launched all along the line. It was too much. Despite tattered uniforms stuffed with straw and newspaper, weapons that jammed in the arctic temperatures and a grave lack of tanks or aircraft, the German Army defended itself with extraordinary professionalism and courage. By March, the great offensive was over. The inexperienced Red Army had been unable to break the Germans' stubborn defence.

protect Moscow, taking the Soviet capital offered the best chance of winning the war. Hitler was adamant, however, and the tanks were diverted. By mid-July, below the Pinsk Marshes, the Germans had come within a few miles of Kiev. The First Panzer Army then went south while the German Seventeenth Army struck east and in between the Germans trapped three Soviet armies near Uman. As the Germans eliminated the pocket, the tanks turned north and crossed the Dnieper.

Before the attack on Moscow could begin, operations in Kiev needed to be finished. The encirclement of Soviet Forces in Kiev was achieved on 16 September. After 10 days of vicious fighting, the Germans claimed the capture of over 600,000 Soviet men, about half a million of whom were frontline soldiers. Nearly 200,000 managed to break out of the pocket, leaving about 300,000 Soviets to be housed in POW camps.

Army Group South

Hitler's staff, the High Command of the German armed forces (OKW), felt that the primary objective of Army Group South had been all but achieved and the bulk of the Soviet armies in the southwest destroyed.

The Soviets were proving to be much tougher opponents than anticipated, and were adept at exploiting the gaps that were forming in the German lines between the fast-moving armoured units in the spearheads and the slower-moving infantry divisions.

The optimism of the high command was not shared by the troops at the front – correctly, as it turned out, when a Soviet counteroffensive began. The Soviet attack was aimed at cutting the main supply route. Though the attacks were beaten off, it was by no means an easy task.

Hand-to-hand fighting with bayonet, knife and entrenching spade was common. Wooded areas, through which much of the fighting raged, brought their own nightmares as shells burst among the trees, showering everyone with lethal splinters of wood. Casualties were heavy on both sides. The battle lines were so fluid that the combatants rarely knew exactly

who had gained the upper hand or who was outmanoeuvring whom.

On 10 July, Hitler unexpectedly altered the whole thrust of the attack in the south, from an advance in the direction of Kiev, to a drive towards Uman, in an attempt to cut off and surround the Soviet armies there. Weeks of savage fighting ensued in this sector.

XXXVIII Corps was tasked with a drive on Novo Archangelsk to close this Uman Pocket. The weight of the Soviet attempts to break out of the German encirclement was falling in this area. Some of these attacks involved massed infantry formations with concentrated armour support, and were barely beaten back. Ultimately the breakthrough attempts weakened as the SS lines held firm. When the Soviets in the Uman Pocket surrendered, over 100,000 men from the Soviet Sixth and Twelfth Armies were taken into captivity.

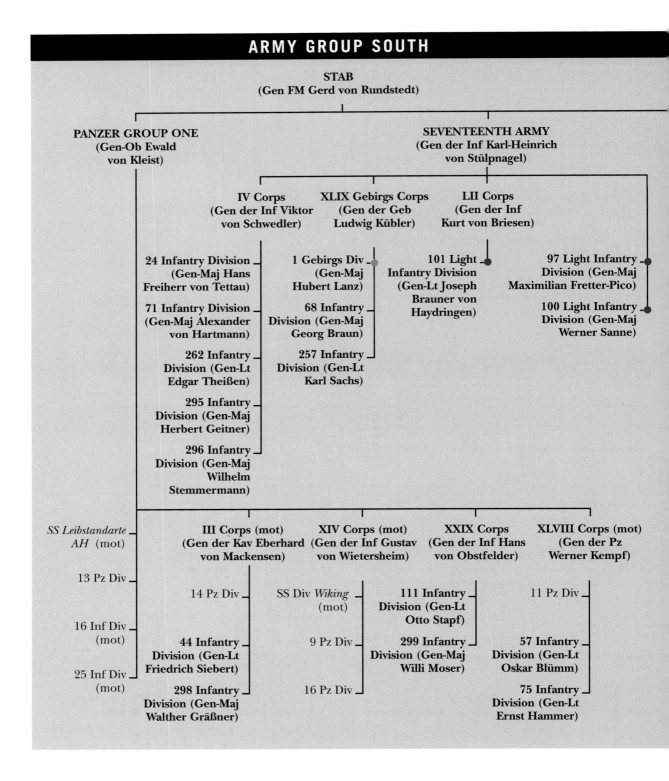

ARMY GROUP SOUTH

STAB
(Gen FM Gerd von Rundstedt)

PANZER GROUP ONE
(Gen-Ob Ewald
von Kleist)

SEVENTEENTH ARMY
(Gen der Inf Karl-Heinrich
von Stülpnagel)

IV Corps
(Gen der Inf Viktor
von Schwedler)

XLIX Gebirgs Corps
(Gen der Geb
Ludwig Kübler)

LII Corps
(Gen der Inf
Kurt von Briesen)

24 Infantry Division
(Gen-Maj Hans
Freiherr von Tettau)

71 Infantry Division
(Gen-Maj Alexander
von Hartmann)

262 Infantry
Division (Gen-Lt
Edgar Theißen)

295 Infantry
Division (Gen-Maj
Herbert Geitner)

296 Infantry
Division (Gen-Maj
Wilhelm
Stemmermann)

1 Gebirgs Div
(Gen-Maj
Hubert Lanz)

68 Infantry
Division (Gen-Maj
Georg Braun)

257 Infantry
Division (Gen-Lt
Karl Sachs)

101 Light
Infantry Division
(Gen-Lt Joseph
Brauner von
Haydringen)

97 Light Infantry
Division (Gen-Maj
Maximilian Fretter-Pico)

100 Light Infantry
Division (Gen-Maj
Werner Sanne)

*SS Leibstandarte
AH* (mot)

13 Pz Div

16 Inf Div
(mot)

25 Inf Div
(mot)

III Corps (mot)
(Gen der Kav Eberhard
von Mackensen)

XIV Corps (mot)
(Gen der Inf Gustav
von Wietersheim)

XXIX Corps
(Gen der Inf Hans
von Obstfelder)

XLVIII Corps (mot)
(Gen der Pz
Werner Kempf)

14 Pz Div

44 Infantry
Division (Gen-Lt
Friedrich Siebert)

298 Infantry
Division (Gen-Maj
Walther Gräßner)

SS Div *Wiking*
(mot)

9 Pz Div

16 Pz Div

111 Infantry
Division (Gen-Lt
Otto Stapf)

299 Infantry
Division (Gen-Maj
Willi Moser)

11 Pz Div

57 Infantry
Division (Gen-Lt
Oskar Blümm)

75 Infantry
Division (Gen-Lt
Ernst Hammer)

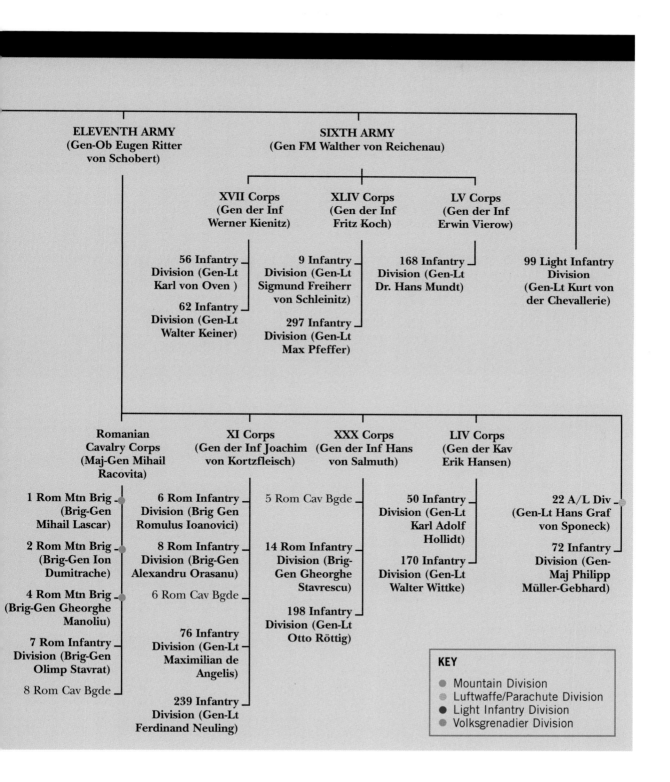

ELEVENTH ARMY
(Gen-Ob Eugen Ritter
von Schobert)

SIXTH ARMY
(Gen FM Walther von Reichenau)

XVII Corps
(Gen der Inf
Werner Kienitz)

XLIV Corps
(Gen der Inf
Fritz Koch)

LV Corps
(Gen der Inf
Erwin Vierow)

56 Infantry
Division (Gen-Lt
Karl von Oven)

62 Infantry
Division (Gen-Lt
Walter Keiner)

9 Infantry
Division (Gen-Lt
Sigmund Freiherr
von Schleinitz)

297 Infantry
Division (Gen-Lt
Max Pfeffer)

168 Infantry
Division (Gen-Lt
Dr. Hans Mundt)

99 Light Infantry
Division
(Gen-Lt Kurt von
der Chevallerie)

**Romanian
Cavalry Corps**
(Maj-Gen Mihail
Racovita)

XI Corps
(Gen der Inf Joachim
von Kortzfleisch)

XXX Corps
(Gen der Inf Hans
von Salmuth)

LIV Corps
(Gen der Kav
Erik Hansen)

1 Rom Mtn Brig
(Brig-Gen
Mihail Lascar)

2 Rom Mtn Brig
(Brig-Gen Ion
Dumitrache)

4 Rom Mtn Brig
(Brig-Gen Gheorghe
Manoliu)

7 Rom Infantry
Division (Brig-Gen
Olimp Stavrat)

8 Rom Cav Bgde

6 Rom Infantry
Division (Brig Gen
Romulus Ioanovici)

8 Rom Infantry
Division (Brig-Gen
Alexandru Orasanu)

6 Rom Cav Bgde

76 Infantry
Division (Gen-Lt
Maximilian de
Angelis)

239 Infantry
Division (Gen-Lt
Ferdinand Neuling)

5 Rom Cav Bgde

14 Rom Infantry
Division (Brig-
Gen Gheorghe
Stavrescu)

198 Infantry
Division (Gen-Lt
Otto Röttig)

50 Infantry
Division (Gen-Lt
Karl Adolf
Hollidt)

170 Infantry
Division (Gen-Lt
Walter Wittke)

22 A/L Div
(Gen-Lt Hans Graf
von Sponeck)

72 Infantry
Division (Gen-
Maj Philipp
Müller-Gebhard)

KEY
● Mountain Division
● Luftwaffe/Parachute Division
● Light Infantry Division
● Volksgrenadier Division

RIFLE COMPANY: 1943

From 1943, the basic German infantry division was reorganized, with reduced manning levels but with increased firepower. Most divisions lost their armoured car battalions, and a bicycle reconnaissance platoon was introduced to every regiment. Some anti-tank units were motorized, and a motorized flak company was added. The divisional engineer battalion was given extra heavy weapons, which should have been motorized but until the end of the war were generally horse-drawn. Infantry regiments were given anti-tank companies, which included one platoon equipped with three 5cm (2in) Pak 38 guns and two platoons equipped with Panzerfausts. The number of standard infantry battalions was reduced from three to two, though towards the end of the war units were given fusilier battalions. These were basically bicycle-mounted infantry, which often served as the divisional reconnaissance unit. Battalion support companies exchanged their six 8.1cm (3.2in) mortars for four of the much heavier 12cm (4.8in) mortars. Some of the 8.1cm (3.2in) mortars were passed down to the rifle platoons in rifle companies, replacing their light 5cm (2in) mortars.

Company HQ (1 officer, 12 men)

Company Supply Train (24 men)

Antitank Rifle Section (7 men)

One Rifle Platoon; Platoon HQ (1 officer, 5 men), Light Mortar Section (3 men), Rifle Squad (10 men) x 4

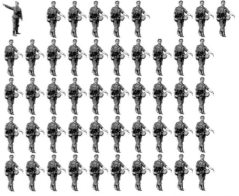

Second Rifle Platoon; Platoon HQ (1 officer, 5 men), Light Mortar Section (3 men), Rifle Squad (10 men) x 4

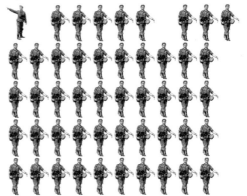

Third Rifle Platoon; Platoon HQ (1 officer, 5 men), Light Mortar Section (3 men), Rifle Squad (10 men) x 4

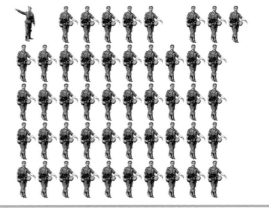

Leningrad and Moscow: 1941–42

The autumn of 1941 saw powerful forces driving hard to capture the cities of Leningrad and Moscow. Hitler ordered the final destruction of Leningrad, the cradle of the hated Bolshevik Revolution. No prisoners were to be taken.

For its final attack on Leningrad, Fourth Panzer Army was reinforced by tanks from Army Group Centre. On 8 August, the tanks broke through the Soviet defences. The German Sixteenth Army attacked to the northeast, while Eighteenth Army cleared Estonia and advanced to Lake Peipus. The Infantry was marching as fast as possible to catch up with the fast moving armour. By the end of August, Fourth Panzer Army was within 50km (30 miles) of Leningrad. The Finns had advanced on both sides of Lake Ladoga, reaching the old Finnish-Soviet frontier.

Driving up the west bank of the Volkhov, the lead German panzers reached Ishora, only 17km (11 miles) from the centre of Leningrad. Motorized infantry swung up to the east towards the River Neva and the shores of Lake Ladoga. The old imperial capital of Russia was now surrounded – but not occupied.

The two leading divisions were soon enmeshed in a labyrinth of anti-tank ditches and straggling earthworks thrown up by the citizens while the Germans had paused to regroup. By the evening of 10 September, the Germans had reached the Dugerdorf Heights, 10km (6 miles) south-east of the city.

But so many panzers had been hit or had broken down that the momentum of attack had been lost. German infantry moved up on their left during the following day, entering the Leningrad suburbs of Slutsk and Pushkin. By evening, they had occupied the Summer Palace of the Tsars at Krasnoye Selo.

Starved, not stormed

Hitler now lost patience and ordered that Leningrad should not be stormed but starved into submission. He needed the tanks of Army Group North transferred to Army Group Centre for an all-out drive to Moscow.

Over the next months, the Red Army made several attempts to break the siege. On 8 February, as part of the series of offensives that had started with the Moscow counterattack in December 1941, the Soviets launched an offensive near Toropets, to the south of Leningrad. The Red Army attack cut off the German II Corps as well as part of the X Corps of Generaloberst Ernst Busch's Sixteenth Army.

Demyansk Pocket

Trapped in the pocket at Demyansk were 90,000 men from the 12th, 30th, 32nd, 123rd and 290th infantry divisions, as well as the SS-Division *Totenkopf*. Some 10,000 auxiliaries from the Reich Labour service, Police and *Todt* organization were also caught in the pocket. Their commander was *General der Infanterie* Walter Graf von Brockdorff-Ahlefeldt, commander of the Second Army Corps.

LENINGRAD AND MOSCOW: 1941–1942		
	Dec 1941	**Mar 1942**
GERMAN ARMY DIVISIONS BY TYPE		
Panzer	24	25
Infantry (mot)	16	17
Cavalry	0	0
Infantry	162	170
Mountain	8	8
Security	9	9
GERMAN ARMY DIVISIONS BY THEATRE		
Germany	6	8
East	146	167
West	42	32
Norway	7	8
Finland	6	7
Southeast	9	5

ARMY GROUP NORTH (SUMMER 1942)

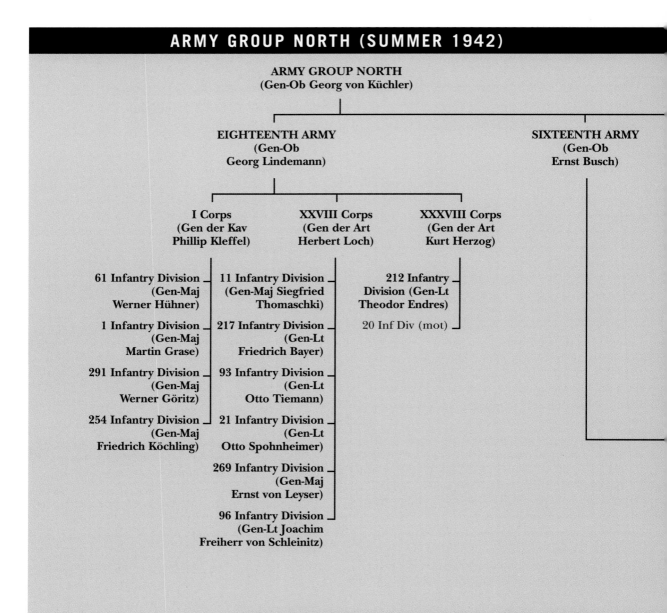

ARMY GROUP NORTH
(Gen-Ob Georg von Küchler)

EIGHTEENTH ARMY
(Gen-Ob
Georg Lindemann)

SIXTEENTH ARMY
(Gen-Ob
Ernst Busch)

I Corps
(Gen der Kav
Phillip Kleffel)

XXVIII Corps
(Gen der Art
Herbert Loch)

XXXVIII Corps
(Gen der Art
Kurt Herzog)

61 Infantry Division
(Gen-Maj
Werner Hühner)

11 Infantry Division
(Gen-Maj Siegfried
Thomaschki)

**212 Infantry
Division (Gen-Lt
Theodor Endres)**

1 Infantry Division
(Gen-Maj
Martin Grase)

217 Infantry Division
(Gen-Lt
Friedrich Bayer)

20 Inf Div (mot)

291 Infantry Division
(Gen-Maj
Werner Göritz)

93 Infantry Division
(Gen-Lt
Otto Tiemann)

254 Infantry Division
(Gen-Maj
Friedrich Köchling)

21 Infantry Division
(Gen-Lt
Otto Spohnheimer)

269 Infantry Division
(Gen-Maj
Ernst von Leyser)

96 Infantry Division
(Gen-Lt Joachim
Freiherr von Schleinitz)

KEY

- Mountain Division
- Luftwaffe/Parachute Division
- Light Infantry Division
- Volksgrenadier Division

After the initial failure to take Leningrad by storm at the end of 1941, Army Group North settled into a siege in the early part of 1942. However, in his plans for the summer offensive of 1942, Hitler restated his intention to take the city. Part of Eleventh Army, along with the heavy siege train which it had used to flatten Sevastopol, was transferred to Army Group North under the command of Generalfeldmarschall Erich von Manstein. Operation *Nordlicht* was to have been launched in September. However, a pre-emptive strike by the Soviet Volkhov Front forced the Germans to use up the supplies and equipment which had been intended for the offensive, and it was cancelled.

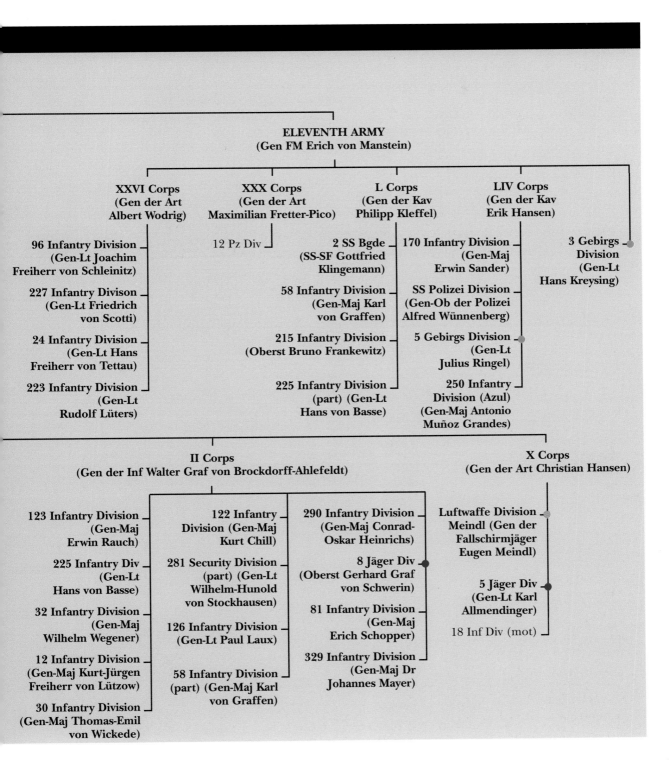

ELEVENTH ARMY
(Gen FM Erich von Manstein)

XXVI Corps
(Gen der Art Albert Wodrig)

96 Infantry Division
(Gen-Lt Joachim Freiherr von Schleinitz)

227 Infantry Divison
(Gen-Lt Friedrich von Scotti)

24 Infantry Division
(Gen-Lt Hans Freiherr von Tettau)

223 Infantry Division
(Gen-Lt Rudolf Lüters)

XXX Corps
(Gen der Art Maximilian Fretter-Pico)

12 Pz Div

L Corps
(Gen der Kav Philipp Kleffel)

2 SS Bgde
(SS-SF Gottfried Klingemann)

58 Infantry Division
(Gen-Maj Karl von Graffen)

215 Infantry Division
(Oberst Bruno Frankewitz)

225 Infantry Division
(part) (Gen-Lt Hans von Basse)

LIV Corps
(Gen der Kav Erik Hansen)

170 Infantry Division
(Gen-Maj Erwin Sander)

SS Polizei Division
(Gen-Ob der Polizei Alfred Wünnenberg)

5 Gebirgs Division
(Gen-Lt Julius Ringel)

250 Infantry Division (Azul)
(Gen-Maj Antonio Muñoz Grandes)

3 Gebirgs Division
(Gen-Lt Hans Kreysing)

II Corps
(Gen der Inf Walter Graf von Brockdorff-Ahlefeldt)

123 Infantry Division
(Gen-Maj Erwin Rauch)

225 Infantry Div
(Gen-Lt Hans von Basse)

32 Infantry Division
(Gen-Maj Wilhelm Wegener)

12 Infantry Division
(Gen-Maj Kurt-Jürgen Freiherr von Lützow)

30 Infantry Division
(Gen-Maj Thomas-Emil von Wickede)

122 Infantry Division (Gen-Maj Kurt Chill)

281 Security Division
(part) (Gen-Lt Wilhelm-Hunold von Stockhausen)

126 Infantry Division
(Gen-Lt Paul Laux)

58 Infantry Division
(part) (Gen-Maj Karl von Graffen)

290 Infantry Division
(Gen-Maj Conrad-Oskar Heinrichs)

8 Jäger Div
(Oberst Gerhard Graf von Schwerin)

81 Infantry Division
(Gen-Maj Erich Schopper)

329 Infantry Division
(Gen-Maj Dr Johannes Mayer)

X Corps
(Gen der Art Christian Hansen)

Luftwaffe Division Meindl (Gen der Fallschirmjäger Eugen Meindl)

5 Jäger Div
(Gen-Lt Karl Allmendinger)

18 Inf Div (mot)

Hitler ordered that the surrounded divisions hold their positions until relieved. The Pocket contained two fairly capable airfields at Demyansk and Peski. The weather was surprisingly cooperative, and despite considerable snow on the ground at this time, resupply operations were generally successful. The *Luftwaffe* managed to deliver daily up to 270 tons of supplies by air, though it required virtually all of the *Luftwaffe's* transports as well as much of their bomber force.

The Soviets increased their attempts to destroy the pocket, and over the winter and spring launched a number of large-scale assaults. Three Soviet Armies, with more than 18 infantry divisions, were tied up for four months.

On 21 March 1942, German forces opened a narrow corridor to the pocket. Over the next weeks, this corridor was widened. The battle group was able to break out of the siege on 21 April, but the battle had taken a toll. Out of about 100,000 men trapped, some 3335 were lost and over 10,000 wounded. However, their struggle had denied the Soviet High Command the use of numerous units at a critical moment.

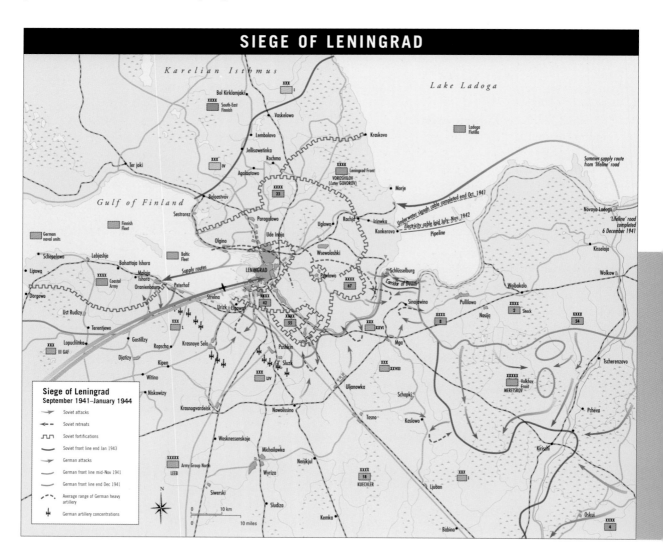

SIEGE OF LENINGRAD

Siege of Leningrad
September 1941–January 1944

- Soviet attacks
- Soviet retreats
- Soviet fortifications
- Soviet front line end Jan 1943
- German attacks
- German front line mid-Nov 1941
- German front line end Dec 1941
- Average range of German heavy artillery
- German artillery concentrations

Operation Typhoon, the drive to Moscow, began on October 2nd. In front of Army Group Centre was a series of elaborate defence lines, the first centred on Vyazma and the second on Mozhaisk.

The first blow took the Soviets completely by surprise as Guderian's 2nd Panzer Group, now renamed Second Panzer Army, took Orel. Three days later, the Panzers pushed on Bryansk while Second Army attacked from the west. Three Soviet armies were now encircled. To the north, Third and Fourth Panzer Armies attacked Vyazma, trapping another five Soviet armies.

Moscow's first line of defence had been shattered. The pocket yielded 663,000 Soviet prisoners, bringing the tally since the start of the invasion to three million Soviet soldiers captured. The Soviets had only 90,000 men and 150 tanks left for the defence of Moscow.

Fighting the mud

On 13 October, Third Panzer Army was within 140km (90 miles) of the capital. But now the weather played a fateful role. While temperatures fell, heavy rainfall turned the roads into mud, and the German advance on Moscow was slowed to as little as 3km (2 miles) a day. On 31 October, a halt was ordered so that the armies could re-organize. The pause gave the Soviets, who

could use their rail network, time to reinforce. In a month, they organized eleven new armies, including 30 divisions of Siberian troops. These had been freed from the Soviet far east, as Soviet intelligence had assured Stalin there was no longer a threat from the Japanese.

On 15 November, the rains slowed, but the first stirring of winter was beginning to make itself felt. The hardening ground allowed the Germans to resume the offensive.

However, the supply position had not improved. On 2 December, the Fourth Panzer Army had penetrated to within 24km (15 miles) of Moscow. Indeed, a reconnaissance patrol from the 258th Infantry Division reported that it had seen the spires of the Kremlin in the distance. By now, however, the first blizzards of the winter had set in.

The *Wehrmacht* was not equipped for winter warfare. Frostbite and disease caused more casualties than combat, and the dead and wounded reached 155,000 in three weeks. Some divisions were now at 50 per cent strength. The bitter cold also caused severe problems for their guns and equipment, and weather conditions grounded the *Luftwaffe*.

Soviet counteroffensive

Under the command of Georgi Zhukhov, the Soviets had built up a force of over 500,000 men for the defence of Moscow. On 5 December, they launched a massive counterattack that pushed the Germans back over 322km (200 miles).

Panzer crews and *Luftwaffe* personnel were forced to fight as infantry as the cold immobilized their equipment. Rifles froze solid as temperatures fell to −40°C: engine cylinder blocks cracked in the cold and axles were frozen solid. For the infantryman in his summer uniform, the only way to fight off the cold was to pad it with newspapers or straw. The ground was frozen solid, and the only way to dig defensive positions was by using explosives.

After the failure to take Moscow, the German Army eventually held the advancing Soviets and by a Herculean effort managed to stabilize the front. The invasion of the USSR would cost the German Army over 250,000 dead and 500,000 wounded, the majority of whom became casualties after 1 October.

September 1941 – January 1944

The failure of the German attempt to take Leningrad by force in September 1941, and Hitler's decision to starve the city into submission, meant that the divisions of Army Group North now settled in for a siege. Tanks played some part in the campaign, but it was essentially an infantry and artillery battle, with troops manning World War I-style trench lines and a massive artillery park bombarding the city incessantly.

For Leningrad, a precarious lifeline was provided by Lake Ladoga, a bare minimum of supplies coming by ship in summer and across the ice in winter.

The Germans did not manage to cut that line, which was enough to ensure that Leningrad survived over 900 days of siege – though more than half a million of its citizens did not.

ARMY GROUP CENTRE (SUMMER 1942)

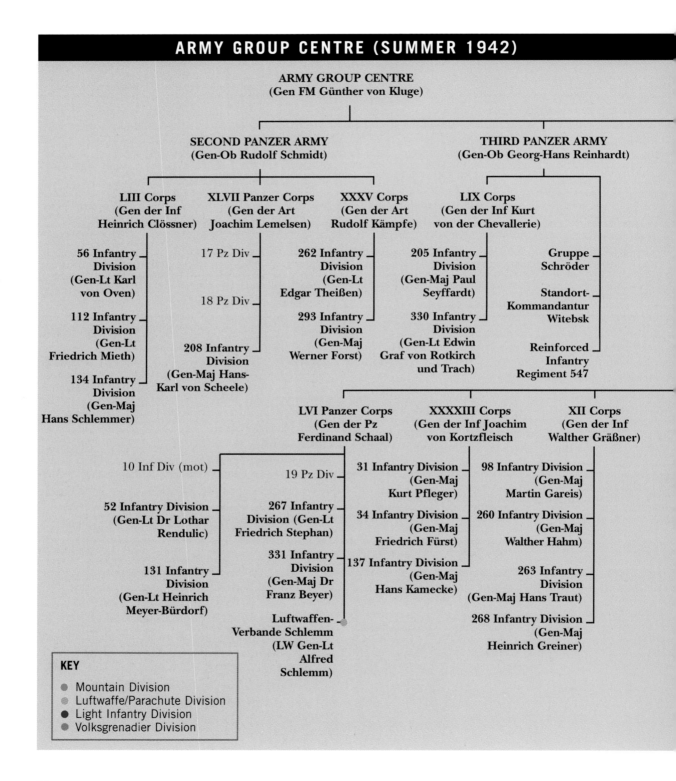

ARMY GROUP CENTRE
(Gen FM Günther von Kluge)

SECOND PANZER ARMY
(Gen-Ob Rudolf Schmidt)

THIRD PANZER ARMY
(Gen-Ob Georg-Hans Reinhardt)

LIII Corps
(Gen der Inf
Heinrich Clössner)

XLVII Panzer Corps
(Gen der Art
Joachim Lemelsen)

XXXV Corps
(Gen der Art
Rudolf Kämpfe)

LIX Corps
(Gen der Inf Kurt
von der Chevallerie)

56 Infantry
Division
(Gen-Lt Karl
von Oven)

17 Pz Div

262 Infantry
Division
(Gen-Lt
Edgar Theißen)

205 Infantry
Division
(Gen-Maj Paul
Seyffardt)

Gruppe
Schröder

112 Infantry
Division
(Gen-Lt
Friedrich Mieth)

18 Pz Div

Standort-
Kommandantur
Witebsk

134 Infantry
Division
(Gen-Maj
Hans Schlemmer)

208 Infantry
Division
(Gen-Maj Hans-
Karl von Scheele)

293 Infantry
Division
(Gen-Maj
Werner Forst)

330 Infantry
Division
(Gen-Lt Edwin
Graf von Rotkirch
und Trach)

Reinforced
Infantry
Regiment 547

LVI Panzer Corps
(Gen der Pz
Ferdinand Schaal)

XXXXIII Corps
(Gen der Inf Joachim
von Kortzfleisch)

XII Corps
(Gen der Inf
Walther Gräßner)

10 Inf Div (mot)

19 Pz Div

31 Infantry Division
(Gen-Maj
Kurt Pfleger)

98 Infantry Division
(Gen-Maj
Martin Gareis)

52 Infantry Division
(Gen-Lt Dr Lothar
Rendulic)

267 Infantry
Division (Gen-Lt
Friedrich Stephan)

34 Infantry Division
(Gen-Maj
Friedrich Fürst)

260 Infantry Division
(Gen-Maj
Walther Hahm)

131 Infantry
Division
(Gen-Lt Heinrich
Meyer-Bürdorf)

331 Infantry
Division
(Gen-Maj Dr
Franz Beyer)

137 Infantry Division
(Gen-Maj
Hans Kamecke)

263 Infantry
Division
(Gen-Maj Hans Traut)

Luftwaffen-
Verbande Schlemm
(LW Gen-Lt
Alfred
Schlemm)

268 Infantry Division
(Gen-Maj
Heinrich Greiner)

KEY
- Mountain Division
- Luftwaffe/Parachute Division
- Light Infantry Division
- Volksgrenadier Division

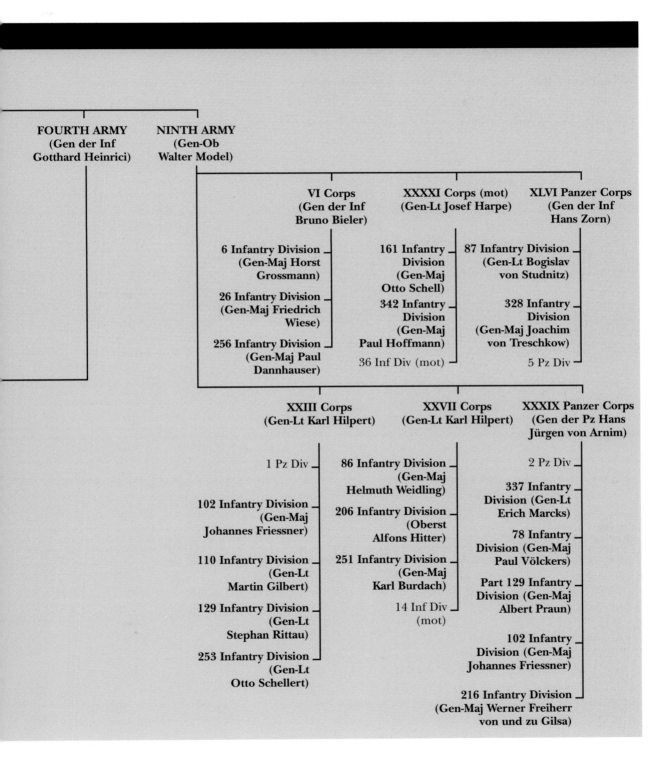

FOURTH ARMY
(Gen der Inf
Gotthard Heinrici)

NINTH ARMY
(Gen-Ob
Walter Model)

VI Corps
(Gen der Inf
Bruno Bieler)

XXXXI Corps (mot)
(Gen-Lt Josef Harpe)

XLVI Panzer Corps
(Gen der Inf
Hans Zorn)

6 Infantry Division
(Gen-Maj Horst
Grossmann)

26 Infantry Division
(Gen-Maj Friedrich
Wiese)

256 Infantry Division
(Gen-Maj Paul
Dannhauser)

161 Infantry
Division
(Gen-Maj
Otto Schell)

342 Infantry
Division
(Gen-Maj
Paul Hoffmann)

36 Inf Div (mot)

87 Infantry Division
(Gen-Lt Bogislav
von Studnitz)

328 Infantry
Division
(Gen-Maj Joachim
von Treschkow)

5 Pz Div

XXIII Corps
(Gen-Lt Karl Hilpert)

XXVII Corps
(Gen-Lt Karl Hilpert)

XXXIX Panzer Corps
(Gen der Pz Hans
Jürgen von Arnim)

1 Pz Div

102 Infantry Division
(Gen-Maj
Johannes Friessner)

110 Infantry Division
(Gen-Lt
Martin Gilbert)

129 Infantry Division
(Gen-Lt
Stephan Rittau)

253 Infantry Division
(Gen-Lt
Otto Schellert)

86 Infantry Division
(Gen-Maj
Helmuth Weidling)

206 Infantry Division
(Oberst
Alfons Hitter)

251 Infantry Division
(Gen-Maj
Karl Burdach)

14 Inf Div
(mot)

2 Pz Div

337 Infantry
Division (Gen-Lt
Erich Marcks)

78 Infantry
Division (Gen-Maj
Paul Völckers)

Part 129 Infantry
Division (Gen-Maj
Albert Praun)

102 Infantry
Division (Gen-Maj
Johannes Friessner)

216 Infantry Division
(Gen-Maj Werner Freiherr
von und zu Gilsa)

Southern Front: 1942

In January 1942, 12 German armies were locked in combat with 22 Soviet armies. On a front stretching from the Crimea to the Gulf of Finland, 141 divisions, including 11 from Axis allies, faced more than 300 Russian formations.

The fighting conditions were appalling, and favoured the Soviets, used to the rigours of the Russian winter. As the petrol froze in their fuel tanks, the Germans came to place greater reliance on horse drawn transport.

As the winter drew on, however, they succeeded in stemming the Soviet hordes. The stubborn German defence exposed the Red Army's lack of experience, its problems exacerbated by shortages of all kinds. By March, even Stalin had to admit that his great offensive was over.

Plan for 1942

With the situation at the front less perilous, the *Führer* began planning his summer offensive. In Directive No 41, dated 5 April, Hitler stated: 'The enemy has suffered enormous losses of men and materiel. In attempting to exploit their apparent initial successes, they have exhausted during this winter the mass of their reserves, which were intended for later operations.'

All available forces were to be concentrated on the southern sector. Their mission was firstly to annihilate the enemy on the Don. Then they were to swing north and take Stalingrad, followed by a combined assault to conquer the oil-producing areas of the Caucasus. Without that oil, German panzers would go nowhere. Lastly, they were to capture the passes through the Caucasus mountains, giving access to the Middle East.

Soviet Spring offensive

The return of warmer weather in the spring of 1942 was the signal for a Soviet offensive in the south, but the attempt to recapture Kharkov failed dismally. Ten days and nights of hectic thrust and counterthrust in open country turned into a master class in *blitzkrieg*.

The advancing Soviets were outmanoeuvred by the superbly coordinated German air and ground forces. The *Luftwaffe* air fleets under Ritter von Greim dominated the skies. Swarms of Ju88s, Stukas and Heinkel 111s pounded the Soviet positions, protected by the world's most experienced fighter pilots, who had been reinforced by Germany's Axis allies.

Three Soviet armies were surrounded and annihilated. Marshal Timoshenko was summoned to Moscow to explain the loss of another 200,000 men.

Army Group A: Early 1942

As the German Sixth and Seventeenth Armies shattered the Soviet offensive at Kharkov, Eleventh Army under the command of General Erich von Manstein broke through the heavily fortified Soviet positions on the Kerch peninsula.

By April 1942, the Soviets had ferried 250,000 men into the Crimea, together with considerable tank and artillery support. However, the sheer weight of German metal forced the Soviets back from Feodosia. The Panzers, supported by screaming Stukas, then drove through the waist of the peninsula towards Kerch itself. Between 15 and 20 May, the Soviets were driven into the Black Sea. They left behind 170,000 prisoners.

With its flank protected, Eleventh Army doubled back to storm Sevastopol, home of the Soviet Black Sea Fleet.

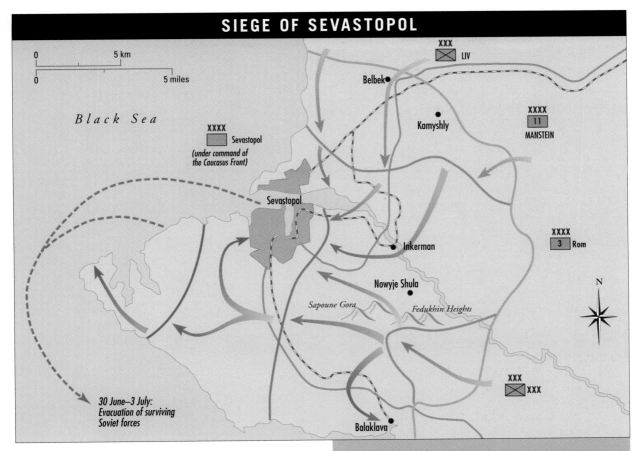

SIEGE OF SEVASTOPOL

0 — 5 km

0 — 5 miles

Black Sea

XXX · LIV

Belbek

XXXX · Sevastopol · (under command of the Caucasus Front)

Kamyshly

XXXX · 11 · MANSTEIN

Sevastopol

Inkerman

XXXX · 3 · Rom

Nowyje Shula

Sapoune Gora

Fedukhin Heights

N

Balaklava

XXX · XXX

30 June–3 July: Evacuation of surviving Soviet forces

Manstein had received strong reinforcements. To oppose the Russian garrison, he could call on 204,000 men, 720 tanks, 600 aircraft, 670 guns and 450 mortars, including Wehrmacht's general reserve of siege artillery.

Battle for Sevastopol

After the initial barrage, the German LIV Corps moved against the defences. The Soviets defended every metre of territory through the first weeks of June, demonstrating a tenacity that would be repeated to devastating effect at Stalingrad later that year.

The Germans finally breached the defences on the night of 28/29 June. During the next three days, the Soviets organized a Dunkirk-style evacuation to rescue as many as possible of the men, women and children who had survived the 250-day siege. The Germans had won, but were left with a gutted city, its buildings destroyed.

December 1941–July 1942

At dawn on 8 May, Manstein's Eleventh Army crossed the Kamenskoye isthmus to assault the positions covering Kerch. The nine German divisions were outnumbered two to one, but as usual the *Wehrmacht* commanders placed their strongest forces against the weakest point in the enemy front line.

Armageddon preceded the assault on the fortress. Operations commenced with a five-day barrage, which reminded some older members of the Army staff of Verdun, 25 years before. Manstein's experts used every piece of artillery they could bring to bear.

Included in the heavy artillery pounding the Russian positions was the massive 'Karl', a siege mortar with a calibre of 60cm (24in), and the largest gun ever made, the 80cm (32in) 'Gustav' railway gun.

ARMY GROUP B (AUGUST 1942)

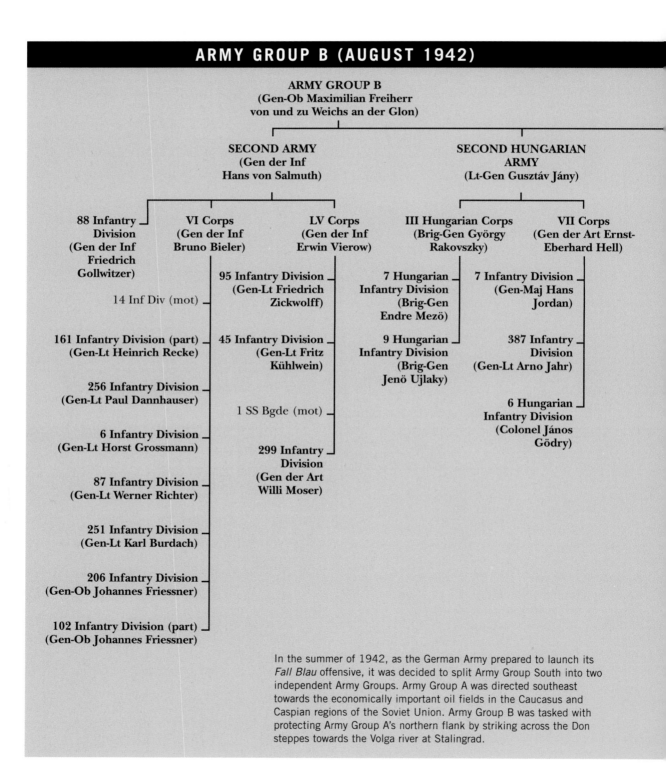

ARMY GROUP B
(Gen-Ob Maximilian Freiherr
von und zu Weichs an der Glon)

SECOND ARMY
(Gen der Inf
Hans von Salmuth)

SECOND HUNGARIAN ARMY
(Lt-Gen Gusztáv Jány)

88 Infantry Division
(Gen der Inf
Friedrich
Gollwitzer)

VI Corps
(Gen der Inf
Bruno Bieler)

LV Corps
(Gen der Inf
Erwin Vierow)

III Hungarian Corps
(Brig-Gen György
Rakovszky)

VII Corps
(Gen der Art Ernst-
Eberhard Hell)

14 Inf Div (mot)

95 Infantry Division
(Gen-Lt Friedrich
Zickwolff)

**7 Hungarian
Infantry Division**
(Brig-Gen
Endre Mezö)

7 Infantry Division
(Gen-Maj Hans
Jordan)

161 Infantry Division (part)
(Gen-Lt Heinrich Recke)

45 Infantry Division
(Gen-Lt Fritz
Kühlwein)

**9 Hungarian
Infantry Division**
(Brig-Gen
Jenö Ujlaky)

**387 Infantry
Division**
(Gen-Lt Arno Jahr)

256 Infantry Division
(Gen-Lt Paul Dannhauser)

1 SS Bgde (mot)

**6 Hungarian
Infantry Division**
(Colonel János
Gödry)

6 Infantry Division
(Gen-Lt Horst Grossmann)

**299 Infantry
Division**
(Gen der Art
Willi Moser)

87 Infantry Division
(Gen-Lt Werner Richter)

251 Infantry Division
(Gen-Lt Karl Burdach)

206 Infantry Division
(Gen-Ob Johannes Friessner)

102 Infantry Division (part)
(Gen-Ob Johannes Friessner)

In the summer of 1942, as the German Army prepared to launch its *Fall Blau* offensive, it was decided to split Army Group South into two independent Army Groups. Army Group A was directed southeast towards the economically important oil fields in the Caucasus and Caspian regions of the Soviet Union. Army Group B was tasked with protecting Army Group A's northern flank by striking across the Don steppes towards the Volga river at Stalingrad.

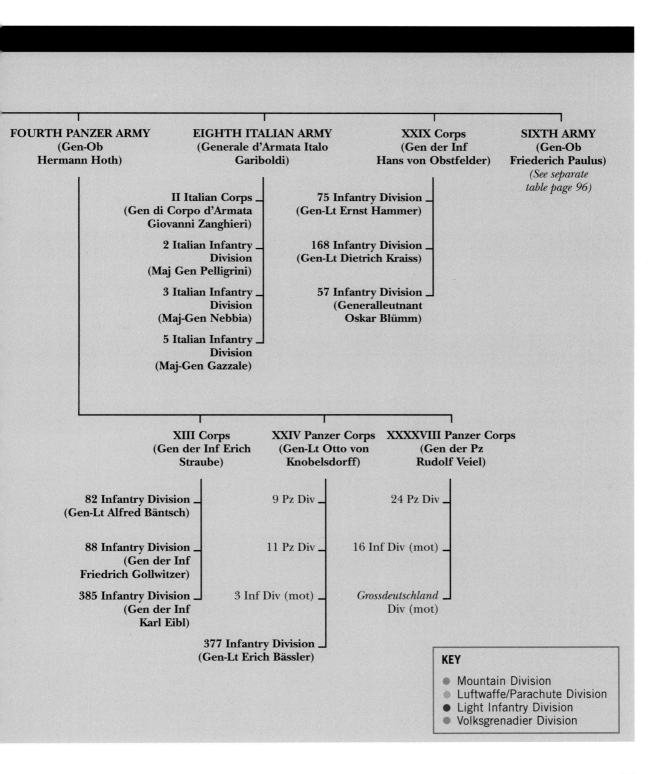

FOURTH PANZER ARMY
(Gen-Ob
Hermann Hoth)

EIGHTH ITALIAN ARMY
(Generale d'Armata Italo
Gariboldi)

XXIX Corps
(Gen der Inf
Hans von Obstfelder)

SIXTH ARMY
(Gen-Ob
Friederich Paulus)
*(See separate
table page 96)*

II Italian Corps
(Gen di Corpo d'Armata
Giovanni Zanghieri)

**2 Italian Infantry
Division**
(Maj Gen Pelligrini)

**3 Italian Infantry
Division**
(Maj-Gen Nebbia)

**5 Italian Infantry
Division**
(Maj-Gen Gazzale)

75 Infantry Division
(Gen-Lt Ernst Hammer)

168 Infantry Division
(Gen-Lt Dietrich Kraiss)

57 Infantry Division
(Generalleutnant
Oskar Blümm)

XIII Corps
(Gen der Inf Erich
Straube)

XXIV Panzer Corps
(Gen-Lt Otto von
Knobelsdorff)

XXXXVIII Panzer Corps
(Gen der Pz
Rudolf Veiel)

82 Infantry Division
(Gen-Lt Alfred Bäntsch)

88 Infantry Division
(Gen der Inf
Friedrich Gollwitzer)

385 Infantry Division
(Gen der Inf
Karl Eibl)

9 Pz Div

11 Pz Div

3 Inf Div (mot)

377 Infantry Division
(Gen-Lt Erich Bässler)

24 Pz Div

16 Inf Div (mot)

Grossdeutschland
Div (mot)

KEY
- ● Mountain Division
- ● Luftwaffe/Parachute Division
- ● Light Infantry Division
- ● Volksgrenadier Division

95

Stalingrad

The German summer offensive of 1942 was known as *Fall Blau*, 'Operation Blue'. Hitler had sacked von Brauchitsch, the commander-in-chief of the Army, and now planned to exercise total military control himself.

Three-quarters of the Soviet Union's oil was produced in the Caucasus, and Stalingrad, which overlooked the River Volga, was an important nexus of transportation.

Army Group A was to advance to the oilfields in the southeast, while Army Group B led by *Generaloberst* M von Weichs would march on and take Stalingrad.

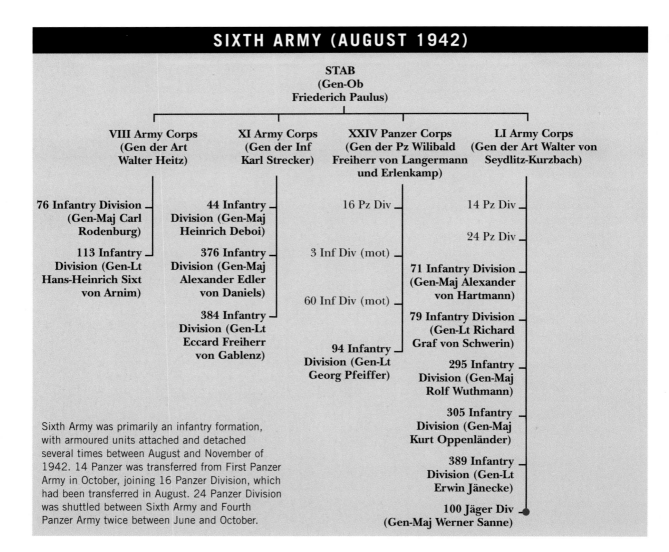

SIXTH ARMY (AUGUST 1942)

STAB
(Gen-Ob Friederich Paulus)

VIII Army Corps (Gen der Art Walter Heitz)

XI Army Corps (Gen der Inf Karl Strecker)

XXIV Panzer Corps (Gen der Pz Wilibald Freiherr von Langermann und Erlenkamp)

LI Army Corps (Gen der Art Walter von Seydlitz-Kurzbach)

76 Infantry Division (Gen-Maj Carl Rodenburg)

113 Infantry Division (Gen-Lt Hans-Heinrich Sixt von Arnim)

44 Infantry Division (Gen-Maj Heinrich Deboi)

376 Infantry Division (Gen-Maj Alexander Edler von Daniels)

384 Infantry Division (Gen-Lt Eccard Freiherr von Gablenz)

16 Pz Div

3 Inf Div (mot)

60 Inf Div (mot)

94 Infantry Division (Gen-Lt Georg Pfeiffer)

14 Pz Div

24 Pz Div

71 Infantry Division (Gen-Maj Alexander von Hartmann)

79 Infantry Division (Gen-Lt Richard Graf von Schwerin)

295 Infantry Division (Gen-Maj Rolf Wuthmann)

305 Infantry Division (Gen-Maj Kurt Oppenländer)

389 Infantry Division (Gen-Lt Erwin Jänecke)

100 Jäger Div (Gen-Maj Werner Sanne)

Sixth Army was primarily an infantry formation, with armoured units attached and detached several times between August and November of 1942. 14 Panzer was transferred from First Panzer Army in October, joining 16 Panzer Division, which had been transferred in August. 24 Panzer Division was shuttled between Sixth Army and Fourth Panzer Army twice between June and October.

Final battle for Stalingrad

Marshal Georgi Zhukhov launched Operation Uranus on 19 November 1942, and within days a massive Soviet pincer movement had isolated Sixth Army fighting in Stalingrad. All attempts to relieve the trapped German soldiers failed, and the *Luftwaffe* was never able to make good Hermann Göring's boasts that he would sustain the city from the air. As January progressed, the noose around Stalingrad was tightened. The German forces retreated to the city, losing control of important airfields. The fighting was less fierce than it had been in September and October: the Soviets could let cold, starvation and disease do most of the work. Stalin ordered the pocket eliminated in January, and by the end of the month the surviving Germans were pressed into two small pockets on the Volga.

The Battle for Stalingrad
September 1942–February 1943

Russian attacks
German counterattacks
German retreats
German front line
Limit of Russian artillery
Russian air support

BATTLE OF STALINGRAD

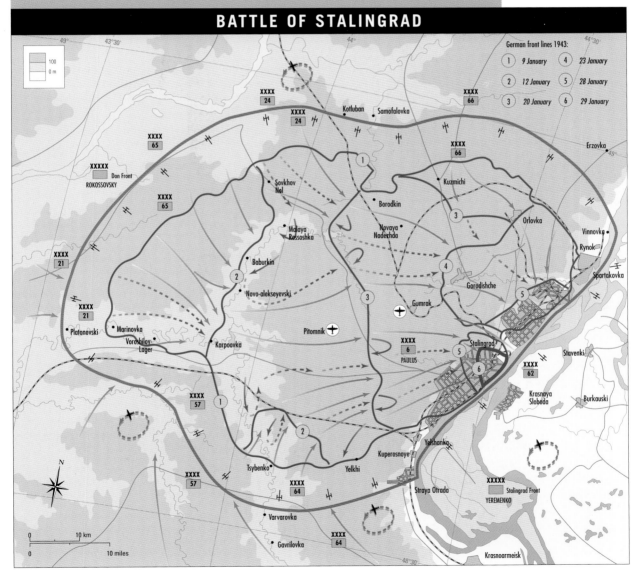

German front lines 1943:
1. 9 January
2. 12 January
3. 20 January
4. 23 January
5. 28 January
6. 29 January

FRIEDERICH PAULUS
(1890–1957)

Born in Hesse, the son of a school teacher, Friedrich Paulus joined the German Army as an officer cadet in 1910. During World War I, he served as an infantry officer. Between the wars, he served primarily as a staff officer. Conscientious and hard-working, he was nevertheless considered indecisive, and senior officers like Guderian had some doubts about his toughness and lack of command experience.

• He was Chief-of-Staff in Tenth Army in Poland (September 1939), and of Sixth Army under von Reichenau in the Low Countries (may 1940).

• As Deputy Chief of the General Staff, he helped to draw up the plans for the invasion of the Soviet Union in 1941.

• Paulus took command of Sixth Army in January 1942 after the death of von Reichenau. He led it to defeat at Stalingrad, surrendering on 31 January 1943, one day after being promoted to Field Marshal by Hitler.

The Stalingrad offensive was intended to secure the flank of Group A and to cut off the Caucasus area entirely from the rest of Russia.

Easy early victories convinced Hitler that taking Stalingrad would be easy, and he ordered several units of the Stalingrad advance to head south to assist the invasion of the Caucasus. The remaining troops of the Sixth Army and the Fourth Panzer Army were to continue and take the city.

Stalingrad attack

German Sixth Army launched its attack on Stalingrad in September. In Berlin, Hitler was already proclaiming victory. However, the Soviets fed in just enough troops to keep the Germans occupied, and to resist their best efforts. Prior to the assault, the *Luftwaffe* had bombed the city heavily.

Unfortunately, the ruined buildings proved to be an advantage to the defenders, and the German infantry became bogged down in a series of battles to take key factories in the city.

The Red Army had built up a massive reserve to the east, but they were not immediately thrown into the battle. The purpose for the delay was finally revealed on 19 November, after the last of six major attacks by Sixth Army had been beaten off.

Surprise was near total when the Soviets unleashed massive barrages north and south of Stalingrad. German divisions were engulfed by wave upon wave of Soviet armour, heavily supported by aircraft and artillery. The next day the Soviets attacked in the south.

Siege and surrender

By 23 November, the encirclement was complete. Some 300,000 Axis soldiers were trapped inside Stalingrad. Stalin ordered the pocket crushed in January, and a renewed Soviet *blitzkrieg* broke into the perimeter west of the city. Something like 25,000 sick and wounded Germans were evacuated by air, but a far greater number of men died as frost-bitten limbs and wounds turned gangrenous.

Of the 300,000 men in the pocket, 91,000 survived to surrender, of whom half would be dead before spring. Survivors were marched off to Siberia: only 5000 would ever return from Soviet captivity.

Army Group A: the Caucasus

For the first few weeks of Operation Blue, the German offensive was a repeat of the lightning advances of Operation *Barbarossa* the previous year. Hitler, frustrated at the lack of opposition, fired Fedor von Bock and split Army Group South into two.

Army Group A, under Field Marshal Wilhelm List, was to turn south, take Rostov and drive into the Caucasus. Army Group B, commanded by Field Marshal Maximilian von Weichs, would thrust east and cut the Volga while screening the left wing of the offensive.

Kleist's panzer spearheads, leading Army Group A, raced across the steppe under an air umbrella that was impenetrable to a Soviet Air Force still woefully short of skilled pilots.

Advance into the Caucasus

On August 9, German troops captured the oil-producing centre of Maikop but found it completely wrecked. As supplies ran low and the Red Army's resistance stiffened, the German advance stalled on August 28 – well short of its objective, the Grozny oil fields. Hitler dismissed the commander responsible at the end of August and began directing Army Group A himself.

As the drive reached the mountains, the emphasis switched from Kleist's panzers to LXXIX Gebirgs Korps (Mountain Corps), led by *General der Gebirgstruppen* Ludwig Kübler. The mountain infantrymen were given a mixed reception by the local inhabitants. Some, hostile to the Soviet regime, welcomed them. Others, local troops in the main, put up a stubborn defence.

The mountain troops fought a war without any fixed lines. Truly defensive positions in the higher ranges were in short supply, and patrols from both sides would penetrate deep into territory that was at least nominally held by the enemy.

Battle for Tuapse

The *Gebirgsjäger* nevertheless pushed through the mountain range, attacking the port of Tuapse on the northeastern shore of the Black Sea. Thus far, the port had resisted capture by Kleist's panzers, which found it difficult to advance through the terrain.

The 1st Mountain Division, the *Edelweiss* division commanded by Hubert Lanz, advanced through the Marukhskiy Pass and the Klukhorskiy Pass.

The 4th Mountain Division, manned primarily by Tyrolean Austrians, pushed further through the mountains in the direction of Tbilisi, getting to within 30km (19 miles) of Sukhumi in Georgia.

Raising the flag

In August, a team of mountaineers climbed Mount Elbruz, which at 5642m (18510ft) is the highest peak in Europe. The German flag was raised at 11.00 a.m. on 21 August. The triumph was not for long: when the Soviets returned later in 1942, the flag's removal was considered a priority.

The German advance began to run out of steam in Chechnya in September, partly as a result of the diversion of reserves to the Stalingrad front. The rout of a Romanian mountain division in the face of a Soviet counterattack forced von Kleist to call off his last attempt to break through the Caucasus late in October.

Early in 1943, the mountain troops in the Caucasus were forced to beat a hasty retreat, after the success of the Soviet counteroffensives at Stalingrad threatened to isolate the whole of Army Group A.

Retreat from the Caucasus

Kleist conducted a masterly retreat in the face of a Soviet attack in the Caucasus. At the same time, Field Marshal Erich von Manstein had been given command of a new formation, Army Group Don. Operation Saturn – a massive Red Army offensive in the southernmost part of the front, aimed at capturing Rostov and thus cutting off the German Army Group A – forced von Manstein to divert his forces to help the hard-pressed Army Group A in its retreat to the Ukraine, thus avoiding the collapse of the entire front.

ARMY GROUP A (AUGUST 1942)

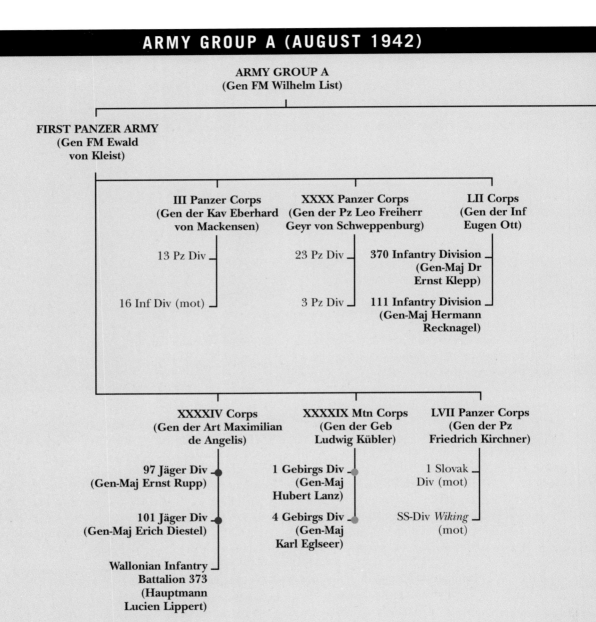

ARMY GROUP A
(Gen FM Wilhelm List)

FIRST PANZER ARMY
(Gen FM Ewald
von Kleist)

III Panzer Corps
(Gen der Kav Eberhard
von Mackensen)

XXXX Panzer Corps
(Gen der Pz Leo Freiherr
Geyr von Schweppenburg)

LII Corps
(Gen der Inf
Eugen Ott)

13 Pz Div

23 Pz Div

370 Infantry Division
(Gen-Maj Dr
Ernst Klepp)

16 Inf Div (mot)

3 Pz Div

111 Infantry Division
(Gen-Maj Hermann
Recknagel)

XXXXIV Corps
(Gen der Art Maximilian
de Angelis)

XXXXIX Mtn Corps
(Gen der Geb
Ludwig Kübler)

LVII Panzer Corps
(Gen der Pz
Friedrich Kirchner)

97 Jäger Div
(Gen-Maj Ernst Rupp)

1 Gebirgs Div
(Gen-Maj
Hubert Lanz)

1 Slovak
Div (mot)

101 Jäger Div
(Gen-Maj Erich Diestel)

4 Gebirgs Div
(Gen-Maj
Karl Eglseer)

SS-Div *Wiking*
(mot)

**Wallonian Infantry
Battalion 373**
(Hauptmann
Lucien Lippert)

Army Group A contained both Kleist's First Panzer Army, which would
spearhead the German drive to the oilfields of the Caucasus, and von
Manstein's Eleventh Army. This would play little part in the early stages
of the campaign, having just completed the gruelling conquest of
Crimea and Sevastopol, and was in need of restoration. In August and
September, the German Seventeenth Army was renamed *Armeegruppe*
Ruoth while it controlled the Romanian Third Army.

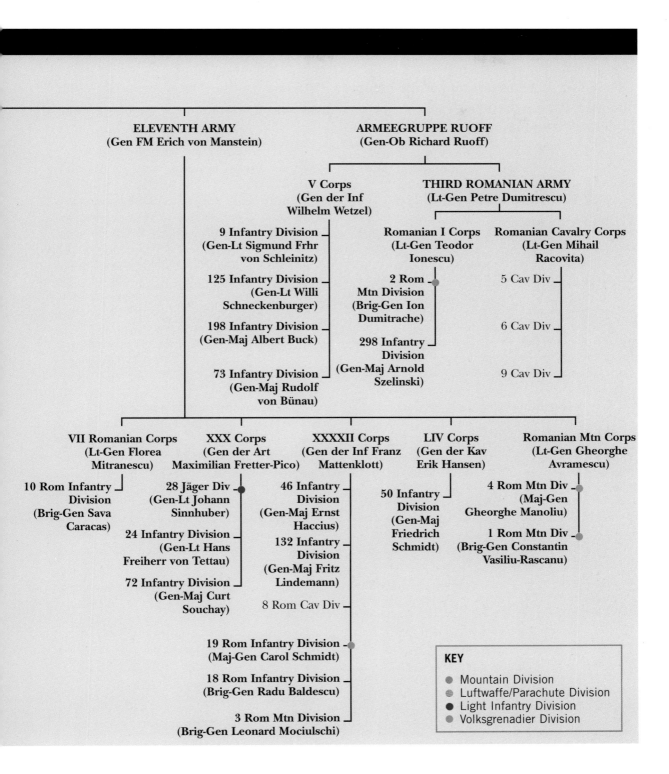

ELEVENTH ARMY
(Gen FM Erich von Manstein)

ARMEEGRUPPE RUOFF
(Gen-Ob Richard Ruoff)

V Corps
(Gen der Inf
Wilhelm Wetzel)

THIRD ROMANIAN ARMY
(Lt-Gen Petre Dumitrescu)

9 Infantry Division
(Gen-Lt Sigmund Frhr
von Schleinitz)

125 Infantry Division
(Gen-Lt Willi
Schneckenburger)

198 Infantry Division
(Gen-Maj Albert Buck)

73 Infantry Division
(Gen-Maj Rudolf
von Bünau)

Romanian I Corps
(Lt-Gen Teodor
Ionescu)

2 Rom
Mtn Division
(Brig-Gen Ion
Dumitrache)

298 Infantry
Division
(Gen-Maj Arnold
Szelinski)

Romanian Cavalry Corps
(Lt-Gen Mihail
Racovita)

5 Cav Div

6 Cav Div

9 Cav Div

VII Romanian Corps
(Lt-Gen Florea
Mitranescu)

XXX Corps
(Gen der Art
Maximilian Fretter-Pico)

XXXXII Corps
(Gen der Inf Franz
Mattenklott)

LIV Corps
(Gen der Kav
Erik Hansen)

Romanian Mtn Corps
(Lt-Gen Gheorghe
Avramescu)

10 Rom Infantry
Division
(Brig-Gen Sava
Caracas)

28 Jäger Div
(Gen-Lt Johann
Sinnhuber)

24 Infantry Division
(Gen-Lt Hans
Freiherr von Tettau)

72 Infantry Division
(Gen-Maj Curt
Souchay)

46 Infantry
Division
(Gen-Maj Ernst
Haccius)

132 Infantry
Division
(Gen-Maj Fritz
Lindemann)

8 Rom Cav Div

50 Infantry
Division
(Gen-Maj
Friedrich
Schmidt)

4 Rom Mtn Div
(Maj-Gen
Gheorghe Manoliu)

1 Rom Mtn Div
(Brig-Gen Constantin
Vasiliu-Rascanu)

19 Rom Infantry Division
(Maj-Gen Carol Schmidt)

18 Rom Infantry Division
(Brig-Gen Radu Baldescu)

3 Rom Mtn Division
(Brig-Gen Leonard Mociulschi)

KEY
- Mountain Division
- Luftwaffe/Parachute Division
- Light Infantry Division
- Volksgrenadier Division

Eastern Front: 1943

The fall of Stalingrad at the end of January 1943 was followed by a series of Soviet offensives along the length of the Eastern Front aimed at smashing the bulk of the *Wehrmacht* and ending the war in 1943.

By 8 February, the Soviet Tank Armies leading the advance had recaptured Kursk and had begun to encircle the Ukrainian industrial city of Kharkov. Taking the railway junction at Sinelnikovo, they threatened to cut off supply lines to the German forces on the Mius River. The Soviet Fifth Shock Army was less than 160km (100 miles) from the Sea of Azov, threatening the encirclement of Erich von Manstein's Army Group Don.

Kharkov counterattack

The German army was far from beaten, however. Hitler ordered that Kharkhov should be held at all costs. The defenders were the recently formed SS Panzer Corps, commanded by *SS-Obergruppenführer* Paul Hausser. Its divisions had recently returned from France, where they had been upgraded to *Panzergrenadier* formations.

Hitler's 'stand fast' order was a mistake. The Germans needed to fight a fast-moving war of manoeuvre to make use of their superior tactical skills, rather than become bogged down in a static war of attrition with the superior numbers of the Red Army.

Hausser, one of the few German commanders with the courage to disobey an order from the *Führer*, decided to abandon Kharkov while a corridor remained open through the encircling Soviet forces. Hitler was furious, especially since it was his own SS troops who had retreated. He came to realize, however, that Hausser's actions had delayed the Soviets long enough to allow other units to form a fragile defensive line further west.

Stalin, interpreting the SS retreat as the start of a general withdrawal, ordered his troops onto the offensive throughout the Ukraine. The Soviet Sixth Army was to advance to the Dniepr, and the Fifth Shock Army to the Sea of Azov. Unfortunately, Field Marshal von Manstein had other ideas.

The flexibility of the German armour and infantry formations let Manstein plan a fast-moving and elastic defensive-offensive campaign, using the *Wehrmacht* in a mobile campaign to outmanoeuvre the Soviets.

Once the Soviet divisions had advanced to the end of their logistical lines, he launched a counterattack. Hoth's Fourth Panzer Army and Army Detachment Kempf isolated a large part of the Soviet South West Front, winning a battle at Krasnograd and Barvenkovo.

Manstein then pushed Hausser's SS Panzer Corps on towards Kharkov, which after an intense period of urban combat was retaken on 14 March. The SS Panzer Corps then captured Belgorod on March 21. The Soviets lost 50,000 dead, a further 20,000 taken prisoner, and the Soviet Ukrainian offensive was stopped in its tracks.

Von Manstein now proposed a 'backhand blow' for the summer: a further attack to outflank the Red Army, pushing it into the Sea of Azov at Rostov. Hitler, however, insisted on Operation Citadel, to crush the Kursk salient.

The battles of Kharkov had been classic examples of mobile warfare. Further north, the forces of Army Group Centre had been fighting more infantry-oriented battles since the Battle of Moscow at the end of 1941.

The Soviet offensives early in 1942 had been fought to a standstill by hastily formed German defensive lines 322km (200 miles) to the west of the Soviet capital.

2–23 March 1943

Kharkov had fallen to the Soviets in February 1943, following the Red Army's offensive at Stalingrad. However, led by Field Marshal Erich von Manstein, the Germans counterattacked and, after destroying Soviet spearheads in a classic battle of manoeuvre, retook the city after some costly street fighting. By 9 March, the *Wehrmacht* had also inflicted a heavy defeat on the Soviets at Krasnograd and Barvenkovo.

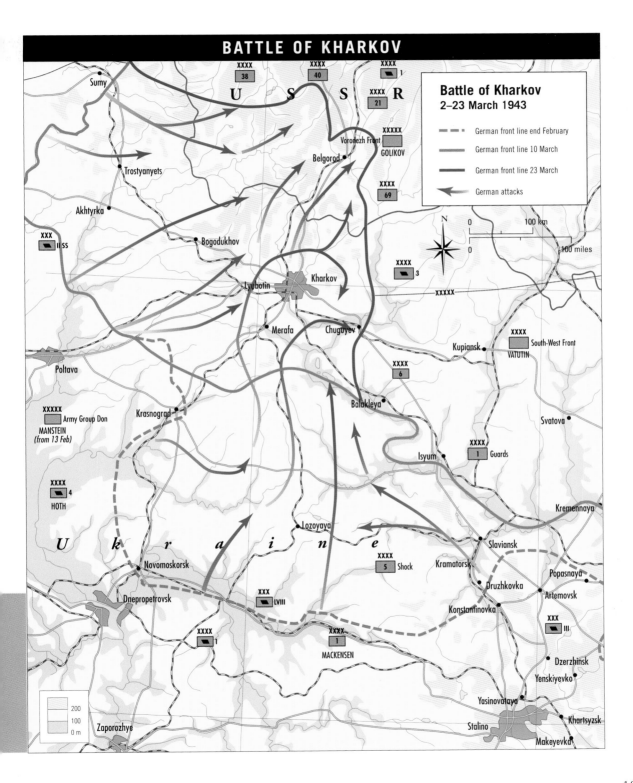

BATTLE OF KHARKOV

Battle of Kharkov
2–23 March 1943

- – – – German front line end February
- ──── German front line 10 March
- ──── German front line 23 March
- ◄──── German attacks

Sumy

U   S   S   R

XXXX
38

XXXX
40

XXXX
1

XXXX
21

Trostyanets

Akhtyrka

Voronezh Front
GOLIKOV
XXXXX

Belgorod

XXX
II SS

Bogodukhov

XXXX
69

N

0   100 km

0   100 miles

XXXX
3

Lyubotin   Kharkov

Poltava

Merafa   Chugayev

Kupiansk

South-West Front
VATUTIN
XXXX

XXXX
6

XXXXX
Army Group Don
MANSTEIN
(from 13 Feb)

Krasnograd

Balakleya

Svatova

XXXX
4
HOTH

XXXX
1   Guards

Isyum

Kremennaya

U   k   r   a   i   n   e

Lozovaya

Slaviansk

Kramatorsk

Popasnaya

XXXX
5   Shock

Druzhkovka

Artemovsk

Novomoskorsk

XXX
LVIII

Konstantinovka

XXX
III

Dnepropetrovsk

XXXX
1

XXXX
1
MACKENSEN

Dzerzhinsk

Yenskiyevko

200
100
0 m

Zaporozhye

Yasinovataya

Stalino

Khartsyzsk

Makeyevka

ARMY GROUP NORTH (JANUARY–FEBRUARY 1943)

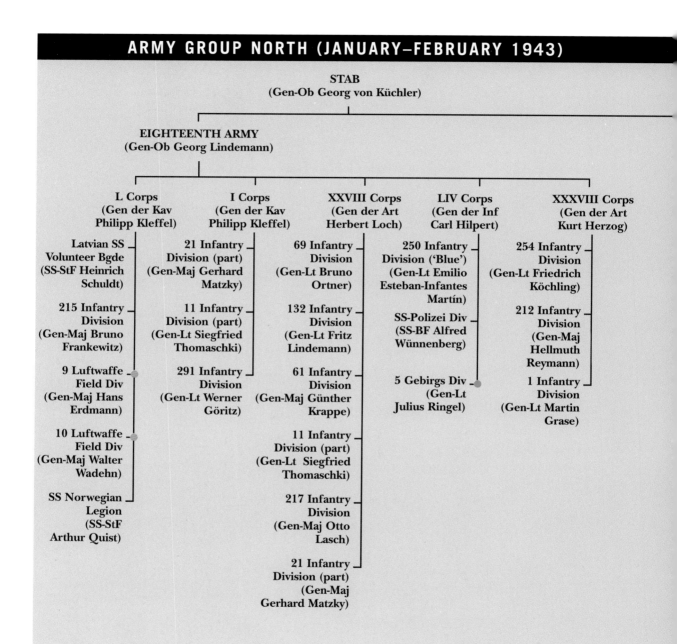

STAB
(Gen-Ob Georg von Küchler)

EIGHTEENTH ARMY
(Gen-Ob Georg Lindemann)

L Corps
(Gen der Kav
Philipp Kleffel)

I Corps
(Gen der Kav
Philipp Kleffel)

XXVIII Corps
(Gen der Art
Herbert Loch)

LIV Corps
(Gen der Inf
Carl Hilpert)

XXXVIII Corps
(Gen der Art
Kurt Herzog)

Latvian SS
Volunteer Bgde
(SS-StF Heinrich
Schuldt)

215 Infantry
Division
(Gen-Maj Bruno
Frankewitz)

9 Luftwaffe
Field Div
(Gen-Maj Hans
Erdmann)

10 Luftwaffe
Field Div
(Gen-Maj Walter
Wadehn)

SS Norwegian
Legion
(SS-StF
Arthur Quist)

21 Infantry
Division (part)
(Gen-Maj Gerhard
Matzky)

11 Infantry
Division (part)
(Gen-Lt Siegfried
Thomaschki)

291 Infantry
Division
(Gen-Lt Werner
Göritz)

69 Infantry
Division
(Gen-Lt Bruno
Ortner)

132 Infantry
Division
(Gen-Lt Fritz
Lindemann)

61 Infantry
Division
(Gen-Maj Günther
Krappe)

11 Infantry
Division (part)
(Gen-Lt Siegfried
Thomaschki)

217 Infantry
Division
(Gen-Maj Otto
Lasch)

21 Infantry
Division (part)
(Gen-Maj
Gerhard Matzky)

250 Infantry
Division ('Blue')
(Gen-Lt Emilio
Esteban-Infantes
Martín)

SS-Polizei Div
(SS-BF Alfred
Wünnenberg)

5 Gebirgs Div
(Gen-Lt
Julius Ringel)

254 Infantry
Division
(Gen-Lt Friedrich
Köchling)

212 Infantry
Division
(Gen-Maj
Hellmuth
Reymann)

1 Infantry
Division
(Gen-Lt Martin
Grase)

In January 1943, Army Group North, which was continuing to besiege Leningrad, was an almost exclusively infantry formation. The German Army was suffering from manpower shortages at the time, and several Luftwaffe field divisions were deployed to serve on the Leningrad Front, as was the Spanish volunteer 'Blue' Division. Eighteenth Army also controlled numerous independent police and security battalions, as well as a number of Russian volunteer formations, the so-called *Ost Bataillonen* ('Eastern battalions').

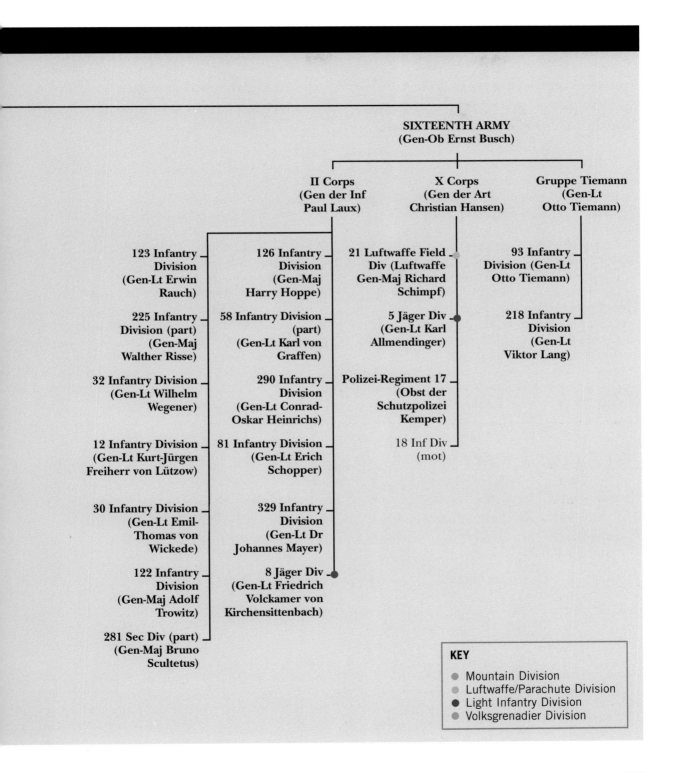

SIXTEENTH ARMY
(Gen-Ob Ernst Busch)

II Corps
(Gen der Inf
Paul Laux)

X Corps
(Gen der Art
Christian Hansen)

Gruppe Tiemann
(Gen-Lt
Otto Tiemann)

123 Infantry
Division
(Gen-Lt Erwin
Rauch)

126 Infantry
Division
(Gen-Maj
Harry Hoppe)

21 Luftwaffe Field
Div (Luftwaffe
Gen-Maj Richard
Schimpf)

93 Infantry
Division (Gen-Lt
Otto Tiemann)

225 Infantry
Division (part)
(Gen-Maj
Walther Risse)

58 Infantry Division
(part)
(Gen-Lt Karl von
Graffen)

5 Jäger Div
(Gen-Lt Karl
Allmendinger)

218 Infantry
Division
(Gen-Lt
Viktor Lang)

32 Infantry Division
(Gen-Lt Wilhelm
Wegener)

290 Infantry
Division
(Gen-Lt Conrad-
Oskar Heinrichs)

Polizei-Regiment 17
(Obst der
Schutzpolizei
Kemper)

12 Infantry Division
(Gen-Lt Kurt-Jürgen
Freiherr von Lützow)

81 Infantry Division
(Gen-Lt Erich
Schopper)

18 Inf Div
(mot)

30 Infantry Division
(Gen-Lt Emil-
Thomas von
Wickede)

329 Infantry
Division
(Gen-Lt Dr
Johannes Mayer)

122 Infantry
Division
(Gen-Maj Adolf
Trowitz)

8 Jäger Div
(Gen-Lt Friedrich
Volckamer von
Kirchensittenbach)

281 Sec Div (part)
(Gen-Maj Bruno
Scultetus)

KEY
- Mountain Division
- Luftwaffe/Parachute Division
- Light Infantry Division
- Volksgrenadier Division

Army Group North: 1943

Further north, as part of the series of Soviet offensives launched along the length of the front after Stalingrad, the Leningrad and Volkhov fronts partially broke the siege of Leningrad in operation *Iskra* (Spark).

In a six day battle starting on 12 January 1943, the Soviets overran the powerful German positions south of Lake Ladoga, opening a land corridor to the besieged city. In most military senses, the battles on the Leningrad Front were less important than the confrontations in the central and southern sectors of the Eastern Front. The Red Army and Army Group North faced each other in sets of fortified lines that prevented the two sides from doing much more than trading artillery barrages. Although the city was still threatened by the Germans, it was actually in no great danger. Enough supplies had been getting through since 1942 to alleviate the danger of starvation.

The main consequence of the Leningrad campaign was to keep Army Group North uselessly pinned down. Generaloberst Georg von Küchler had seen his command regularly lose troops to campaigns further south. It made no sense to remain where he was and be worn down by attrition.

In the summer of 1943 he began to plan an orderly withdrawal to a fortified line known as the 'Panther Position' about 210km (150 miles) southwest. Considerable work had been done to build up the Panther Position in the second half of 1943. By the end of the year it was very strong, and well-supplied with large stockpiles of food, fuel and ammunition. He expected to move back early in 1944, but in a meeting with Hitler on December 1943 the Führer, who hated retreats of any kind, refused to allow any withdrawal.

In the event, Army Group North was forced to retreat less than a month later when the final Soviet offensive to relieve Leningrad opened in January 1944.

Army Group Centre: Kursk 1943

By the time the Soviet offensives mounted after the fall of Stalingrad had ground to a halt, the Germans had been forced back all along the Eastern Front. One of the key features in the line was a large Soviet-held salient around the city of Kursk.

The Kursk salient offered the Germans a number of strategic opportunities. A battle of encirclement to eliminate the bulge could destroy a huge part of the Red Army. Later, the retaken ground might offer the Germans a chance to go back onto the offensive, either striking north towards Moscow or south to make a second attempt on the Caucasus oilfields.

Hitler realized that time was running out for the *Wehrmacht* in the East. The Red Army was growing both in quantity and quality, and if not stopped might be able to take the initiative. Hitler also pinned great hopes on new weapons about to enter service, especially the powerful Panzer V Panther and the Panzer VI Tiger.

Hitler postponed the offensive, codenamed Operation *Zitadelle* (Citadel), several times in order to build up his forces as much as possible. Many of his generals, most notably von Manstein, felt that this was a mistake. If an offensive was to be launched, it should be as soon as possible, before the Soviets had a chance to build their strength in the battle area. Finally, Hitler ordered the launch of *Zitadelle* in the first week of July. Ninth Army from Army Group Centre would strike from the north,

NORTHERN FRONT (SUMMER 1943)

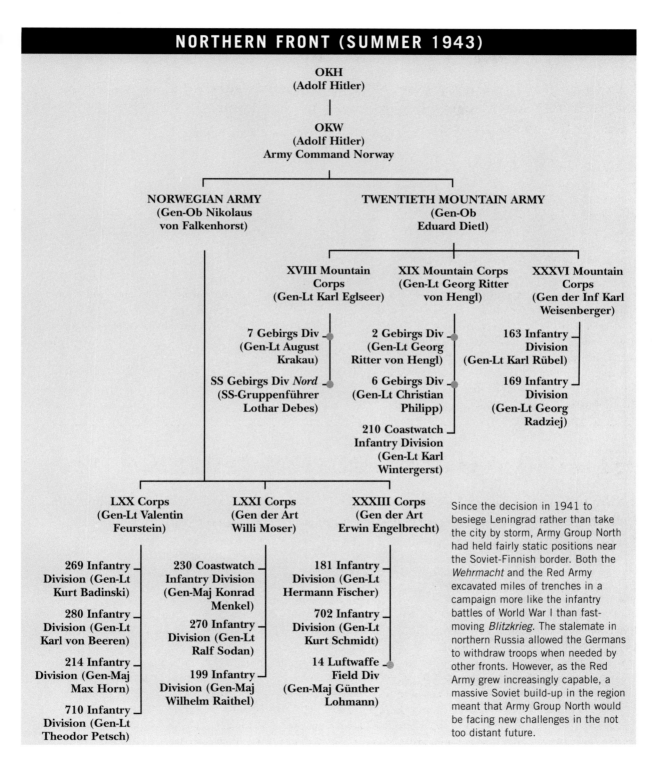

OKH
(Adolf Hitler)

OKW
(Adolf Hitler)
Army Command Norway

NORWEGIAN ARMY
(Gen-Ob Nikolaus
von Falkenhorst)

TWENTIETH MOUNTAIN ARMY
(Gen-Ob
Eduard Dietl)

**XVIII Mountain
Corps**
(Gen-Lt Karl Eglseer)

XIX Mountain Corps
(Gen-Lt Georg Ritter
von Hengl)

**XXXVI Mountain
Corps**
(Gen der Inf Karl
Weisenberger)

7 Gebirgs Div
(Gen-Lt August
Krakau)

SS Gebirgs Div *Nord*
(SS-Gruppenführer
Lothar Debes)

2 Gebirgs Div
(Gen-Lt Georg
Ritter von Hengl)

6 Gebirgs Div
(Gen-Lt Christian
Philipp)

210 Coastwatch
Infantry Division
(Gen-Lt Karl
Wintergerst)

163 Infantry
Division
(Gen-Lt Karl Rübel)

169 Infantry
Division
(Gen-Lt Georg
Radziej)

LXX Corps
(Gen-Lt Valentin
Feurstein)

LXXI Corps
(Gen der Art
Willi Moser)

XXXIII Corps
(Gen der Art
Erwin Engelbrecht)

269 Infantry
Division (Gen-Lt
Kurt Badinski)

280 Infantry
Division (Gen-Lt
Karl von Beeren)

214 Infantry
Division (Gen-Maj
Max Horn)

710 Infantry
Division (Gen-Lt
Theodor Petsch)

230 Coastwatch
Infantry Division
(Gen-Maj Konrad
Menkel)

270 Infantry
Division (Gen-Lt
Ralf Sodan)

199 Infantry
Division (Gen-Maj
Wilhelm Raithel)

181 Infantry
Division (Gen-Lt
Hermann Fischer)

702 Infantry
Division (Gen-Lt
Kurt Schmidt)

14 Luftwaffe
Field Div
(Gen-Maj Günther
Lohmann)

Since the decision in 1941 to besiege Leningrad rather than take the city by storm, Army Group North had held fairly static positions near the Soviet-Finnish border. Both the *Wehrmacht* and the Red Army excavated miles of trenches in a campaign more like the infantry battles of World War I than fast-moving *Blitzkrieg*. The stalemate in northern Russia allowed the Germans to withdraw troops when needed by other fronts. However, as the Red Army grew increasingly capable, a massive Soviet build-up in the region meant that Army Group North would be facing new challenges in the not too distant future.

ARMY GROUP CENTRE (EARLY 1943)

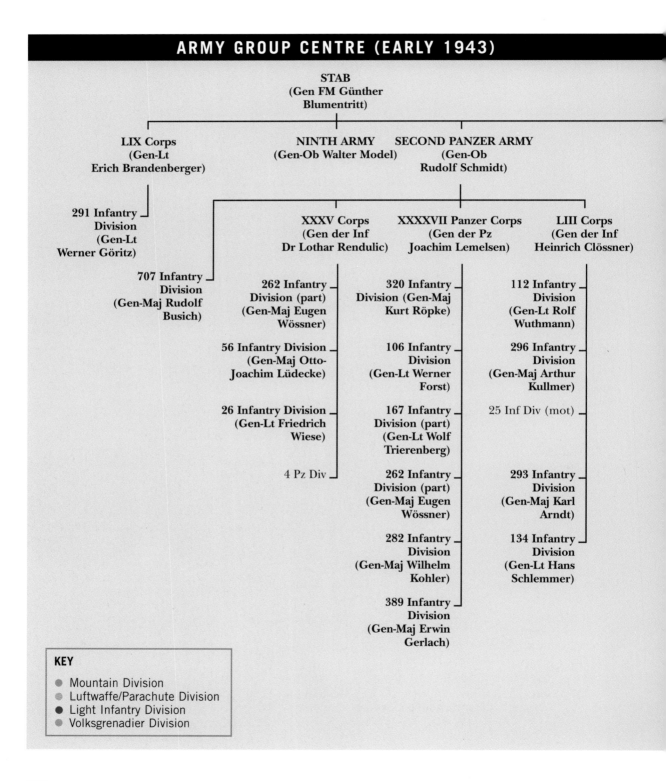

STAB
(Gen FM Günther Blumentritt)

LIX Corps
(Gen-Lt Erich Brandenberger)

NINTH ARMY
(Gen-Ob Walter Model)

SECOND PANZER ARMY
(Gen-Ob Rudolf Schmidt)

291 Infantry Division
(Gen-Lt Werner Göritz)

XXXV Corps
(Gen der Inf Dr Lothar Rendulic)

XXXXVII Panzer Corps
(Gen der Pz Joachim Lemelsen)

LIII Corps
(Gen der Inf Heinrich Clössner)

707 Infantry Division
(Gen-Maj Rudolf Busich)

262 Infantry Division (part)
(Gen-Maj Eugen Wössner)

320 Infantry Division (Gen-Maj Kurt Röpke)

112 Infantry Division
(Gen-Lt Rolf Wuthmann)

56 Infantry Division
(Gen-Maj Otto-Joachim Lüdecke)

106 Infantry Division
(Gen-Lt Werner Forst)

296 Infantry Division
(Gen-Maj Arthur Kullmer)

26 Infantry Division
(Gen-Lt Friedrich Wiese)

167 Infantry Division (part)
(Gen-Lt Wolf Trierenberg)

25 Inf Div (mot)

4 Pz Div

262 Infantry Division (part)
(Gen-Maj Eugen Wössner)

293 Infantry Division
(Gen-Maj Karl Arndt)

282 Infantry Division
(Gen-Maj Wilhelm Kohler)

134 Infantry Division
(Gen-Lt Hans Schlemmer)

389 Infantry Division
(Gen-Maj Erwin Gerlach)

KEY
- ● Mountain Division
- ● Luftwaffe/Parachute Division
- ● Light Infantry Division
- ● Volksgrenadier Division

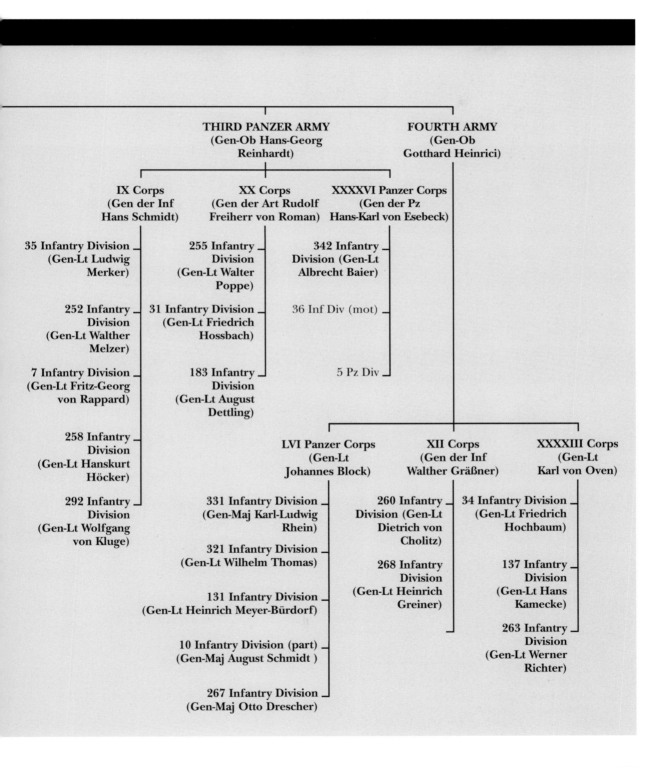

while Fourth Panzer Army and Army Detachment Kempf would attack from Army Group South's positions.

Battle of Kursk

Kursk would be the largest armoured and aerial battle of the war. The Nazis amassed 3000 tanks, including the Panthers and Tigers, and 1800 tactical aircraft. The Soviets had 3600 tanks and 1.3 million soldiers. More to the point, the delays had allowed the Soviets to develop several lines of defences all around the salient, incorporating infantry, artillery, anti-tank units and minefields. The battle began on 5 July 1943. Progress was slow, as the German forces battered their way through the Soviet lines, and by 11 July all progress had

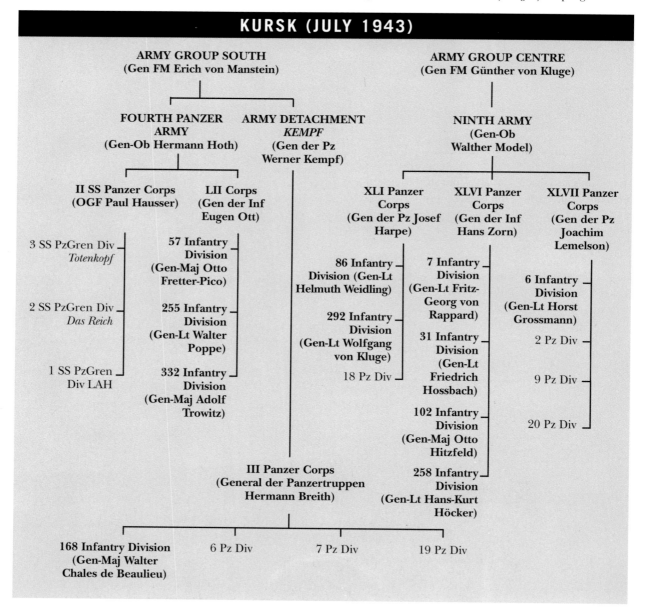

slowed to a crawl. Hitler's generals had been right to fear a Soviet build-up. The Soviets were becoming much more adept at mobile warfare, and their plan involved more than stopping the Germans. They intended to counterattack around the flanks of the German positions. In the battle of Prokhorovka on 12 July, 600 German tanks and 850 Red Army tanks clashed while a furious air battle raged overhead. The battle became a nightmare of attrition, as tanks were burned out in fierce tank-on-tank fighting. Both sides called in reinforcements.

Withdrawal from Kursk

On 13 July, Hitler began to order a withdrawal, as the Western Allies began to make their presence felt with the Anglo-American landings on Sicily. On 17 July, the Germans began a full-scale withdrawal, leaving behind 70,000 dead and 2950 wrecked tanks on the battlefield. The Soviets also lost many tanks, but since they claimed the battlefield, many of their losses were repaired and returned to battle within a few months. The Soviets immediately began a counteroffensive.

These losses, coming so soon after Stalingrad, ended the German initiative in the East. It would take time for the Soviets to go over to the full offensive, but the Germans had mounted their last drive to conquer the Red Army and were now on the defensive.

July 1943

Kursk was such an obvious objective that the Soviets began fortifying it almost as soon as the Germans decided to attack it. As early as March, Marshal Georgi Zhukhov and his front commanders were presenting Stalin with their expectations on likely German plans for the coming campaigning season. Their predictions proved to be remarkably accurate when the battle started in July.

In addition, the Red Army planned new offensives of its own, scheduled to open the moment the German attack stalled. Stalin and his most senior commanders gambled that they could hold Kursk against the elite panzer divisions, absorb the full strength of the German blow, then unleash a multi-front offensive that would liberate the Ukraine.

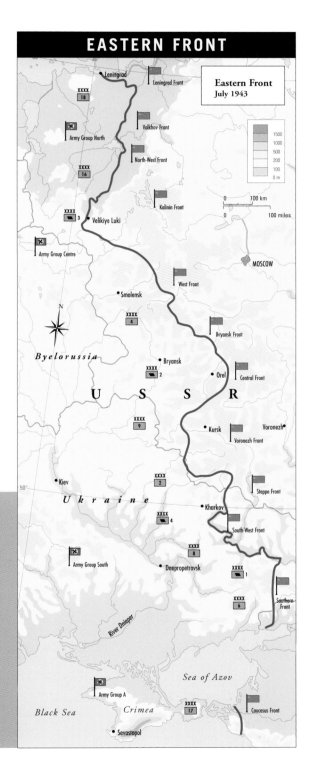

EASTERN FRONT

Eastern Front
July 1943

Southern Front: 1943

Following the failure at Kursk, Hitler called off *Zitadelle* and ordered the SS panzer corps to be transferred to the west. The *Ostheer* would go over to the defensive and contain the Russian drive on Orel.

Walter Model, commander of the German Ninth Army, was one of Hitler's favourite generals. But he was unable to prevent the loss of Orel, which fell on 5 August. The Soviet Briansk and Kalinin Fronts began new offensives in the north. Another major attack developed south of Kursk, forcing Manstein back to the scene of his triumph in the spring.

This time there was no power available for a Manstein-style backhand blow: all that the Germans could do was to fight a succession of rearguard actions as they withdrew, giving up Belgorod on 5 August and eventually abandoning Kharkov itself. On 23 August, the city changed hands for the last time.

General German retreat
Army Group South retreated to prepared positions running from Zaporezhe to the Black Sea. The Soviets reached the isthmus connecting the Crimea to the mainland. The German Seventeenth Army was isolated.

At Stalingrad, the Red Army had learned how to stop the German Army. After Kursk, it was to show that it could drive them backwards.

Soviet techniques had improved considerably thanks to the harsh lessons taught by their German instructors. They now practised better field reconnaissance. Camouflage techniques were improved and when the battle started, cooperation among infantry, tanks and cavalry was good.

Superior Soviet resources
Although the Red Army would never approach the levels of professionalism and efficiency that marked out the German war machine, the Soviets were always willing and able to overcome their shortcomings by employing vastly superior reserves of men and material.

As Soviet confidence burgeoned, that of the Germans declined. Before Stalingrad, they went into battle with the stout belief that German efficiency and courage would inevitably bring victory. After that great defeat, the ordinary German soldier knew that if the Soviets weren't stopped, the eastern hordes would soon reach the German homelands.

Kursk had been the *Wehrmacht's* last supreme effort to reverse months of withdrawals. But even before the ill-fated offensive, the writing was on the wall. In addition to the great losses between the Don and the Donetz following the fall of Stalingrad, almost the whole of von Kleist's Army Group had been hastily withdrawn.

Only the previous year, Kleist had been poised to capture the vital Caucasian oilfields and perhaps even break down into Persia and the Middle East. Now he had pulled his Army group out through Rostov by only the narrowest of margins.

The defeat at Kursk merely accelerated the pace of the Soviet recovery. When the German attack stalled, the Red Army offensives continued, one beginning as its predecessor slowed.

Offensives from south to north
As Kharkov fell in the south, General Popov launched an attack out of the newly won ground around Orel towards Bryansk. Further north, the Kalinin Front under Eremenko drove down towards Smolensk. Two drives were launched in the direction of Kiev – from the Central Front under Rokossovsky and from the Voronezh Front under Vatutin.

At the far south of the line, Tolbukhin's Southern Front crossed the River Mius, outflanked Taganrog (from which the last of Kleist's men hastily withdrew) and drove along the Azov coast to Mariupol.

By mid-September, the whole Soviet front from Smolensk down to the Black Sea was on the move. Within days, Central Front had swept through Sevsk as far as Konotop, Voronezh Front was through Piryatin,

ARMY GROUP DON (JANUARY 1943)

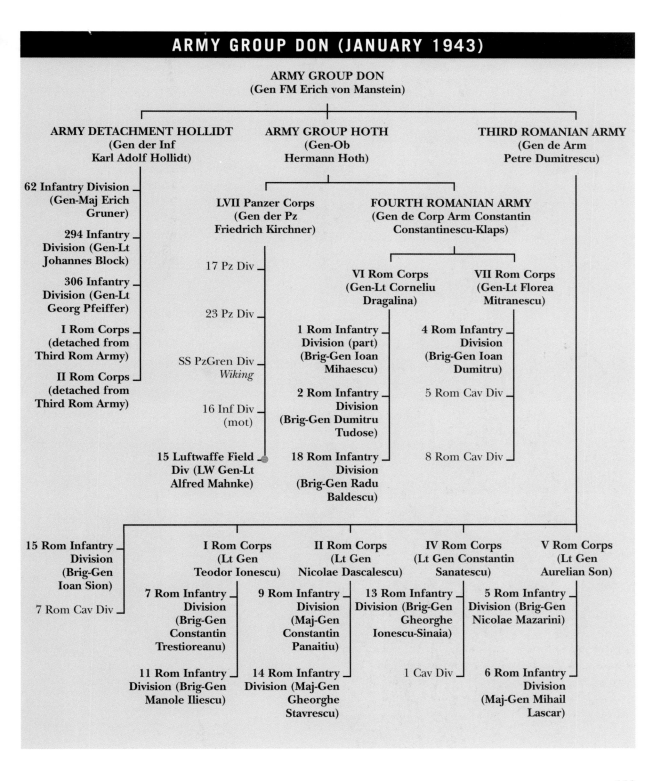

ARMY GROUP DON
(Gen FM Erich von Manstein)

ARMY DETACHMENT HOLLIDT
(Gen der Inf
Karl Adolf Hollidt)

ARMY GROUP HOTH
(Gen-Ob
Hermann Hoth)

THIRD ROMANIAN ARMY
(Gen de Arm
Petre Dumitrescu)

62 Infantry Division
(Gen-Maj Erich
Gruner)

294 Infantry
Division (Gen-Lt
Johannes Block)

306 Infantry
Division (Gen-Lt
Georg Pfeiffer)

I Rom Corps
(detached from
Third Rom Army)

II Rom Corps
(detached from
Third Rom Army)

LVII Panzer Corps
(Gen der Pz
Friedrich Kirchner)

17 Pz Div

23 Pz Div

SS PzGren Div
Wiking

16 Inf Div
(mot)

15 Luftwaffe Field
Div (LW Gen-Lt
Alfred Mahnke)

FOURTH ROMANIAN ARMY
(Gen de Corp Arm Constantin
Constantinescu-Klaps)

VI Rom Corps
(Gen-Lt Corneliu
Dragalina)

VII Rom Corps
(Gen-Lt Florea
Mitranescu)

1 Rom Infantry
Division (part)
(Brig-Gen Ioan
Mihaescu)

4 Rom Infantry
Division
(Brig-Gen Ioan
Dumitru)

2 Rom Infantry
Division
(Brig-Gen Dumitru
Tudose)

5 Rom Cav Div

18 Rom Infantry
Division
(Brig-Gen Radu
Baldescu)

8 Rom Cav Div

15 Rom Infantry
Division
(Brig-Gen
Ioan Sion)

7 Rom Cav Div

I Rom Corps
(Lt Gen
Teodor Ionescu)

7 Rom Infantry
Division
(Brig-Gen
Constantin
Trestioreanu)

11 Rom Infantry
Division (Brig-Gen
Manole Iliescu)

II Rom Corps
(Lt Gen
Nicolae Dascalescu)

9 Rom Infantry
Division
(Maj-Gen
Constantin
Panaitiu)

14 Rom Infantry
Division (Maj-Gen
Gheorghe
Stavrescu)

IV Rom Corps
(Lt Gen Constantin
Sanatescu)

13 Rom Infantry
Division (Brig-Gen
Gheorghe
Ionescu-Sinaia)

1 Cav Div

V Rom Corps
(Lt Gen
Aurelian Son)

5 Rom Infantry
Division (Brig-Gen
Nicolae Mazarini)

6 Rom Infantry
Division
(Maj-Gen Mihail
Lascar)

SOVIET ADVANCE TO THE DNIEPER

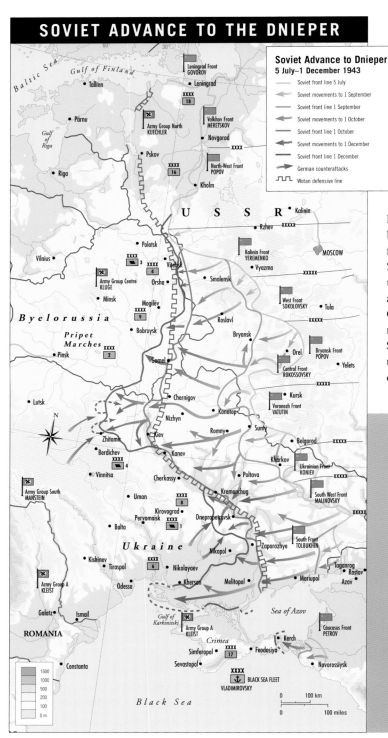

Soviet Advance to Dnieper
5 July–1 December 1943

— Soviet front line 5 July
← Soviet movements to 1 September
— Soviet front line 1 September
← Soviet movements to 1 October
— Soviet front line 1 October
← Soviet movements to 1 December
— Soviet front line 1 December
➤ German counterattacks
⊥⊥⊥ Wotan defensive line

and Steppe Front had reached Poltava. The South West and Southern Fronts between them had cleared all enemy forces from the Donetz Basin and were within striking distance of the Dnieper at Zaporozhye.

Kiev falls

By September, the Red Army had bridgeheads across the Dnieper to the north and south of Kiev. Reinforced by units of the Thirty-Eighth Army, these liberation of Kiev was launched from the bridgeheads. On 3 November, the German forces were shattered by the fire of some 2000 guns. Soviet tanks broke through to threaten Kiev with encirclement. Artillery and heavy mortars were pounding the German defences, and Soviet infantry – many of whom had learned their trade at Stalingrad – were fighting their way through the city streets. On 6 November, Kiev was once more in Soviet hands.

5 July–1 December 1943

After the recapture of Kiev, the Red Army was content to clear the rest of the Dnieper in the south, and recapture a few significant places to the north. Now the ground was frozen, the Russian winter again chilled the hearts of the German forces. The Steppe and South West fronts drove across the river and formed a wide and deep penetration pointing at Krivoi Rog and Kirovograd. Southern Front reached the mouth of the Dnieper, and effectively shut off all German forces left in the Crimea. To the north, generals Vatutin and Rokossovsky had driven their fronts as far as Korosten and the eastern edge of the Pripet Marshes, and Sokolovski had taken – at great cost – the massive defensive bastion that the Germans had made of Smolensk.

Eastern Front: 1944

In spite of the distasters that had overtaken his forces in 1943, Hitler still had designs on the east. The *Führer* still believed that the *Wehrmacht* could retain control of the Ukraine, with its vast grain fields.

The German Army was on the defensive, the Red Army getting stronger by the day, but with a change of luck, his Panzers would storm forwards, retaking the Donets Basin with its supplies of iron ore and manganese.

From there, he could push southwest in the spring of 1944, using Kleist's Army Group A in the Crimea as a bridgehead to take the Caucasus oilfields. Even if that proved impossible, holding the Crimea would enable the *Luftwaffe* and the *Kriegsmarine* to dominate the Black Sea, protecting the Romanian oilfields at Ploesti.

On the defensive

His generals knew better. After the failure of Operation Citadel, General Zeitzler, the Army Chief of Staff, wanted to establish the Panther Line, or the East Wall, running from Leningrad down to the Dnieper and the Sea of Azov. Manstein, in command of the forces in the Ukraine, also urged a retreat to the Dnieper. Hitler would have none of it: 'If I let them build defences to the rear, it will only encourage the Generals to retreat if things get too tough.' In the event, Soviet successes compelled him to change his mind within two months.

Since they told him what he did not want to hear, Hitler now began to refuse meetings with his generals. And now the best were gone. Von Kluge had been injured in a car crash at the end of 1943. Ernst Busch had replaced him at Army Group Centre. And von Manstein was out of favour.

The Soviets now took time to consolidate the gains made since Kursk. The pause in the continuous string of offensives did not last long, however.

Korsun-Shevchenkovsky

At the turn of the year, the Germans still held a small stretch of the Dnieper around Kanev, where they had thrown back the Soviet bridgehead. Behind them to the west they occupied a salient nearly 30km (19 miles) deep and, at its base, more than 140km (87 miles) wide. Such distances were beginning to mean nothing on the scale of Red Army movements, and on 24 January the battle of 'Korsun-Shevchenkovsky' began.

On 24 January, General Koniev's Second Ukrainian Front smashed through the eastern end of the salient, driving forwards 12km (7 miles) in a day. Koniev exploited the breakthrough with the Fifth Guards Tank Army. On 26 January, Vatutin's First Ukrainian Front attacked from the north. On the 28th, the two forces met, trapping 10 German divisions in the pocket, from which all attempts to escape were doomed. The equipment of four panzer and six infantry divisions plus 18,000 men were wiped from the strength of von Manstein's Army Group South. Yet this was just the beginning of a far greater strategic move.

General Chuikov's Eighth Guards Army took Krivoi Rog on 22 February, and in some desperation Manstein transferred divisions down from the central sector.

Zhukov attacks

Zhukov struck these weakened central positions almost immediately. By 10 March, he had reached the valley of the Dniester.

Army Group South was still trapped in a pocket to the southeast. Here they were attacked by armies of the Second Ukrainian Front, under Marshal Koniev. The Soviets drove clear of the base of the German salient to reach the Dniester between Mogilev Podolsky and Rybnitsa. By the end of March, the whole length of the Bug had gone. Malinovsky's armies had driven from Krivoi Rog to take Nikolayev and reach the lower Dniester, while Chuikov had swung his army further south to attack Odessa. He captured it on 10 April – and by this time, Koniev's troops were across the Pruth and into Bessarabia. The whole of the Ukraine except the area around Lvov was back under Soviet rule.

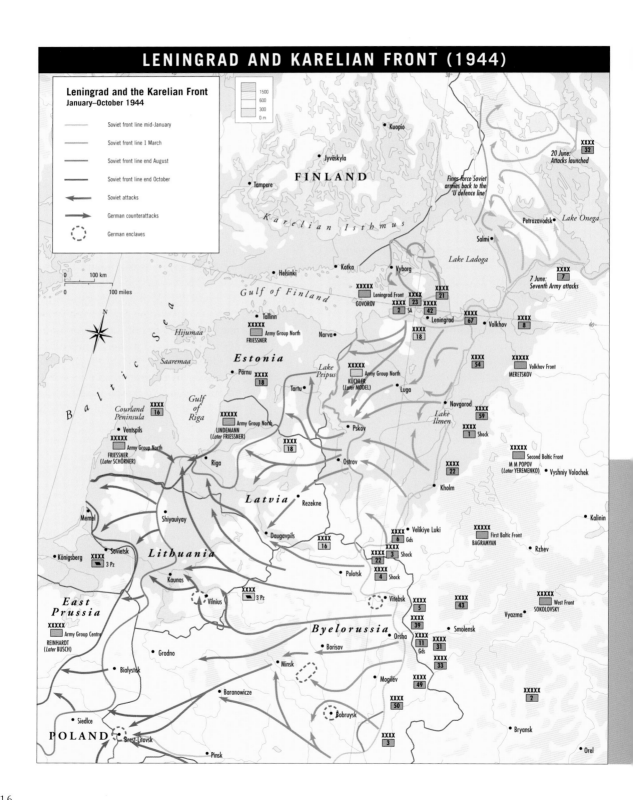

LENINGRAD AND KARELIAN FRONT (1944)

Leningrad and the Karelian Front
January–October 1944

Soviet front line mid-January
Soviet front line 1 March
Soviet front line end August
Soviet front line end October
Soviet attacks
German counterattacks
German enclaves

1500
600
300
0 m

Kuopio

20 June:
Attacks launched

XXXX
32

Jyväskylä

FINLAND

Finns force Soviet
armies back to the
'U defence line'

Tampere

Karelian Isthmus

Petrozavodsk Lake Onega

Salmi

Lake Ladoga

7 June:
Seventh Army attacks

XXXX
7

Helsinki Kotka Vyborg

Gulf of Finland

XXXXX
Leningrad Front
GOVOROV

XXXX
23
XXXX
2 SA
XXXX
42

XXXX
21

Leningrad

XXXX
67
Volkhov

XXXX
8

100 km

0

100 miles

N

Tallinn

Hijumaa

Army Group North
FRIESSNER

Narva

XXXX
18

XXXX
54

XXXXX
Volkhov Front
MERETSKOV

Saaremaa

Estonia

Pärnu
XXXX
18

Lake
Peipus

Tartu

XXXXX
Army Group North
KÜCHLER
(Later MODEL)

Luga

Novgorod

Lake
Ilmen

XXXX
59

XXXX
1 Shock

Courland
Peninsula

XXXX
16

Gulf
of
Riga

XXXXX
Army Group North
LINDEMANN
(Later FRIESSNER)

Pskov

XXXX
18

Ostrov

XXXX
22

XXXXX
Second Baltic Front
M M POPOV
(Later YEREMENKO) Vyshniy Volochek

Ventspils

XXXXX
Army Group North
FRIESSNER
(Later SCHÖRNER)

Riga

Kholm

Baltic Sea

Latvia

Rezekne

Velikiye Luki

XXXX
6 Gds

XXXXX
First Baltic Front
BAGRAMYAN

Kalinin

Rzhev

Memel

Shiyauiyay

Daugavpils

XXXX
16

XXXX
22
XXXX
3 Shock

XXXX
4 Shock

Polotsk

Königsberg

XXXX
3 Pz

Sovietsk

Lithuania

Kaunas

XXXX
3 Pz

Vilnius

Vitebsk

XXXX
5

XXXX
43

XXXXX
West Front
SOKOLOVSKY

Vyazma

East
Prussia

XXXXX
Army Group Centre
REINHARDT
(Later BUSCH)

Gradno

Byelorussia

Orsha

Smolensk

XXXX
39

XXXX
11
Gds
XXXX
31

XXXX
33

XXXXX
2

Bialystok

Baranowicze

Borisov

Minsk

Mogilёv

XXXX
49

XXXX
50

Bobruysk

Siedlce

Brest-Litovsk

POLAND

Pinsk

XXXX
3

Bryansk

Orel

Northern Front: 1944

The carefully planned German withdrawal to the Panther Line around Lake Peipus and along the Narva River became a headlong retreat in the face of renewed Soviet attacks early in 1944.

The Soviet northern offensives did not end with the relief of Leningrad. Luga fell on 12 February. The Second Baltic Front under General Popov drove west below Lake Ilmen, and when on 1 March the Soviet High Command called a halt, Soviet troops had reached Pskov and the shores of Lakes Peipus.

The rapid Soviet advance threatened to isolate the hundreds of thousands of German troops in the Baltic States. To avoid being cut off, the Germans began planning for the withdrawal from the Narva bridgehead to the Tannenberg Line. A series of bloody battles were fought that became known as the 'Battle of the European SS' because of the large number of *Waffen* SS foreign volunteer units engaged in the area.

On 14 September, a huge offensive was launched by the Soviets, aimed at capturing Riga and cutting off Army Group North in the Courland area. Hitler finally agreed to allow the evacuation of all troops in Estonia.

Arctic operations

Further north, a little known campaign was also coming to a climax. Operations in the Karelian Isthmus and further into the Arctic were intended to finally knock the Finns out of the war. Vastly outnumbered by the Soviets, the Finns were also facing an enemy who was better trained, better equipped and better led than during the Winter War of 1940. Soviet pressure quickly told: not surprisingly, the Finns had to fall back as the Red Army retook territory that it had lost in 1941. An armistice followed on 4 September 1944, leaving German troops on the Arctic Front to fight their way back to northern Norway.

Retreat of Army Group North

By the end of the January 1944 the Siege of Leningrad was over, and for the first time in 900 days the people of the city could walk their streets without fear of *Wehrmacht* shells or *Luftwaffe* bombs.

Now the Red Army stood poised in the wilderness of forests and lakes that runs along the Estonian border. Army Group North strove to keep the Soviets out of the Baltic but they were undone as a side product of Operation *Bagration* in July 1944. Having taken Minsk, the Red Army pushed on into Lithuania, and by the end of August the Soviets were on the Prussian borders, trapping most of Army Group North in the Courland Peninsula west of Riga.

On the Arctic Front, the Red Army slowly regained the territory it had lost in 1940, forcing the Finnish to sign an armistice in September 1944. The German Twentieth Mountain Army was forced to retreat back into Norway.

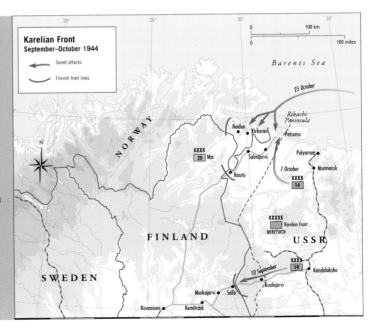

ARMY GROUP NORTH (OCTOBER 1944)

ARMY GROUP NORTH
(Gen-Ob Ferdinand Schörner)

ARMY GROUP GRASSER
(Gen der Inf
Anton Grasser)

SIXTEENTH ARMY
(Gen der Inf
Carl Hilpert)

VI SS Corps
(OGF
Walther Krüger)

XVI Corps
(Gen der Kav
Philipp Kleffel)

XXXXIII Corps
(Gen der Geb
Kurt Versock)

19 SS Grenadier Div
(Latvian)
(SS-GF Bruno
Steckenbach)

81 Infantry
Division
(Gen-Maj Franz-
Eccard von
Bentivegni)

58 Infantry Division
(Gen-Lt Curt
Siewert)

15 SS Grenadier Div
(Latvian)
(SS-BF Herbert von
Obwurzer)

93 Infantry
Division
(Gen-Maj Kurt
Domansky)

225 Infantry
Division
(Gen-Lt Walther
Risse)

389 Infantry
Division
(Gen-Lt Fritz
Becker)

52 Sec Div
(Gen-Lt Albrecht Baron
Digeon von Monteton)

XXVIII Corps
(Gen der Inf
Hans Gollnick)

31 Volks Gren Div
(Gen-Maj Hans-Joachim
von Stolzmann)

21 Infantry Division
(Gen-Maj Heinrich Götz)

30 Infantry Division
(Gen-Maj Otto Barth)

61 Infantry Division
(Gen-Lt Günther Krappe)

12 Luftwaffe Field Div
(Gen-Lt Gottfried Weber)

On 14 September, a huge offensive was launched by the Soviet First, Second and Third Baltic fronts. The offensive was aimed at capturing Riga and cutting off Army Group North in the Courland area. Realizing the situation was critical, Hitler finally agreed to evacuate all German troops from Estonia. On 22 September, Tallinn, the Estonian capital, was abandoned. By the beginning of October, Army Group North had become isolated in what became known as the Courland Pocket. The Narva defenders would see action in the battles to hold this pocket before being withdrawn late in 1944 to defend Berlin and the Oder.

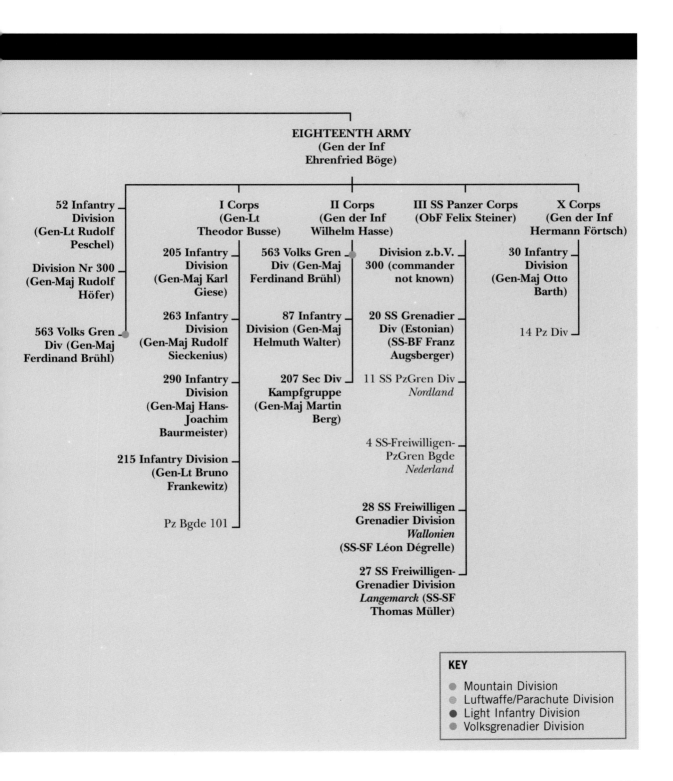

EIGHTEENTH ARMY
(Gen der Inf
Ehrenfried Böge)

52 Infantry Division
(Gen-Lt Rudolf Peschel)

Division Nr 300
(Gen-Maj Rudolf Höfer)

563 Volks Gren Div (Gen-Maj Ferdinand Brühl)

I Corps
(Gen-Lt Theodor Busse)

205 Infantry Division
(Gen-Maj Karl Giese)

263 Infantry Division
(Gen-Maj Rudolf Sieckenius)

290 Infantry Division
(Gen-Maj Hans-Joachim Baurmeister)

215 Infantry Division
(Gen-Lt Bruno Frankewitz)

Pz Bgde 101

II Corps
(Gen der Inf Wilhelm Hasse)

563 Volks Gren Div (Gen-Maj Ferdinand Brühl)

87 Infantry Division (Gen-Maj Helmuth Walter)

207 Sec Div Kampfgruppe (Gen-Maj Martin Berg)

III SS Panzer Corps
(ObF Felix Steiner)

Division z.b.V. 300 (commander not known)

20 SS Grenadier Div (Estonian) (SS-BF Franz Augsberger)

11 SS PzGren Div *Nordland*

4 SS-Freiwilligen-PzGren Bgde *Nederland*

28 SS Freiwilligen Grenadier Division *Wallonien* (SS-SF Léon Dégrelle)

27 SS Freiwilligen-Grenadier Division *Langemarck* (SS-SF Thomas Müller)

X Corps
(Gen der Inf Hermann Förtsch)

30 Infantry Division
(Gen-Maj Otto Barth)

14 Pz Div

KEY
- Mountain Division
- Luftwaffe/Parachute Division
- Light Infantry Division
- Volksgrenadier Division

Army Group Centre: 1944

Even before the end of the successful Soviet spring offensive, the Soviet High Command was planning the next stage of its campaign to drive the Nazi invaders from the soil of the Soviet Union.

After some debate, it was decided that an attack should be mounted against Army Group Centre. Initially with the aim of liberating the city of Minsk, Operation *Bagration* took its codename from a Russian general of the Napoleonic Wars. The attack was to be made with such force that if the initial offensive suceeded in crumbling the German lines, the Red Army would have enough power to push forward into Poland and Romania. Operation *Bagration* began shortly after the Allied invasion of Normandy, with the aim of stretching the Germans to breaking point.

On 23 June 1944, four Soviet Fronts attacked the central sector of the Eastern Front. The aim of the attack was simple, though vast in scale. The Red Army intended to encircle – and crush – the bulk of Army Group Centre in a triangle that was bounded by Minsk, Vitebsk and Rogachev.

Bagration is launched

A massive two-hour artillery bombardment across the entire depth of the German positions marked the start of the offensive. Within 24 hours, German forces in Vitebsk had been cut off and destroyed by the First Baltic Front and the Third Byelorussian Front.

The Soviets enjoyed air superiority, and had considerably more men, artillery and tanks than the Germans. Successively they encircled the German LIII Corps, and then the bulk of the German Fourth Army.

In each case, Hitler gave his by now customary order that the troops must stand fast. On those occasions when it became clear even to the *Führer* that a withdrawl was necessary, he gave his reluctant permission, usually when it was too late to save the troops on the ground.

As a result of Hitler's refusal to allow any retreat, the German Army suffered a series of disasters in quick succession. First, the German IX Corps was destroyed at Vitebsk. On 29 June, 70,000 men of the German Ninth Army were trapped in the Bobruisk pocket, most being killed or captured when the Soviets stormed the city.

Fourth Army surrounded

Following a further Soviet breakthrough at Orsha, the German Fourth Army was in danger of being surrounded at Mogilev by elements of the Second Byelorussian Front. In an attempt to remedy the situation, Hitler fired Field Marshal Busch, replacing him with Field Marshal Walter Model. But even the man known as 'the *Führer's* Fireman' could do nothing to stem the Soviet tide. Although the commander of XII Corps, *General der Infanterie* Kurt von Tippelskirch, disobeyed orders and withdrew his command, by 30 June his forces had been penned in on the east bank of the River Berezhina. Most of the troops were killed or captured.

June–July 1944

The Soviet summer offensive of 1944 was the most decisive single campaign of World War II. Launched three years to the day after the German invasion, and three weeks after the Western Allies landed in Normandy, it involved the largest military force in history: more than 2.7 million men smashed into the German front lines. More than one million men attacked Army Group Centre alone.

By the end of August, Soviet forces were in the Baltic states, across the Polish border and about to cross into Romania. Army Group Centre had been annihilated. From the 97 German divisions and 13 separate brigades that had been in place in Army Group Centre, or which had been rushed into action as reinforcements throughout the two-month operation, 17 divisions and three brigades were destroyed completely. Another 50 divisions lost between 60 and 70 per cent of their manpower.

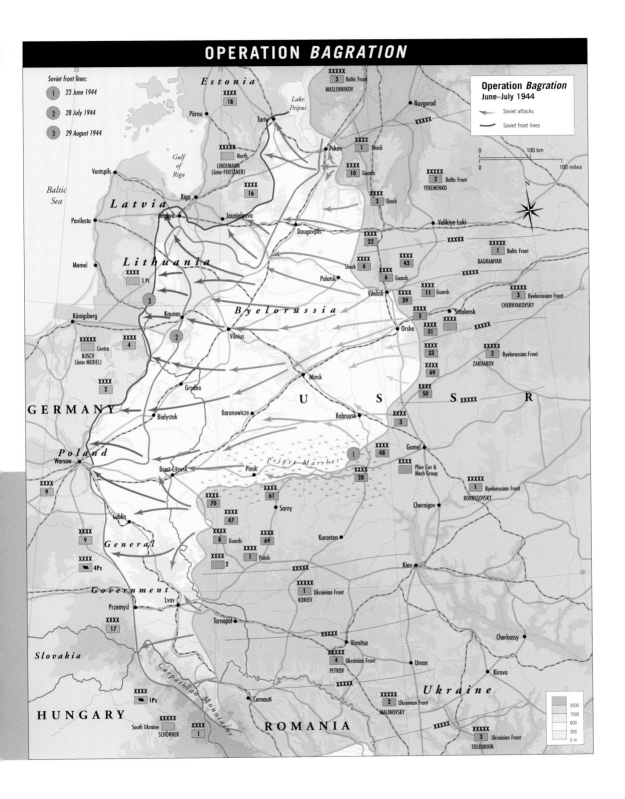

OPERATION *BAGRATION*

Soviet front lines:

1 23 June 1944

2 28 July 1944

3 29 August 1944

Operation *Bagration*
June–July 1944

→ Soviet attacks

⌒ Soviet front lines

0   100 km
0   100 miles

Estonia

Lake Peipus

XXXXX **3** Baltic Front MASLENNIKOV

Navgorod

XXXX **18**

Pärnu

Tartu

XXXXX **1** Shock

XXXXX

Gulf of Riga

North LINDEMANN (*later* FRIESSNER)

Pskov

XXXXX **10** Guards

XXXXX **2** Baltic Front YEREMENKO

Ventspils

Riga

XXXX **16**

XXXX **3** Shock

Baltic Sea

Latvia

Jelgava

Jaunjelgava

Daugavpils

Velikiye Luki

Pavilosta

XXXX **22**

XXXXX **1** Baltic Front BAGRAMYAN

Memel

Lithuania

XXXX Shock **4**

XXXX **43**

XXXX Guards **6**

XXXXX **3** Byelorussian Front CHERNYAKOVSKY

XXXX **3 Pz**

3

Polotsk

Königsberg

Kaunas

Byelorussia

Vitebsk

XXXX **39**

XXXX **11** Guards

2

Vilnius

XXXX **5**

Smolensk

XXXXX Centre BUSCH (*later* MODEL)

XXXX **4**

Orsha

XXXX **31**

XXXXX **2** Byelorussian Front ZAKHAROV

XXXX **33**

Grodno

Minsk

XXXX **49**

XXXX **2**

GERMANY

U   **S**

XXXX **50**

S   XXXXX   **R**

Bialystok

Baranowicze

Bobruysk

XXXX **3**

Pripet Marshes

XXXX **48**

Gomel

Poland

Warsaw

1

XXXX Pliev Cav & Mech Group

Brest-Litovsk

Pinsk

XXXX **28**

XXXX **9**

XXXX **70**

XXXX **61**

Sarny

Chernigov

XXXXX **1** Byelorussian Front ROKOSSOVSKY

Lublin

XXXX **47**

XXXX **9**

General

XXXX **8** Guards

XXXX **69**

Korosten

Kiev

XXXX **4Pz**

XXXX **2**

XXXX **1** Polish

Government

Lvov

XXXXX **1** Ukrainian Front KONIEV

Cherkassy

Przemysl

Tarnopol

XXXX **17**

XXXXX Vinnitsa

XXXXX **4** Ukrainian Front PETROV

Uman

Kirovo

XXXX **1Pz**

Slovakia

Carpathian Mountains

Cernauti

XXXXX

Ukraine

XXXXX **2** Ukrainian Front MALINOVSKY

HUNGARY

XXXXX South Ukraine SCHÖRNER

XXXX **1**

ROMANIA

XXXXX

XXXXX **3** Ukrainian Front TOLBUKHIN

3000
1500
600
300
0 m

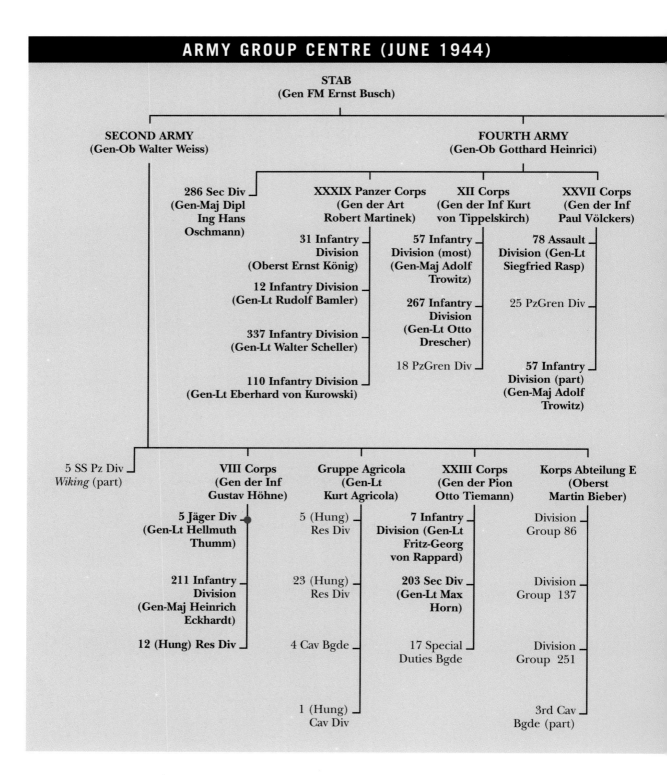

ARMY GROUP CENTRE (JUNE 1944)

STAB
(Gen FM Ernst Busch)

SECOND ARMY
(Gen-Ob Walter Weiss)

FOURTH ARMY
(Gen-Ob Gotthard Heinrici)

286 Sec Div
(Gen-Maj Dipl
Ing Hans
Oschmann)

XXXIX Panzer Corps
(Gen der Art
Robert Martinek)

XII Corps
(Gen der Inf Kurt
von Tippelskirch)

XXVII Corps
(Gen der Inf
Paul Völckers)

31 Infantry
Division
(Oberst Ernst König)

57 Infantry
Division (most)
(Gen-Maj Adolf
Trowitz)

78 Assault
Division (Gen-Lt
Siegfried Rasp)

12 Infantry Division
(Gen-Lt Rudolf Bamler)

267 Infantry
Division
(Gen-Lt Otto
Drescher)

25 PzGren Div

337 Infantry Division
(Gen-Lt Walter Scheller)

18 PzGren Div

57 Infantry
Division (part)
(Gen-Maj Adolf
Trowitz)

110 Infantry Division
(Gen-Lt Eberhard von Kurowski)

5 SS Pz Div
Wiking (part)

VIII Corps
(Gen der Inf
Gustav Höhne)

Gruppe Agricola
(Gen-Lt
Kurt Agricola)

XXIII Corps
(Gen der Pion
Otto Tiemann)

Korps Abteilung E
(Oberst
Martin Bieber)

5 Jäger Div
(Gen-Lt Hellmuth
Thumm)

5 (Hung)
Res Div

7 Infantry
Division (Gen-Lt
Fritz-Georg
von Rappard)

Division
Group 86

211 Infantry
Division
(Gen-Maj Heinrich
Eckhardt)

23 (Hung)
Res Div

203 Sec Div
(Gen-Lt Max
Horn)

Division
Group 137

12 (Hung) Res Div

4 Cav Bgde

17 Special
Duties Bgde

Division
Group 251

1 (Hung)
Cav Div

3rd Cav
Bgde (part)

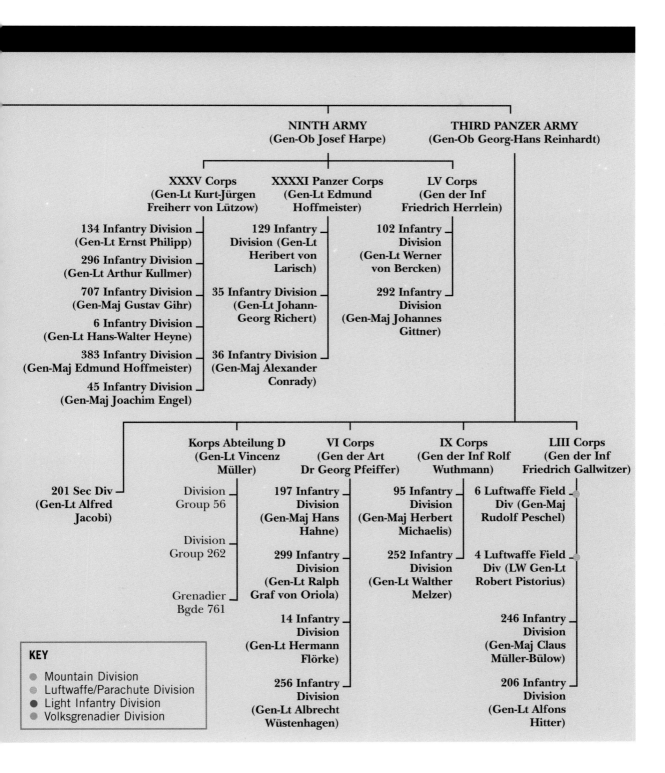

NINTH ARMY
(Gen-Ob Josef Harpe)

THIRD PANZER ARMY
(Gen-Ob Georg-Hans Reinhardt)

XXXV Corps
(Gen-Lt Kurt-Jürgen
Freiherr von Lützow)

XXXXI Panzer Corps
(Gen-Lt Edmund
Hoffmeister)

LV Corps
(Gen der Inf
Friedrich Herrlein)

134 Infantry Division
(Gen-Lt Ernst Philipp)

296 Infantry Division
(Gen-Lt Arthur Kullmer)

707 Infantry Division
(Gen-Maj Gustav Gihr)

6 Infantry Division
(Gen-Lt Hans-Walter Heyne)

383 Infantry Division
(Gen-Maj Edmund Hoffmeister)

45 Infantry Division
(Gen-Maj Joachim Engel)

129 Infantry
Division (Gen-Lt
Heribert von
Larisch)

35 Infantry Division
(Gen-Lt Johann-
Georg Richert)

36 Infantry Division
(Gen-Maj Alexander
Conrady)

102 Infantry
Division
(Gen-Lt Werner
von Bercken)

292 Infantry
Division
(Gen-Maj Johannes
Gittner)

Korps Abteilung D
(Gen-Lt Vincenz
Müller)

VI Corps
(Gen der Art
Dr Georg Pfeiffer)

IX Corps
(Gen der Inf Rolf
Wuthmann)

LIII Corps
(Gen der Inf
Friedrich Gallwitzer)

201 Sec Div
(Gen-Lt Alfred
Jacobi)

Division
Group 56

Division
Group 262

Grenadier
Bgde 761

197 Infantry
Division
(Gen-Maj Hans
Hahne)

299 Infantry
Division
(Gen-Lt Ralph
Graf von Oriola)

14 Infantry
Division
(Gen-Lt Hermann
Flörke)

256 Infantry
Division
(Gen-Lt Albrecht
Wüstenhagen)

95 Infantry
Division
(Gen-Maj Herbert
Michaelis)

252 Infantry
Division
(Gen-Lt Walther
Melzer)

6 Luftwaffe Field
Div (Gen-Maj
Rudolf Peschel)

4 Luftwaffe Field
Div (LW Gen-Lt
Robert Pistorius)

246 Infantry
Division
(Gen-Maj Claus
Müller-Bülow)

206 Infantry
Division
(Gen-Lt Alfons
Hitter)

KEY
- Mountain Division
- Luftwaffe/Parachute Division
- Light Infantry Division
- Volksgrenadier Division

ERNST BUSCH (1885–1945)

Born in Essen-Steele, Ernst Busch joined the German army in 1904. He served on the Western Front in World War I, winning the Pour le Merite for bravery. Serving in the Inspectorate of Transport Troops between the wars, he was a supporter of Hitler, and was promoted rapidly after the Nazis came to power.

• Busch served in Poland, then was appointed commander of Sixteenth Army in the Western campaign in 1940.

• He served with Army Group North during Operation *Barbarossa* in 1941, leading Sixteenth Army in the siege of Leningrad.

• As Field Marshal, he commanded Army Group Centre, which was destroyed during Operation *Bagration* in 1944.

• Busch commanded Army Group North West, fighting the British, in the last months of the war.

The Second Belorussian Front was within 80km (50 miles) of the Prussian border by the end of August. At the same time, First Byelorussian Front had punched its way into Poland and crossed the Vistula River.

Ten days after the fall of Minsk, the Red Army reached the pre-war Polish border. The subsequent Lublin-Brest and Lvov-Sandomierz operations further exploited the collapse of Army Group Centre, as German forces were hastily transferred back from Army Group North Ukraine, weakening it in the process.

Annihilation of Army Group Centre

By the time *Bagration* officially ended on 29 August, the Red Army had advanced over 545km (340 miles) along a 1120km (700 mile) front. The offensive had inflicted near irreparable damage to Army Group Centre, and had severed any contact between German forces in the Ukraine and those serving with Army Group North.

Overall, the annihilation of Army Group Centre cost the Germans 2000 tanks and 57,000 other vehicles. German losses are estimated at 300,000 dead, with about 250,000 wounded and 120,000 captured. Soviet losses were 60,000 killed, 110,000 wounded and a further 8000 missing, with 2957 tanks, 2447 artillery pieces and 822 aircraft also lost.

1 August–2 October 1944

The massive Soviet summer offensive of 1944 saw the Germans pushed out of Russia and into Poland and East Prussia. The approaching Red army prompted the Polish Home Army to rise against the Germans.

The Red Army, which had just finished a major campaign with now exhausted troops, low supplies and unserviceable equipment, stopped short of Warsaw. By 16 September 1944, Soviet forces had reached a point a few hundred metres from the city, across the Vistula River. Their reluctance to help the Poles may have come from Stalin himself: the Home Army was Nationalist and anti-Communist, and it was in the Soviet dictator's interest to see it wiped out – which it was, brutally. Polish losses amounted to 18,000 combatants killed and 25,000 wounded, in addition to between 120,000 and 200,000 civilian deaths, mostly from massacres conducted by retreating German troops.

THE WARSAW RISING

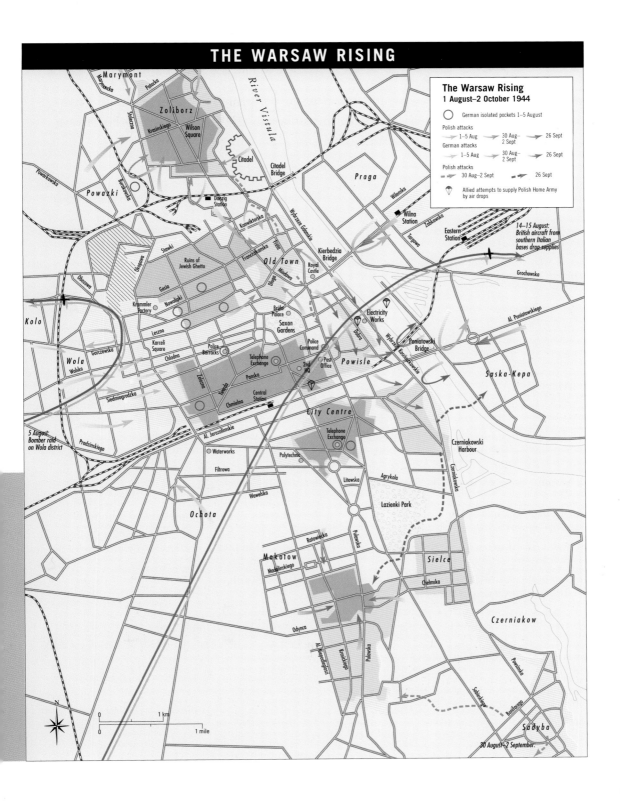

The Warsaw Rising
1 August–2 October 1944

○ German isolated pockets 1–5 August

Polish attacks
→ 1–5 Aug   → 30 Aug–2 Sept   → 26 Sept

German attacks
→ 1–5 Aug   → 30 Aug–2 Sept   → 26 Sept

Polish attacks
--→ 30 Aug–2 Sept   --→ 26 Sept

Allied attempts to supply Polish Home Army by air drops

*14–15 August:
British aircraft from
southern Italian
bases drop supplies*

*5 August:
Bomber raid
on Wola district*

30 August–2 September

N

0   1 km

0   1 mile

Army Group North Ukraine: 1944

The *Oberkommando des Heeres* expected the Soviets to launch a major Eastern Front offensive in the summer of 1944, either in the Baltic against Army Group North, in Byelorussia against Army Group Centre, or as an attack in the Ukraine.

Duped by an effective Soviet *maskirova*, or deception plan, the German High Command decided that the third option was most likely. By early June 1944, the forces of *General Feldmarschall* Walter Model's Army Group North Ukraine had been pushed back beyond the Dniepr and were desperately clinging to the north-western corner of Ukraine.

Stalin ordered the liberation of Ukraine, and the Soviet High Command set in motion plans that would become the Lvov–Sandomierz Operation. The objective of the offensive was for Konev's 1st Ukrainian Front to occupy Lvov and clear the Germans from Ukraine.

Ukraine is strengthened

Though several German commanders were concerned about increased Soviet activity opposite Army Group Centre, German forces were transferred southwards to Army Group North Ukraine throughout the summer, in order to meet an attack there. This left Army Group Centre dangerously weakened, as Stavka, the Soviet high command, had intended.

When Operation *Bagration* was launched, it came as a complete surprise. Model was removed from command of Army Group North Ukraine and replaced by *Generaloberst* Josef Harpe.

Harpe's force comprised two panzer armies, the First Panzer Army, under *Generaloberst* Gotthard Heinrici, and Fourth Panzer Army, under *General der Panzertruppen* Walther Nehring. Attached to the First Panzer Army was the Hungarian First Army.

The Soviet forces under Konev outnumbered the Germans considerably. The First Ukrainian Front could muster over 1,200,000 men, 2050 tanks, 16,000 guns and mortars and over 3250 aircraft. Additionally, the morale of Konev's troops was extremely high. They had been on the offensive for almost a year, and were witnessing the collapse of Army Group Centre to their

North. The Soviet attack was to have two main thrusts. The first, aiming towards Rawa Ruska, was to be led by the Third Guards, First Guards Tank and Thirteenth armies. The second pincer was aimed at Lvov itself, and was to be led by the Sixtieth, Thirty-Eighth, Third Guards Tank and Fourth Tank armies.

The Soviets achieved a massive local superiority against the Germans by limiting their attacks to a front of just of 26km (42 miles). Konev employed roughly 240 guns and mortars per kilometre of front.

The attack is launched

On 13 July, they drove forwards against strong resistance from Army Group North Ukraine. This was where the *Wehrmacht* had expected the Soviet onslaught, and where the strongest German forces had been deployed.

It was not until two more tank armies had been brought up from reserve on 16 July, and this immense weight of men and firepower began to tell, that the defences cracked.

Some 40,000 Germans were surrounded near Brody. Rokossovsky's right-hand army drove straight to the Vistula, crossed it and formed a bridgehead at Sandomir. One tank army flanked Lvov to the north and another was thrown into a direct assault which captured the city on 27 July.

Into Poland

By the end of August, the Carpathians had been reached along their main length. The Red Army had now driven right through Poland and was closing on the prewar borders with Czechoslovakia and Hungary.

In two months, the Soviet troops had advanced over 700km (435 miles) and now the time had again come to reorganize the supply lines. Their advance had been immensely costly – but it had inflicted even greater losses on the Germans.

VOLKSGRENADIER COMPANY: 1944

The crippling defeats suffered by the German Army in the summer of 1944 caused a real manpower shortage, necessitating a more economical infantry divisional structure, which emphasized defensive strength over offensive power. The Volksgrenadier divisions – not to be confused with the poorly-equipped *Volkssturm*, or home guard – had only six infantry battalions instead of nine. The most striking feature of the Volksgrenadier battalion was the substitution of traditional rifle fire with a massive allocation of submachine guns. This reflected the growing German obsession with overwhelming automatic firepower, which was seen as the key to resisting enemy assaults. The theory has some defensive justification, but the Volksgrenadiers were ill-suited to the offensive operations to which they were sometimes committed – such as in the Ardennes Offensive of December 1944 – and they consequently suffered heavy losses.

Headquarters (2 machine gunners, 2 riflemen)

1st (SMG) Platoon

1st SMG Squad (9 sub-machine gunners)

2nd SMG Squad (9 sub-machine gunners)

Rifle Squad (5 sub-machine gunners, 1 machine gunner, 1 assistant gunner, 2 riflemen)

2nd (SMG) Platoon

1st SMG Squad (9 sub-machine gunners)

2nd SMG Squad (9 sub-machine gunners)

Rifle Squad (5 sub-machine gunners, 1 machine gunner, 1 assistant gunner, 2 riflemen)

3rd (Rifle) Platoon

1st Rifle Squad (2 sub-machine gunners, 1 machine gunner, 1 assistant gunner, 5 riflemen)

2nd Rifle Squad (2 sub-machine gunners, 1 machine gunner, 1 assistant gunner, 5 riflemen)

3rd Rifle Squad (2 sub-machine gunners, 1 machine gunner, 1 assistant gunner, 5 riflemen)

ARMY GROUP NORTH UKRAINE (SUMMER 1944)

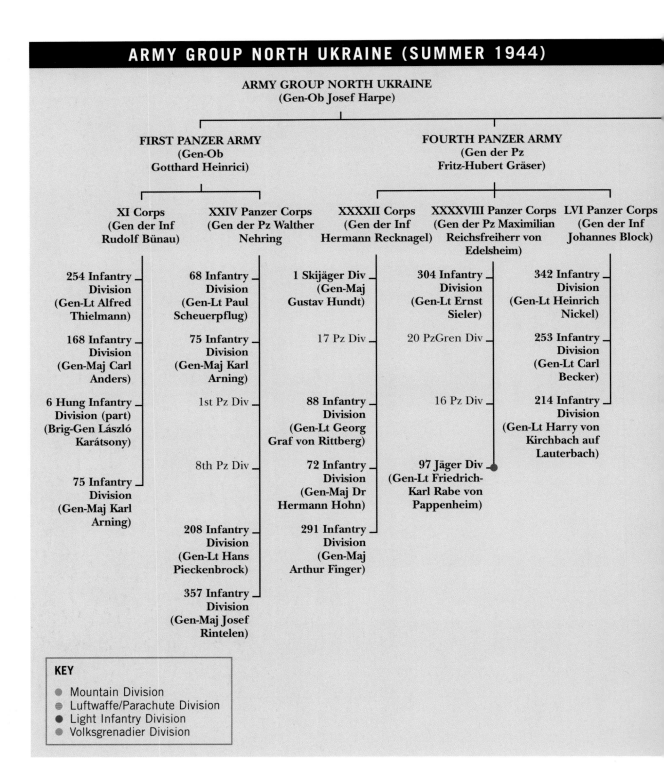

ARMY GROUP NORTH UKRAINE
(Gen-Ob Josef Harpe)

FIRST PANZER ARMY
(Gen-Ob
Gotthard Heinrici)

FOURTH PANZER ARMY
(Gen der Pz
Fritz-Hubert Gräser)

XI Corps
(Gen der Inf
Rudolf Bünau)

XXIV Panzer Corps
(Gen der Pz Walther
Nehring

XXXXII Corps
(Gen der Inf
Hermann Recknagel)

XXXXVIII Panzer Corps
(Gen der Pz Maximilian
Reichsfreiherr von
Edelsheim)

LVI Panzer Corps
(Gen der Inf
Johannes Block)

254 Infantry
Division
(Gen-Lt Alfred
Thielmann)

68 Infantry
Division
(Gen-Lt Paul
Scheuerpflug)

1 Skijäger Div
(Gen-Maj
Gustav Hundt)

304 Infantry
Division
(Gen-Lt Ernst
Sieler)

342 Infantry
Division
(Gen-Lt Heinrich
Nickel)

168 Infantry
Division
(Gen-Maj Carl
Anders)

75 Infantry
Division
(Gen-Maj Karl
Arning)

17 Pz Div

20 PzGren Div

253 Infantry
Division
(Gen-Lt Carl
Becker)

6 Hung Infantry
Division (part)
(Brig-Gen László
Karátsony)

1st Pz Div

88 Infantry
Division
(Gen-Lt Georg
Graf von Rittberg)

16 Pz Div

214 Infantry
Division
(Gen-Lt Harry von
Kirchbach auf
Lauterbach)

75 Infantry
Division
(Gen-Maj Karl
Arning)

8th Pz Div

72 Infantry
Division
(Gen-Maj Dr
Hermann Hohn)

97 Jäger Div ●
(Gen-Lt Friedrich-
Karl Rabe von
Pappenheim)

208 Infantry
Division
(Gen-Lt Hans
Pieckenbrock)

291 Infantry
Division
(Gen-Maj
Arthur Finger)

357 Infantry
Division
(Gen-Maj Josef
Rintelen)

KEY
● Mountain Division
◑ Luftwaffe/Parachute Division
● Light Infantry Division
● Volksgrenadier Division

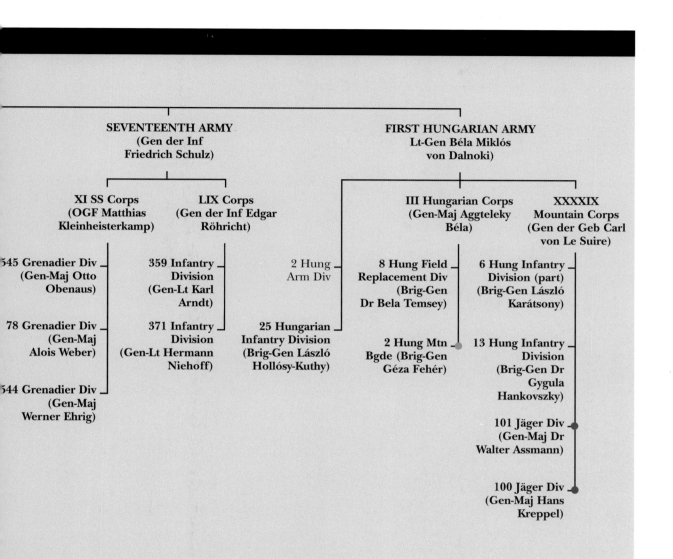

SEVENTEENTH ARMY
(Gen der Inf
Friedrich Schulz)

FIRST HUNGARIAN ARMY
Lt-Gen Béla Miklós
von Dalnoki)

XI SS Corps
(OGF Matthias
Kleinheisterkamp)

LIX Corps
(Gen der Inf Edgar
Röhricht)

III Hungarian Corps
(Gen-Maj Aggteleky
Béla)

XXXXIX
Mountain Corps
(Gen der Geb Carl
von Le Suire)

545 Grenadier Div
(Gen-Maj Otto
Obenaus)

359 Infantry
Division
(Gen-Lt Karl
Arndt)

2 Hung
Arm Div

8 Hung Field
Replacement Div
(Brig-Gen
Dr Bela Temsey)

6 Hung Infantry
Division (part)
(Brig-Gen László
Karátsony)

78 Grenadier Div
(Gen-Maj
Alois Weber)

371 Infantry
Division
(Gen-Lt Hermann
Niehoff)

25 Hungarian
Infantry Division
(Brig-Gen László
Hollósy-Kuthy)

2 Hung Mtn
Bgde (Brig-Gen
Géza Fehér)

13 Hung Infantry
Division
(Brig-Gen Dr
Gygula
Hankovszky)

544 Grenadier Div
(Gen-Maj
Werner Ehrig)

101 Jäger Div
(Gen-Maj Dr
Walter Assmann)

100 Jäger Div
(Gen-Maj Hans
Kreppel)

In February 1943, Army Group Don and the existing Army Group B were combined and re-designated Army Group South. On 4 April 1944, Army Group South was again re-designated Army Group North Ukraine. Army Group North Ukraine existed from 4 April to 28 September of that year. The Army Group's panzer strength was increased dramatically in April and May, anticipating that the major thrust of the Soviet Summer Offensive would be through the Ukraine. In the event, many of the panzer formations were sent north after the opening of Operation *Bagration* against Army Group Centre in Byelorussia. In September 1944, Army Group North Ukraine was re-designated Army Group A.

Army Group South Ukraine: 1944

Army Group South Ukraine was formed in March 1944 when Army Group A was divided in two. Initially commanded by *Generaloberst* Ferdinand Schörner, it was led by *Generaloberst* Johannes Friessner when the Soviets launched their Summer Offensive.

The southern sector of the Soviet attack was perhaps more politically motivated than the attacks against Army Groups North Ukraine and Centre. The Balkans were as great an attraction to Stalin as they had been for centuries to his imperial predecessors.

The Soviet plan of attack called for the Second Ukrainian Front to break through north of Jassi, and then seize the Prut River crossings before the withdrawing German formations of Sixth Army could escape. Third Ukrainian Front was to attack out of its bridgehead across the Dniester River near Tiraspol, and then insert mobile formations with a mission to head north and meet the mobile formations of Second Ukrainian Front.

Soviet breakthrough

The initial stages of the attack into Romania saw two Soviet fronts opposed by two Axis corps, XXX Corps and XXIX Corps, which controlled the 15th and 306th German infantry divisions, the 4th Romanian Mountain Division and the 21st Romanian Infantry Division. The 13th Panzer Division, which was up to strength in manpower but was short of tanks and artillery, was held in reserve. At the end of the first day of the Soviet offensive, both Romanian divisions had been almost completely destroyed, while the German infantry divisions suffered heavy casualties. At the end of the second day, the Red Army stood deep in the rear of German Sixth Army. Their supplies were cut off, and Sixth Army was doomed to be encircled and eventually destroyed. By the end of the third day, the 13th Panzer Division was no longer combat effective.

The Axis disintegrates

By the end of the month, Romania was in the process of being occupied by the Red Army. To the south, Bulgaria was about to be invaded by one of Tolbukhin's armies,

driving down the Black Sea coast through Constanta. Perhaps influenced by events in their northern neighbour, a group of pro-Allied officers now seized control in Sofia and welcomed the Red Army. The invasion therefore became 'a visit by friendly forces', who raced through the capital on 15 September. Collecting two Bulgarian armies, they pressed on to the Yugoslav border opposite Bor in the north and Skopje in the south.

Into the Balkans

The Soviet advance into Yugoslavia, which was possible following the battle, forced the rapid withdrawal of German formations in Greece and Yugoslavia to rescue them from being cut off. By 8 September, Malinovsky's armies had joined Tolbukhin's. On 28 September, they moved forward together to link up with Marshal Tito's partisans, while the Second Ukrainian Front drove over the Romanian border north of the Danube.

January–May 1944

On 20 August, Malinovsky's Second Ukrainian Front broke through the defences of Army Group South Ukraine in the Pruth valley opposite Jassi. By the 24th they were near Leovo, where they met two of Tolbukhin's mechanized corps that had forced a path along the lower Dniester into Bessarabia. Tolbukhin's forces had isolated the German Sixth Army, reconstituted after Stalingrad, when political events intervened.

A coup d'état took place in Bucharest. The Romanian leader, Marshal Antonescu, was overthrown. King Michael took his place, the government sued for peace with the Allies, and two Romanian armies laid down their arms. Southern Bessarabia, the Danube delta and the Carpathian passes to the north lay open to the advancing Soviet armies.

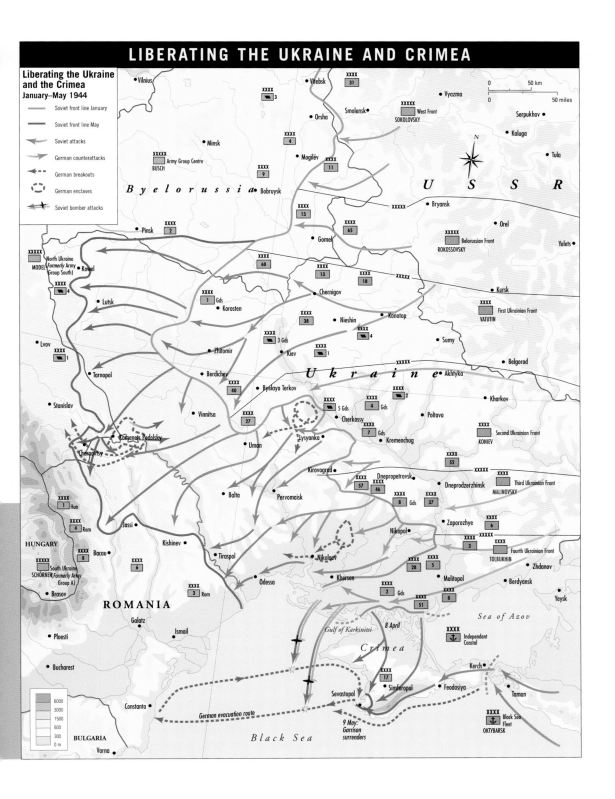

LIBERATING THE UKRAINE AND CRIMEA

Liberating the Ukraine and the Crimea
January–May 1944

— Soviet front line January
— Soviet front line May
→ Soviet attacks
→ German counterattacks
←-- German breakouts
⬭ German enclaves
✈ Soviet bomber attacks

Vilnius

Vitebsk — XXXX 31

XXXX 3

Minsk

Orsha

Smolensk

West Front SOKOLOVSKY — XXXXX

Vyazma

Serpukhov

Kaluga

Tula

Mogilëv — XXXX 4

XXXX 11

U S S R

Army Group Centre BUSCH — XXXXX

XXXX 9

B y e l o r u s s i a — Bobruysk

Pinsk

XXXX 2

XXXX 13

Bryansk — XXXXX

Orel

Gomel — XXXX 65

Belorussian Front ROKOSSOVSKY — XXXXX

Yelets

North Ukraine (Formerly Army Group South) MODEL — XXXXX — Kowel

XXXX 4

Lutsk

XXXX 60

XXXX 13

XXXX 18 — XXXXX

Kursk

Korosten — XXXX 1 Gds

Chernigov

Nieshin

Konotop

Sumy

First Ukrainian Front VATUTIN — XXXX

XXXX 38

Lvov

XXXX 1

Tarnopol

Zhitomir

XXXX 3 Gds

Kiev — XXXX 4

XXXX 1

U k r a i n e — Akhtyka — XXXXX

Belgorod

Stanislav

Berdichev

Byelaya Terkov — XXXX 40

XXXX 2

Kharkov

Vinnitsa — XXXX 27

XXXX 5 Gds

XXXX 4 Gds

Cherkassy — XXXX 7 Gds

Poltava

Second Ukrainian Front KONIEV — XXXX

Uman

Lysanka

Kremenchug

XXXX 52

Kamenets Podolsky

Chernovtsy

Kirovograd

Dnepropetrovsk — XXXX 57 / XXXX 46

Dneprodzerzhinsk — Third Ukrainian Front MALINOVSKY — XXXXX

Balta

Pervomaisk

XXXX 8 Gds

XXXX 37

XXXX 1 Hun

XXXX 4 Rom

Jassi

Zaporozhye — XXXX 6

Nikopol — XXXX 3 — XXXXX

HUNGARY

XXXX 8 — Bacau

XXXX 6

Kishinev

Tiraspol

Njkolaev — XXXX 28 / XXXX 5

Fourth Ukrainian Front TOLBUKHIN — XXXX

Melitopol

Berdyansk

Zhdanov

South Ukraine (Formerly Army Group A) SCHÖRNER — XXXXX

Brasov

XXXX 3 Rom

Odessa

Kherson — XXXX 2 Gds / XXXX 51

XXXX 8

Yeysk

ROMANIA

Galatz

Ismail

Sea of Azov

8 April

Gulf of Karkinitsi

Independent Coastal — XXXX ⚓

Ploesti

C r i m e a

Kerch

Bucharest

XXXX 17

Simferopol

Feodosiya

Taman

Constanta

Sevastopol

9 May: Garrison surrenders

Black Sea Fleet OKTYBARSK — XXXX ⚓

German evacuation route

BULGARIA

Black Sea

Varna

6000
3000
1500
600
300
0 m

ARMY GROUP SOUTH UKRAINE (SEPTEMBER 1944)

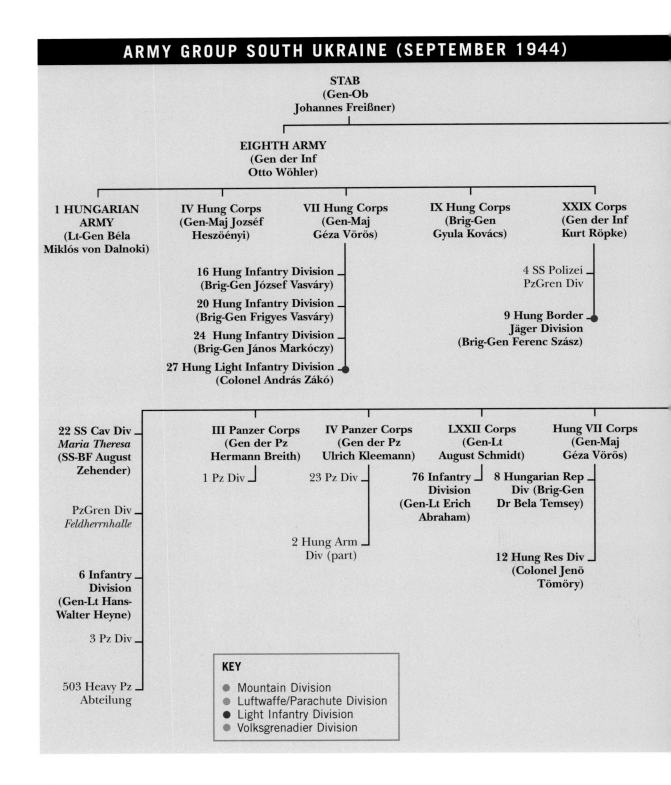

STAB
(Gen-Ob
Johannes Freißner)

EIGHTH ARMY
(Gen der Inf
Otto Wöhler)

1 HUNGARIAN ARMY
(Lt-Gen Béla
Miklós von Dalnoki)

IV Hung Corps
(Gen-Maj Jozséf
Heszöényi)

VII Hung Corps
(Gen-Maj
Géza Vörös)

IX Hung Corps
(Brig-Gen
Gyula Kovács)

XXIX Corps
(Gen der Inf
Kurt Röpke)

16 Hung Infantry Division
(Brig-Gen József Vasváry)

20 Hung Infantry Division
(Brig-Gen Frigyes Vasváry)

24 Hung Infantry Division
(Brig-Gen János Markóczy)

27 Hung Light Infantry Division
(Colonel András Zákó)

4 SS Polizei
PzGren Div

9 Hung Border
Jäger Division
(Brig-Gen Ferenc Szász)

22 SS Cav Div
Maria Theresa
(SS-BF August
Zehender)

III Panzer Corps
(Gen der Pz
Hermann Breith)

IV Panzer Corps
(Gen der Pz
Ulrich Kleemann)

LXXII Corps
(Gen-Lt
August Schmidt)

Hung VII Corps
(Gen-Maj
Géza Vörös)

1 Pz Div

23 Pz Div

76 Infantry
Division
(Gen-Lt Erich
Abraham)

8 Hungarian Rep
Div (Brig-Gen
Dr Bela Temsey)

PzGren Div
Feldherrnhalle

2 Hung Arm
Div (part)

12 Hung Res Div
(Colonel Jenö
Tömöry)

6 Infantry
Division
(Gen-Lt Hans-
Walter Heyne)

3 Pz Div

503 Heavy Pz
Abteilung

KEY
- Mountain Division
- Luftwaffe/Parachute Division
- Light Infantry Division
- Volksgrenadier Division

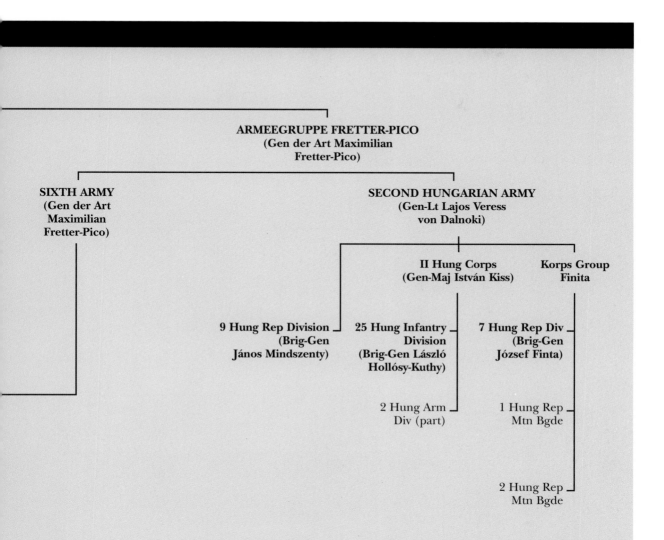

ARMEEGRUPPE FRETTER-PICO
(Gen der Art Maximilian
Fretter-Pico)

SIXTH ARMY
(Gen der Art
Maximilian
Fretter-Pico)

SECOND HUNGARIAN ARMY
(Gen-Lt Lajos Veress
von Dalnoki)

II Hung Corps
(Gen-Maj István Kiss)

**Korps Group
Finita**

9 Hung Rep Division
(Brig-Gen
János Mindszenty)

**25 Hung Infantry
Division**
(Brig-Gen László
Hollósy-Kuthy)

7 Hung Rep Div
(Brig-Gen
József Finta)

2 Hung Arm
Div (part)

1 Hung Rep
Mtn Bgde

2 Hung Rep
Mtn Bgde

Until the beginning of June 1944, Army Group South Ukraine had been one of the most powerful German formations in terms of armour. However, it lost most of its panzers during the summer – transferred to the northern and central front, in order to stem Red Army advances in the Baltic states, Byelorussia, northern Ukraine and Poland. On the eve of the Soviet offensive into Romania, the only armoured formations left were 1st Romanian Armoured Division, the German 13th Panzer Division and the 10th Panzergrenadier Division. Some panzers were returned in the autumn, but for most of its time in combat the army group was largely an infantry formation, made up in the most part from politically unreliable units of Germany's Hungarian and Romanian allies.

Sicily and Italy: 1943–45

In July 1943, the Allies landed on Sicily. It quickly became clear to the Germans that the island could not be held. Unusually, Hitler conceded that only a timely withdrawal from Sicily would avoid a second debacle as had occurred in Tunisia.

The German armies in Italy fought one of the hardest defensive campaigns of the war at places like Anzio, Cassino (pictured) and the Gothic Line.

On 10 July 1943, British and American forces invaded Sicily. While Montgomery's British Eighth Army made slow progress up the east of the island, the dynamic General Patton and his Seventh Army were sent on a roundabout route to the north coast. He took grave risks and suffered one shock defeat, but once past Palermo he turned eastwards and raced towards Messina.

Stubborn defensive fighting held the Allies back until the beginning of August, when Kesselring ordered the evacuation to begin. On 11 August, every available vessel was employed to ferry the remaining defenders to the mainland.

Mussolini overthrown

The Italian people had never been enthusiastic about the war. The Fascist Grand Council, which had not met since 1939, was convened on 24 July 1943. A motion against Mussolini was carried by 19 votes to 8. The dictator was arrested in the name of King Victor Emmanuel and Marshal Pietro Badoglio was appointed head of a new government.

Badoglio assured the Germans that Italy would remain faithful. Just in case, however, Rommel's Operation Alaric – named after the Gothic king who sacked Rome – was ready to be implemented. Pressed by the British and Americans to surrender immediately, the Italian leaders prevaricated, giving the Germans time to transfer additional troops to Italy.

On the Eastern Front, the battle of Kursk had been going badly. Its continuation was already in doubt when news reached Hitler's headquarters that the Allies were ashore in Sicily. The cancellation of Operation Citadel on 13 July enabled some units to be withdrawn, including the 1st SS Panzergrenadier Division *Leibstandarte,* which travelled by train to northern Italy.

Salerno landings

The Allies hoped that Italy would cooperate in surrender: they demanded that the Italian fleet sail to Malta and that Italian army units support an airborne drop on Rome. At length, weary of Badoglio's manoeuvrings, the Allies conducted an amphibious assault south of Naples at Salerno on 9 September. At the same time, Montgomery blasted his way across the straits of Messina to arrive at the toe of Italy. As naval units ferried British airborne troops to seize the naval base of Taranto, Italy belatedly surrendered.

The surrender was a disaster for most ordinary Italian soldiers. Across Italy, the Balkans and Greece, German garrisons turned on their former allies. Italian units were disarmed and hauled off to Germany for use as slave labour.

The Salerno landings seemed to go well at first. British commandos and US Rangers seized Salerno, while the British advanced inland to occupy the airfield at Montecorvino. On the southern bank of the Sele, two inexperienced US infantry divisions held a beachhead 5km (3 miles) deep and 15km (9 miles) across.

German attack

The Allies failed to expand or reinforce their beachhead, while the Germans rushed in every available formation they could scrape together. On 12 September, they commenced an all-out attack, supported by strong *Luftwaffe* elements.

The US divisions were driven back, but held on short of the beach The two British divisions held where they were down, their corps artillery supplemented by naval bombardment.

Lavish air support and continued shore bombardment missions by the warships offshore helped sustain the battered defenders. *Generaloberst* Heinrich von Vietinghoff-Scheel, commander of the German Tenth Army, knew he could only delay the inevitable, and Kesselring recognized that to persist with the attacks risked defeat.

Retreat north

On 16 September, the Germans withdrew into the surrounding mountains as suddenly as they had come. The same day, US patrols in the south encountered elements of the British Eighth Army advancing from the toe of Italy.

The Germans pulled back north of Naples. However, the prospect of taking Rome before winter had disappeared. The terrain lent itself to defence, with towering mountain ranges dominating narrow valleys. The Germans demonstrated time and again the ease with which narrow mountain passes could be defended.

Army Group B

With the defection of Italy, Hitler had three strategic alternatives in the Mediterranean: Germany could assume the defence of Italy and Greece; surrender all of Italy to the Allies; or defend in Italy south of the Po Valley.

Hitler never seriously considered evacuating all of Italy. In addition to giving up the resources of the Po Valley, withdrawal from Italy would have meant placing Allied armies on the southern border of Germany. Though the Alps provided an obstacle to invasion, the Allies would be able to establish air bases within easy striking distance

of south and central Germany, and northern Italy would give the Allies an ideal staging area for amphibious operations against southern France or southeastern Europe.

The plan to occupy and defend all of Italy and the Balkans was the first plan adopted by Hitler. He charged

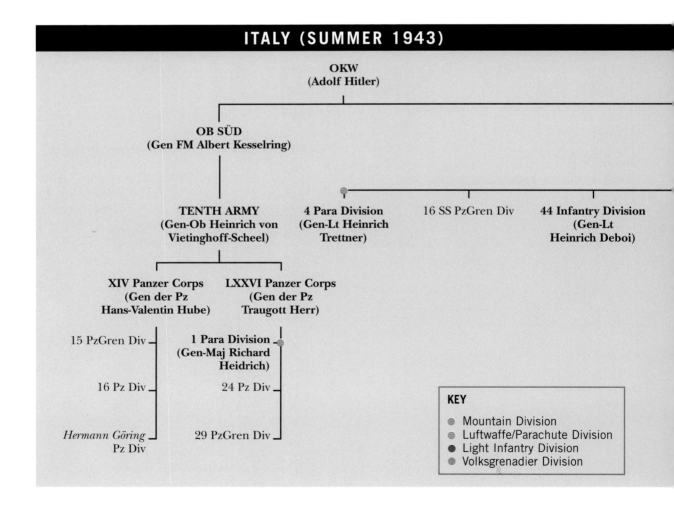

ITALY (SUMMER 1943)

OKW
(Adolf Hitler)

OB SÜD
(Gen FM Albert Kesselring)

TENTH ARMY
(Gen-Ob Heinrich von Vietinghoff-Scheel)

4 Para Division
(Gen-Lt Heinrich Trettner)

16 SS PzGren Div

44 Infantry Division
(Gen-Lt Heinrich Deboi)

XIV Panzer Corps
(Gen der Pz Hans-Valentin Hube)

LXXVI Panzer Corps
(Gen der Pz Traugott Herr)

15 PzGren Div

1 Para Division
(Gen-Maj Richard Heidrich)

16 Pz Div

24 Pz Div

Hermann Göring Pz Div

29 PzGren Div

KEY
● Mountain Division
● Luftwaffe/Parachute Division
● Light Infantry Division
● Volksgrenadier Division

Field Marshal Rommel with the activation of a skeleton army group headquarters in Munich to work out plans to occupy and defend Italy. On 23 July 1943, Rommel moved to Greece as commander of Army Group E, to defend the Greek coast against a possible Allied landing that never happened, only to return to Germany two days later, upon the overthrow of Mussolini. On 17 August 1943, Rommel moved his headquarters from Munich to Lake Garda, as commander of a new Army Group B, created to defend the north of Italy.

Where to defend Italy
Rommel believed that Germany should abandon southern Italy to the Allies, while Field Marshal Albert

Kesselring, the *Oberbefehlshaber Süd*, felt that all of Italy could and should be defended, even if Sicily had to be given up. Kesselring's resourcefulness and unexpected success in coping with the Italians and the two Allied armies during the first days after Salerno gained him at least temporary control over the conduct of operations.

On 12 September, Hitler informed Kesselring and Rommel that Rommel was not authorized to issue directives to Kesselring; this authorization was to be issued by Hitler personally only after the forces of Commander-in-Chief South came within close proximity to the territory of Army Group B along the line from Pisa to Ancona.

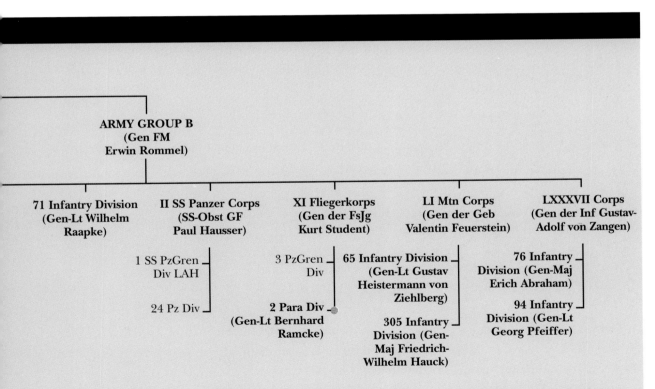

The major German command in the Mediterranean was *Oberbfehlshaber Süd*, which was nominally under the Italian supreme command. Under *Luftwaffe* Field Marshal Albert Kesselring, German forces defended Sicily and southern Italy. In November 1943, after the Italian armistice and the German takeover of the peninsula, units reporting to OB Süd were reorganized into Army Group C, comprising Tenth Army and Fourteenth Army. Meanwhile, a new formation, Army Group B, was established in northern Italy under Field Marshal Erwin Rommel in 1943, to defend against a possible Allied attack there, and was subsequently moved to northern France to defend against the D-Day landings in 1944.

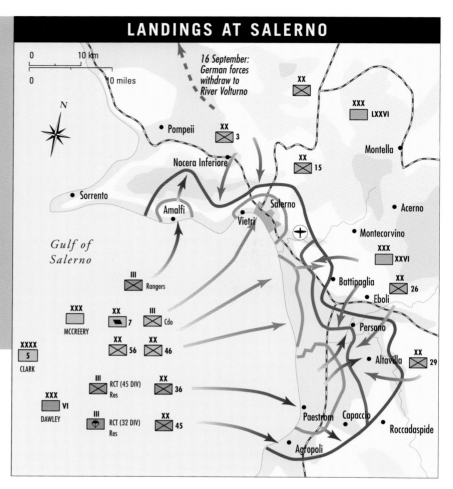

LANDINGS AT SALERNO

9–16 September 1943

The Allied landings at Salerno nearly failed as soon as they started. A ring of hills surrounding the port provided cover for the German 29th Panzergrenadier Division, which struck the Allied beachhead hard. Field Marshal Kesselring rushed reinforcements to Salerno, and soon the Germans had a ring of steel around the landing force. Only after six days of bitter struggle, which saw the American 82nd Airborne Division deployed to reinforce the beachhead, did the tide begin to turn. The approach of the British Eighth Army from the south forced the Germans to withdraw, which they did in good order.

Landings at Salerno
9–16 September 1943

German front line 14 Sept.
Allied front line 11 Sept.
Allied front line 9 Sept.
German movements
British movements
US movement

Anzio and Cassino: 1944

In January 1944, Allied forces under the command of General Mark Clark struck across the Liri Valley towards Monte Cassino, which was the hub of the powerfully fortified series of German defences known as the Gustav Line.

The aim of the attack was partly an attempt to breach the Gustav Line, and partly an attempt to draw German attention away from the major amphibious assault that was to take place at Anzio. Monte Cassino, topped by a historic Benedictine Abbey, was strongly defended.

When the Fifth Army attacked the position in January, the assault quickly came to grief.

However, the attack had in part achieved its aim: the Anzio landings, which began on 22 January, surprised the German defenders. The plan called for the US VI

Corps to strike out from the beachhead towards the Alban Hills, outflanking the Gustav Line. Unfortunately, Clark allowed General Lucas, the commander at Anzio, time to build up his strength, and by the time he was ready to move Kesselring had gathered nine divisions around the beachhead. Instead of being a threat to the Gustav Line, the Allied forces at Anzio were under siege.

With the Anzio force locked in place, Alexander, the Allied commander in Italy, had no choice but to authorize a frontal attack on the Gustav Line. However, further attempts to cross the Liri and Rapido were repelled at great cost.

January–February 1944

Convinced that the Germans were using the ancient Benedictine abbey on top of Monte Cassino as an observation point, the Allies launched a massive air raid in February, smashing the monastery to rubble. The Germans, who had not been using the site, promptly moved into the ruins, which proved to be an almost perfect defensive position, and they pushed back a major Allied ground assault. In March, Alexander ordered the town of Cassino to be destroyed by 500 bombers, but Allied forces were still unable to advance through the ruined town. Eventually, in May, Juin's French Corps penetrated the line west of the Liri River. Fearing being outflanked, the Germans withdrew.

MONTE CASSINO (JANUARY–FEBRUARY 1944)

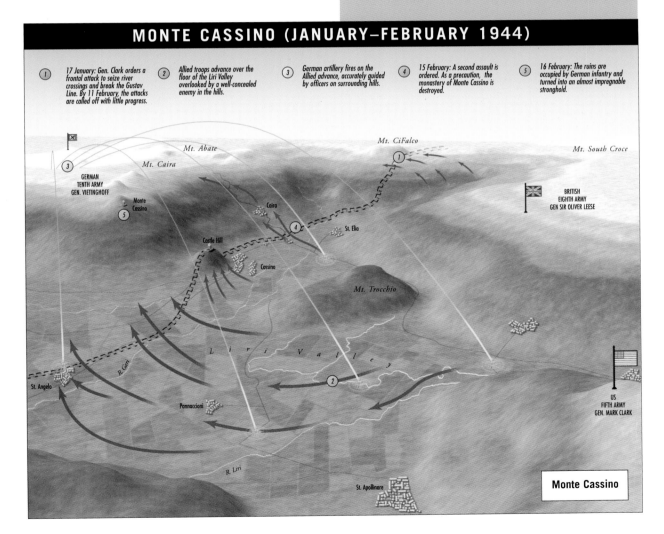

① 17 January: Gen. Clark orders a frontal attack to seize river crossings and break the Gustav Line. By 11 February, the attacks are called off with little progress.

② Allied troops advance over the floor of the Liri Valley overlooked by a well-concealed enemy in the hills.

③ German artillery fires on the Allied advance, accurately guided by officers on surrounding hills.

④ 15 February: A second assault is ordered. As a precaution, the monastery of Monte Cassino is destroyed.

⑤ 16 February: The ruins are occupied by German infantry and turned into an almost impregnable stronghold.

Mt. CiFalco

Mt. Abate

Mt. South Croce

Mt. Caira

GERMAN TENTH ARMY GEN. VIETINGHOFF

Monte Cassino

Caira

St. Elia

BRITISH EIGHTH ARMY GEN SIR OLIVER LEESE

Castle Hill

Cassino

Mt. Trocchio

Liri Valley

R. Garri

St. Angelo

Pannaccioni

US FIFTH ARMY GEN. MARK CLARK

R. Liri

St. Apollinare

Monte Cassino

Army Group C

Originally established in 1939 for the campaigns in Poland and France, Army Group C became Army Group North in Russia in 1941. With the transfer of Army Group B to France in November 1943, a new Army Group C was established in Italy.

Army Group C was commanded by *General-Feldmarschall* Albert Kesselring. At the same time, his title of *Oberfehlshaber Süd* (Commander-in-Chief South) was changed to *Oberbefehlshaber Südwest* (Commander-in-Chief Southwest).

Experienced troops

The principal fighting units of Army Group C were the German Tenth Army under *Generaloberst* Heinrich von Vietinghoff-Scheel, and the German Fourteenth Army,

17 January – 26 May 1944

The hard-fought victory at Cassino should have freed the Allied forces at Anzio to attack inland to Valmontane, which would cut off the retreating German Tenth Army as they struggled northwards. Clark, however, had other ideas. He wanted to be known as the liberator of Rome, so he sent most of Fifth Army northwards to seize the Italian capital, which had been declared an open city. The small force he sent to Valmontane could do nothing to impede the German retreat, and von Vietinghoff-Scheel's Tenth Army managed to escape northwards largely intact.

LANDINGS AT ANZIO

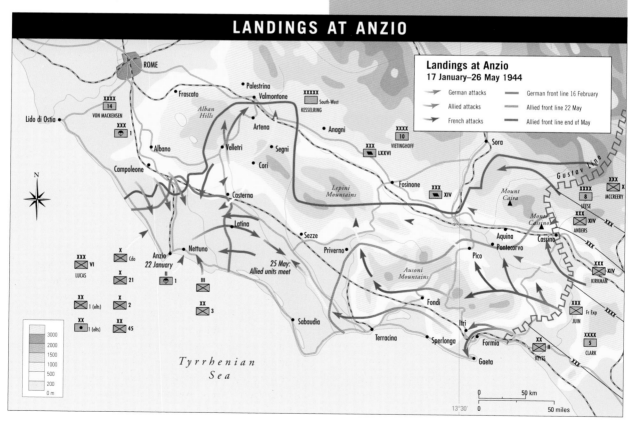

Landings at Anzio
17 January–26 May 1944

- → German attacks
- → Allied attacks
- → French attacks
- German front line 16 February
- Allied front line 22 May
- Allied front line end of May

commanded from July 1944 by *General der Panzertruppen* Joachim Lemelsen. Both were highly experienced formations, and both would prove experts at the bitter defensive fighting which was to come.

Fighting retreat

After the fall of the Gustav Line, Tenth Army retreated northwards, fighting skilful delaying actions in the rugged terrain. Held at arms length by the German rearguards, the Allies contributed to their own slow advance by turning aside to capture important Italian cities like Livorno and Florence. This made good copy for the press, but it meant that they could not close with and destroy the Germans.

The Germans first halted at the temporary defensive positions of the Viterbo Line, north of Rome. They then moved on to the Albert Line near Perugia. Each defensive position forced the Allies to fight battles on difficult terrain chosen by the defenders.

Gothic Line

While the Allies made their slow progress, battering their way through skilfully held defences only to find that the Germans had slipped away, the *Wehrmacht* was building up a new defensive line along the Apennines, known as the Gothic Line. German reinforcements were streaming into Italy from the Eastern Front, with eight divisions being used to build up the strength of the Gothic Line.

By the time Tenth Army reached the line, it had made a fighting retreat across 241km (150 miles) of rugged terrain to the northern Apennine Mountains, holding off and delaying vastly superior Allied forces all the way.

Allied delays

Although General Alexander hoped to smash through the Gothic Line by autumn, perhaps even advancing into the Alps and southern Germany, he was unable to make the decisive breakthrough. The Italian campaign had always been a secondary theatre, and this became much more obvious after the capture of Rome and the Normandy Invasion. Many experienced units, such as the US 3rd, 36th and 45th Infantry Divisions and the French Expeditionary Corps, were pulled out of Italy to participate in Operation Dragoon, the Allied invasion of the South of France.

Through the Gothic Line

Following the breaking of the Gustav Line and the capture of Rome, some Allied commanders expected progress up Italy to be swift. But the hard-bitten, experienced troops of the German Army Group C had other ideas.

The Germans, masters of delaying tactics through the use of demolitions, booby traps and minefields, had to contend with the ever-present threat of Allied air attacks. While medium bombers struck road and rail communications, fighters attacked convoys and vehicles. Night-time brought an additional threat from partisans. Based in the Apennines, they attacked soft targets such as isolated vehicles and small groups of troops. Local resistance also gave invaluable help recovering Allied aircrew whose aircraft had been shot down behind enemy lines.

General Alexander, with the benefit of up-to-the-minute ULTRA decryptions, was convinced that the Gothic Line would be broken with ease. At dawn on 25 August 1944, British, Canadian and Polish troops launched the first probing attacks on the Gothic Line. However, it was not until 12 September that the battle began in earnest. The first move was Operation Olive – an attack on the right flank along the Adriatic Coast by three corps. By 29 August, they had reached the Foglia and the Gothic Line. Although the Canadians managed to break through the defences and reach the River

Conca a day later, the British were held in front of Clemente. Kesselring moved his forces to block these moves, and they and heavy autumn rain brought the attack to a halt.

On 12 September, the US II and British XIII Corps were launched against the centre of the Gothic Line high on the Apennines. They were attacking at the junction between the German Tenth and Fourteenth Armies just east of the Giogo di Scarperia pass. On the west coast, the US IV Corps kept the pressure on the Germans and prevented reinforcements moving to the mountains. In the Apennines, the Americans became involved in a desperate fight for the two peaks, Montecelli and Monte Altuzzo, that dominated Il Giogo Pass. But these did not fall until 17 September.

Slow pace

On the coast, the British Eighth Army resumed its attacks on Cariano on the night of the 12 September. They looked close to a major breakthrough. However, the elements once again contrived against them as heavy autumn rains prevented tanks from being brought forward. The advance was not resumed until a day later. A week's hard fighting followed and the Germans were finally forced back to the Rimini Line.

Up in the mountains, American troops captured Fiorenzuola on 21 September, which presented Kesselring with the threat that they might break through to Route 9. On the Eighth Army front, the Greek Brigade took Rimini and the Canadians crossed the Marecchia River. The next obstacle was the River Po about 100km (62 miles) to the north, but in between were no fewer than nine rivers to be crossed.

Through the Line

The German Army had fought hard. By 27 September, however, the Allies were through the Gothic Line. By 7 October, Eighth Army began to attack towards the River Rubicon, and in five days they were across this symbolic barrier. At the end of October, the campaigning season in the central sector was over. In one month, the Fifth Army had suffered 15,700 casualties, but it was still trapped in the mountains.

On 24 November, General Mark Clark relinquished his command of the US Fifth Army. He was succeeded by General Lucien 'Old Gravel Guts' Truscott. Clark, in turn, took over from General Harold Alexander as C-in-C of the Fifteenth Army Group and thus commander of Allied ground forces in Italy. Alexander was promoted to Supreme Allied Commander in the Mediterranean.

Kesselring's plan

Kesselring had considered that the valleys of the Rivers Po and the Adige could be used as intermediate defence lines as his forces fell back to strong positions in the southern Alps. At this point, Hitler issued one of his disastrous stand-fast orders. He refused Kesselring permission to withdraw into more defensible positions and insisted that Army Group C should stand and fight.

An uneasy stalemate now set in. With heavy frosts and snow, the struggle on both sides was against the elements – not each other. Allied supply routes were kept open only by the daily and unremitting efforts of thousands of civilians and all but those units in the most forward positions. Whilst the Germans were forced to hoard their meagre stocks of petrol and ammunition, the Allies finally began to receive some of the specialized equipment they had for so long been denied. Throughout the remaining winter months, training began in earnest in preparation for the Allied spring offensive. The Germans could only build up their defences as best they could and wait for the strike.

June–December 1944

Italy lent itself to defensive fighting and the Germans fought a series of masterful withdrawals. The country was a narrow peninsula with steep mountains, narrow winding roads, deep river valleys and grim winter weather that produced ribald jokes about 'sunny Italy'. Rome fell on 4 June 1944. German forces in Italy were forced to fall back on the intermediate Albert Line that ran from Grosseto in the west, past Lake Trasimene to the river Chienti and to the Adriatic east coast. Besides the Albert Line, the Germans had established blocking positions on the main roads from Rome to Sienna and Perugia to Arezzo. North of these positions, they established the Arno Line along the valley of the River Arno. The Gothic Line was the Germans' last major defensive barrier. Kesselring utilized the natural obstacles afforded by the Apennines and the rivers Foglia and Pesaro and added strong, in-depth manmade defences.

LIBERATION OF ROME AND ADVANCE NORTH

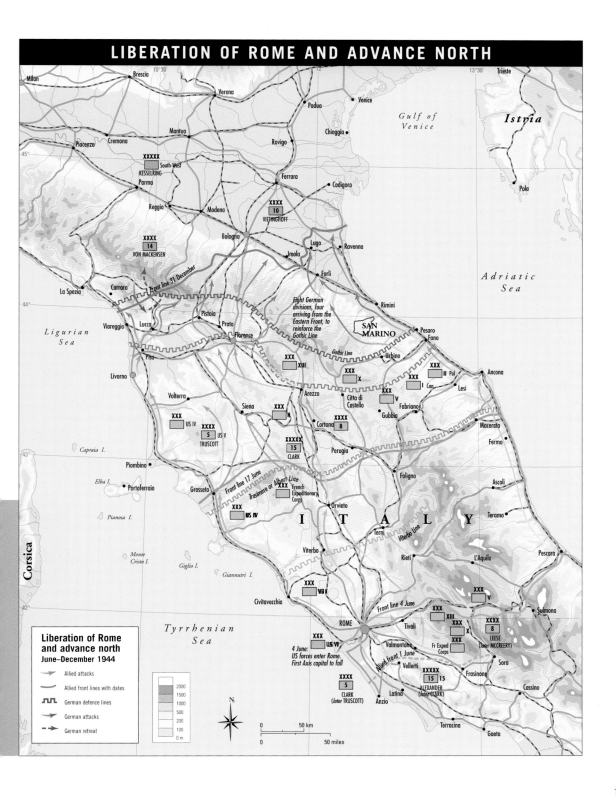

Milan
Brescia
10°30'
Verona
Padua
Venice
Gulf of Venice
Istria
Piacenza
Cremona
Mantua
Rovigo
Chioggia
Pola
45°
XXXXX
South-West
KESSELRING
Parma
Reggio
Modena
Ferrara
Codigoro
XXXX
10
VIETINGHOFF
XXXX
14
VON MACKENSEN
Bologna
Imola
Lugo
Ravenna
Forli
Rimini
Adriatic Sea
La Spezia
Carrara
Front line 31 December
44°
Ligurian Sea
Viareggio
Lucca
Pistoia
Prato
Florence
Pisa
Eight German
divisions, four
arriving from the
Eastern Front, to
reinforce the
Gothic Line
SAN MARINO
Pesaro
Fano
Gothic Line
Urbino
Ancona
Livorno
Volterra
XXX
XIII
Arezzo
XXX
X
Citta di
Castello
XXX
II Pol
XXX
I Can
Lesi
XXX
V
Fabriano
Gubbia
Macerata
Fermo
Siena
XXX
II
XXXXX
15
CLARK
Cortona
XXXX
8
Perugia
XXX
US IV
XXXX
5 US V
TRUSCOTT
Capraia I.
43°
Piombino
Elba I.
Portoferraio
Grosseto
Front line 17 June
Trasimene or Albert Line
XXX
French
Expeditionary
Corps
Foligno
Ascoli
Teramo
Orvieto
Terni
Viterbo Line
XXX
US IV
Pianosa I.
Monte
Cristo I.
Giglio I.
Giannutri I.
Viterbo
Rieti
L'Aquila
Pescara
XXX
VII
XXX
V
Civitavecchia
Front line 4 June
XXX
XIII
XXX
X
XXXX
8
LEESE
(later McCREERY)
Corsica
Tyrrhenian Sea
ROME
Tivoli
XXX
US VI
4 June:
US forces enter Rome.
First Axis capital to fall
Valmontone
Fr Exped
Corps
XXX
Sora
Allied front 1 June
Velletri
XXXXX
15 15
ALEXANDER
(later CLARK)
Frasinone
Cassino
XXXX
5
CLARK
(later TRUSCOTT)
Latina
Anzio
Terracina
Gaeta
Sulmona

Liberation of Rome and advance north
June–December 1944

→ Allied attacks

⌢ Allied front lines with dates

⊓⊔⊓ German defence lines

→ German attacks

⇢ German retreat

2000
1500
1000
500
200
100
0 m

N

0   50 km

0   50 miles

ITALY

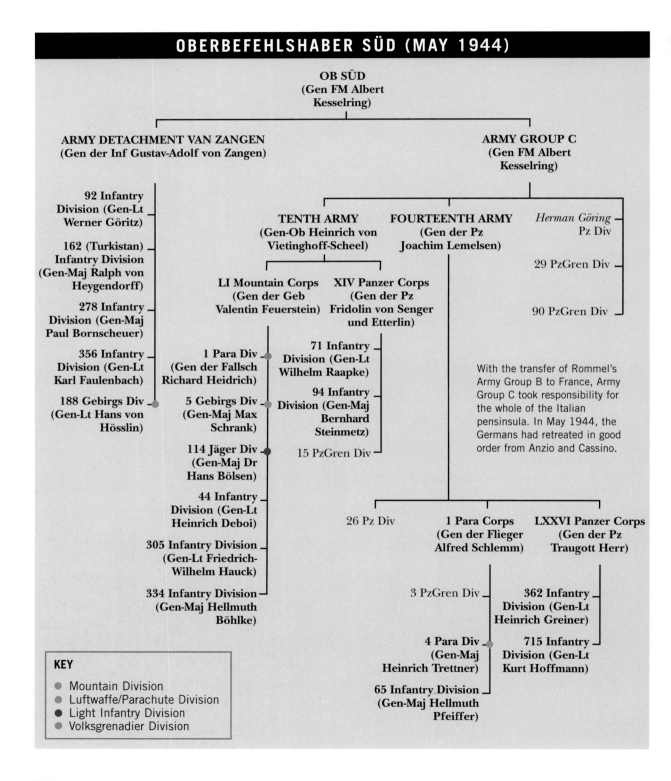

OBERBEFEHLSHABER SÜD (MAY 1944)

OB SÜD
(Gen FM Albert Kesselring)

ARMY DETACHMENT VAN ZANGEN
(Gen der Inf Gustav-Adolf von Zangen)

ARMY GROUP C
(Gen FM Albert Kesselring)

92 Infantry Division (Gen-Lt Werner Göritz)

162 (Turkistan) Infantry Division (Gen-Maj Ralph von Heygendorff)

278 Infantry Division (Gen-Maj Paul Bornscheuer)

356 Infantry Division (Gen-Lt Karl Faulenbach)

188 Gebirgs Div (Gen-Lt Hans von Hösslin)

TENTH ARMY
(Gen-Ob Heinrich von Vietinghoff-Scheel)

FOURTEENTH ARMY
(Gen der Pz Joachim Lemelsen)

Herman Göring Pz Div

29 PzGren Div

90 PzGren Div

LI Mountain Corps
(Gen der Geb Valentin Feuerstein)

XIV Panzer Corps
(Gen der Pz Fridolin von Senger und Etterlin)

71 Infantry Division (Gen-Lt Wilhelm Raapke)

94 Infantry Division (Gen-Maj Bernhard Steinmetz)

15 PzGren Div

1 Para Div (Gen der Fallsch Richard Heidrich)

5 Gebirgs Div (Gen-Maj Max Schrank)

114 Jäger Div (Gen-Maj Dr Hans Bölsen)

44 Infantry Division (Gen-Lt Heinrich Deboi)

305 Infantry Division (Gen-Lt Friedrich-Wilhelm Hauck)

334 Infantry Division (Gen-Maj Hellmuth Böhlke)

With the transfer of Rommel's Army Group B to France, Army Group C took responsibility for the whole of the Italian pensinula. In May 1944, the Germans had retreated in good order from Anzio and Cassino.

26 Pz Div

1 Para Corps
(Gen der Flieger Alfred Schlemm)

LXXVI Panzer Corps
(Gen der Pz Traugott Herr)

3 PzGren Div

362 Infantry Division (Gen-Lt Heinrich Greiner)

4 Para Div (Gen-Maj Heinrich Trettner)

715 Infantry Division (Gen-Lt Kurt Hoffmann)

65 Infantry Division (Gen-Maj Hellmuth Pfeiffer)

KEY
- Mountain Division
- Luftwaffe/Parachute Division
- Light Infantry Division
- Volksgrenadier Division

Italian Theatre: 1945

By 1945, the Allies had an overwhelming materiel advantage in Italy. Although they had broken through the Gothic Line the previous autumn, the weather, the terrain and fierce German defence meant that the final assault would not come until the spring.

The final Allied offensive was launched on 9 April. In preparation for this, on the night of 1 April, British Commandos had attacked the spit running between Lake Comacchio and the Adriatic. The fighting around the Lake area was intended to tie down the German flank, in order to give the major assault a greater chance of success.

Eighth Army attack

The key to a decisive Allied victory was for the Eighth Army to strike across the Senio, exploiting its mobility to capture Ferrara quickly and thus cutting the enemy's lines of supply and retreat across the Po. On the US Fifth Army front, II Corps prepared to take Bologna, while the US IV Corps on its left would attack towards Route 9 between Bologna and, to its left, Modena.

The first phase of the attack was by the Eighth Army, where Indians and New Zealanders of V Corps attacked across the Senio towards Lugo. By 11 April, a bridgehead had been established over the Santerno; and a day earlier, an amphibious operation at Menate across Lake Comacchio had turned the German position in front of the Argenta Gap.

Mixed force

General Mark Clark had a force that was not only depleted but was one of the most heterogeneous field armies of the war, with contingents from more than 25 countries. The French Expeditionary Corps and the US VI Corps, some 86,000 men, had been deployed the previous year in Operation Anvil/Dragoon – the landings in southern France on 15 August 1944. Their place was taken by 2500 men of the Brazilian Corps under General Joao Mascarenhas de Moraes and the US 92nd Division composed of black soldiers. Clark had the added problem that more than one-third of his artillery had been detached to support the Dragoon landings.

On 14 April, Truscott's Fifth Army launched its attack, two days behind schedule because of bad weather. A day later, the Polish II Corps under General Anders began to cross the Sillario River and drove northwest towards the town of Bologna.

Bologna captured

Despite tough fighting in mountainous terrain, Fifth Army broke through to the suburbs of Bologna on 20 April. General Vietinghoff, staring defeat in the face, ordered his troops to retreat across the Po. He succeeded by 23 April, but left most of his heavy equipment behind.

On 25 April, the US Fifth Army, faced with little opposition, took Parma and Verona, and a day later the Allies reached the Adige River. On the west coast, the US advance had been slower, and it was not until 27 April that Genoa was liberated.

With the situation desperate, Vietinghoff asked if he could withdraw his beleaguered forces across the natural defensive line of the Po River. As usual, Hitler refused his permission. Vietinghoff was desperate, however, and ordered a retreat anyway – but it was too late. Allied armoured spearheads raced towards the Po, reaching the river ahead of the retreating Germans.

Unconditional surrender

Vietinghoff, whose headquarters in Bolzano in Northern Italy was under siege by partisans, sent emissaries to Allied Army headquarters on April 28. On 29 April, the Germans signed an unconditional surrender at Caserta. It came into effect at 13.00 GMT on 2 May, just six days before Victory in Europe Day.

In over 20 months of some of the most savage fighting of the war, the Germans had proved the lie to Churchill's famous maxim that Italy was the 'soft underbelly' of Europe.

The end in Italy

The final Allied victories in the Po Valley meant that the last vestiges of Fascism had been smashed in Italy, where it had achieved its first great triumph. Now they could advance into Austria, leaving only loose ends like Mussolini to clear up.

As the situation in Italy fell apart, Mussolini, the once mighty dictator, fled for his life. Imprisoned in 1943, he had been freed by the Germans. The *Führer* maintained a high regard for Mussolini long after it became clear that Italy could offer little to the Axis cause, and ordered his friend's rescue.

A specially picked team of SS and *Luftwaffe* parachutists commanded by Otto Skorzeny made a daring descent on the Gran Sasso on 12 September. After his dramatic rescue, Mussolini was bundled into a tiny Fieseler Storch reconnaissance plane and flown off the mountain. From German-occupied territory, he was flown immediately to see Hitler.

Salo Republic

The *Führer* set up a fascist puppet state in northern Italy, which would continue to fight alongside the Germans. He installed the 'cardboard Caesar' under heavy SS protection as head of the 'Salo Republic'. Its seat was the village of Gargnano on the western shore of Lake Garda. As an early item of business, Mussolini established a tribunal to avenge the coup d'état of 1943 . His son-in-law Count Ciano was among those ordered executed on 11 January 1944.

Although a titular head of state, Mussolini remained a somewhat pathetic figure for the remainder of his life. He continued to inspect military formations, and went about the business of running his Republic with the aid of Marshal Graziani. But he was a broken man.

Mussolini's Salo Republic survived little more than a year. As Allied forces entered the Po Valley in 1945, Mussolini moved his rump government to Milan on 18 April. Forced out after less than a week, he fled northward in hopes of taking refuge in the Tyrol. Wearing a German greatcoat and helmet, he was found hiding in a German army truck at a partisan checkpoint near Lake Como.

Communist leaders in Milan sent one 'Colonel Valerio' – Walter Audisio – to take charge of the captive. On 28 April 1945, *Il Duce* and his mistress, Clara Petacci, were driven to the nearby Villa Belmontone. There they were machine-gunned to death.

Secret negotiations

By then, his former Allies had already negotiated a surrender. On 3 March 1945, an OSS agent met SS General Eugen Dollmann at Lugano, Switzerland. It was the first of a series of secret contacts that had been initiated by General Karl Wolff, the 39-year-old military governor and SS chief in northern Italy. Wolff had acted as the liaison officer between Hitler and Mussolini.

He recognized that although Germany's cause was beyond hope, he could perhaps save his own skin. Accordingly, on 8 March, he met Allen Dulles, the head of intelligence at the Office of Strategic Services (OSS) – later the CIA – and started the process, codenamed 'Sunrise', that would lead to the surrender of German forces in Italy.

On 25 March 1945, von Vietinghoff succeeded Kesselring as Commander-in-Chief in Italy. *Reichsführer* Heinrich Himmler now ordered Wolff not to leave Italy. The head of the SS had picked up rumours of the meetings, and since he was himself involved in tentative negotiations with the Allies, he did not want Wolff to upstage him.

Final surrender

On 23 April, Wolff again approached the Allies. Von Vietinghoff had agreed that an armistice could be signed without reference to Berlin. It was not until 27 April that Dulles was given authority from Alexander's HQ to resume negotiations. The Germans signed a formal surrender document on 29 April, to come into effect on 2 May 1945.

OBERBEFEHLSHABER SÜD (APRIL 1945)

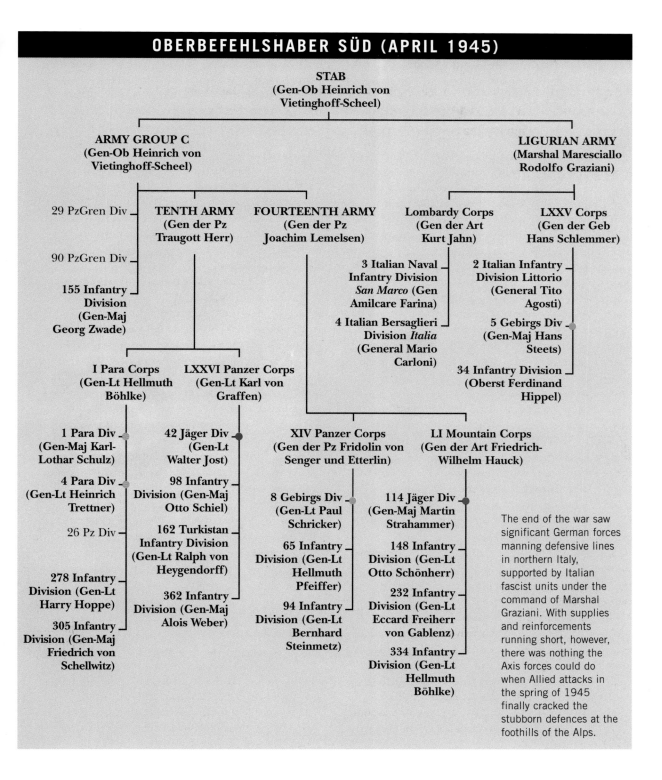

STAB
(Gen-Ob Heinrich von
Vietinghoff-Scheel)

ARMY GROUP C
(Gen-Ob Heinrich von
Vietinghoff-Scheel)

LIGURIAN ARMY
(Marshal Maresciallo
Rodolfo Graziani)

29 PzGren Div

TENTH ARMY
(Gen der Pz
Traugott Herr)

FOURTEENTH ARMY
(Gen der Pz
Joachim Lemelsen)

Lombardy Corps
(Gen der Art
Kurt Jahn)

LXXV Corps
(Gen der Geb
Hans Schlemmer)

90 PzGren Div

155 Infantry
Division
(Gen-Maj
Georg Zwade)

3 Italian Naval
Infantry Division
San Marco (Gen
Amilcare Farina)

2 Italian Infantry
Division Littorio
(General Tito
Agosti)

4 Italian Bersaglieri
Division *Italia*
(General Mario
Carloni)

5 Gebirgs Div
(Gen-Maj Hans
Steets)

34 Infantry Division
(Oberst Ferdinand
Hippel)

I Para Corps
(Gen-Lt Hellmuth
Böhlke)

LXXVI Panzer Corps
(Gen-Lt Karl von
Graffen)

1 Para Div
(Gen-Maj Karl-
Lothar Schulz)

42 Jäger Div
(Gen-Lt
Walter Jost)

XIV Panzer Corps
(Gen der Pz Fridolin von
Senger und Etterlin)

LI Mountain Corps
(Gen der Art Friedrich-
Wilhelm Hauck)

4 Para Div
(Gen-Lt Heinrich
Trettner)

98 Infantry
Division (Gen-Maj
Otto Schiel)

8 Gebirgs Div
(Gen-Lt Paul
Schricker)

114 Jäger Div
(Gen-Maj Martin
Strahammer)

26 Pz Div

162 Turkistan
Infantry Division
(Gen-Lt Ralph von
Heygendorff)

65 Infantry
Division (Gen-Lt
Hellmuth
Pfeiffer)

148 Infantry
Division (Gen-Lt
Otto Schönherr)

278 Infantry
Division (Gen-Lt
Harry Hoppe)

362 Infantry
Division (Gen-Maj
Alois Weber)

94 Infantry
Division (Gen-Lt
Bernhard
Steinmetz)

232 Infantry
Division (Gen-Lt
Eccard Freiherr
von Gablenz)

305 Infantry
Division (Gen-Maj
Friedrich von
Schellwitz)

334 Infantry
Division (Gen-Lt
Hellmuth
Böhlke)

The end of the war saw
significant German forces
manning defensive lines
in northern Italy,
supported by Italian
fascist units under the
command of Marshal
Graziani. With supplies
and reinforcements
running short, however,
there was nothing the
Axis forces could do
when Allied attacks in
the spring of 1945
finally cracked the
stubborn defences at the
foothills of the Alps.

Normandy, France and the Low Countries: 1944

The German occupation of France left the south of the country in the hands of the Vichy regime of Marshal Henri Pétain. However, although many Frenchmen collaborated with the Nazis, a powerful resistance movement quickly arose.

The battles for northwest Europe in 1944 came to a climax with the abortive German offensive in the Ardennes in December.

In October 1942, any claims that Pétain might still have had to legitimacy evaporated when the Germans extended the occupied zone into the Vichy area. They feared that the overwhelming Allied forces in North Africa would soon be invading southern France.

The single biggest factor in the growth of opposition to the Vichy regime was the introduction of forced labour (*Service Travail Obligatoire,* or STO) in February 1943. By this time, the Germans were suffering from manpower shortages on the home front, caused by the insatiable demands of the Army. Vichy complied with German demands and drafted young French men aged between 21 and 23 into compulsory work.

Reluctant to leave for Germany, many of the draftees literally took to the hills, hiding in the maquis or bush. The growing resistance movement in the Southern zone became known as the Maquis, to distinguish them from the Resistance proper, which was principally an urban-based phenomenon.

Laval, now concerned at Germany's deteriorating war situation and with an eye to improving his post-war chances of survival, attempted to secure the return of some of the still-exiled French POWs by complying with the STO requirements.

The Atlantic Wall

He obtained permission for some workers to be exempted from work in Germany, and instead to work on the Atlantic Wall defences in France. Many of these men were in contact with the Resistance, who ensured that plans of the works were sent promptly to London.

By early 1943, Germany had extended her total exclusion zone along the whole of the French coastline. After Rommel returned from North Africa via Italy, he was appointed by Hitler to prepare in-depth defences to counter an Allied invasion of France, wherever it might happen. It was a daunting task, but Rommel's energy and keen eye, combined with the exploitation of tens of thousands of labourers, meant that the work proceeded quickly.

Even so, there was not enough time. The massive concrete emplacements may have provided excellent propaganda footage, but by the time the Allies invaded Normandy in June 1944, some of the largest anti-shipping guns were still not in place.

Rommel thought that the best way of maintaining the integrity of Fortress Europe was to station the majority of German forces as close to the coast as possible. Field Marshal von Rundstedt and others, backed by Hitler, disagreed. When the Allies began their assault on 6 June 1944, the mobile reserve was far to the rear, and the chance to force the Allies back into the sea was lost.

The difficulties that the Germans faced in deploying their panzers was due to a mixture of Allied air superiority and the efforts of the resistance movements, by this time united under the title *Force Francaises de l'Interior* (FFI). They succeeded in causing serious disruption to the German rail network.

In spite of the initial German failure, the liberation of France proceeded at a slow pace. The advance fell behind schedule as the Allies became embroiled in the bloody protracted business of clearing Normandy. But there could only be one outcome. As July followed August, the British broke the siege of Caen, and with the destruction of the panzer armies at Falaise, the Allies achieved the long-awaited breakout into open country.

Reprisals

The brutality that had been the hallmark of the German occupation continued during the retreat to the borders of Germany. More than 50,000 French civilians were to die between D-Day and the final expulsion of the invader. Acts of barbarism were seen in villages and towns throughout the length and breadth of the country, especially where French resistance fighters attempted to liberate settlements still behind the German frontline.

The most notorious acts accompanied the passage of the Waffen SS Division *Das Reich* as it made its way from the south of France towards the Normandy beachheads in June 1944. At Tulle, the SS hanged 99 men from trees and telegraph poles; and at Oradour-sur-Glane, a company – which included many recruits from French Alsace – killed 642 men, women and children. Oradour remains a symbol of the helplessness of France and her people, even at the hour of liberation.

The Germans held onto their remaining French territory for as long as possible, but with the fall of Paris, the centre of the German occupation, the *Reich's* cause in France was lost.

Normandy: 1944

The Germans knew that the Western Allies were coming. They knew that the British and the Americans were preparing the largest amphibious invasion in history. But where would they land? And how would the *Wehrmacht* beat them?

Hitler could not stop the Allies from landing. By early 1944, the *Luftwaffe* was losing control of the skies over the *Reich* itself. *Luftflotte 3* had 820 aircraft on 6 June, of which 170 were serviceable; the Allies committed more than 5000, flying some 10,000 sorties on that day alone. The *Kriegsmarine* readied its submarine flotillas at Brest and Lorient for what was recognized to be a suicide mission; the bulk of the submarine force had already been withdrawn to Norway. S-boats and a handful of destroyers stood no chance of obstructing an invasion fleet 5000 vessels strong, manned by more than a quarter of a million men. Nine Allied battleships, 23 cruisers and 73 destroyers were assigned to shore bombardment missions alone.

Target Normandy

So the Allies would have to be beaten ashore. But where? And how? Field Marshal Gerd von Rundstedt, Commander-in-Chief of the German Army in the west, believed the invasion would take place in the Pas de Calais area, where the Channel is at its narrowest. The Germans would have less time to react once the invasion fleet had been detected, and, once a beachhead had been secured, Rundstedt feared the enemy could reach the Rhine in four days. Inland lay good tank country.

Normandy he ruled out because inland it was dominated by the bocage: narrow lanes and high hedgerows ideal for defence. And there were no major ports, which were assumed to be essential. The Allies' 'Mulberry' artificial harbours would come as a disagreeable surprise.

His conclusion was reinforced by German intelligence, which reported a major concentration of Allied troops in the south-east of England. The First US Army Group, or FUSAG, was commanded by none other than General George S Patton – the one general in the British and American armies that the Germans really feared.

Hitler agreed with his commanders, and the Pas de Calais sector received the bulk of the new fortifications and the strongest concentration of troops.

Swept from the skies

But it would be difficult to beat the Allies since they would have uncontested control of the air. Although the *Luftwaffe* could still make devastating local attacks in the East, it could do very little to contribute to the ground battle in France. Field Marshal Rommel, who had endured similar conditions for more than a year in Africa, believed the Allies had to be destroyed on the beaches. Once a beachhead was established, under that all-powerful air umbrella, he had little confidence that the German Army could throw the invaders back into the sea. He wanted panzer divisions positioned near enough to the coast to intervene within hours, not days.

Von Rundstedt disagreed. He planned a conventional defence, which accepted that the Allies would probably succeed in landing. Once the Germans had identified the enemy's main thrust, he would counterattack with a concentrated blow led by the panzer divisions.

Moving under fire

He accepted that movement behind the lines by day would be vulnerable to air attack, but most divisions received additional anti-aircraft gun batteries. In May 1944, an officer from the 12th SS Panzerdivision *Hitlerjugend* had the idea of mounting the *Flakvierling* quadruple 20mm (0.78in) anti-aircraft gun system onto a Panzer IV chassis: the resulting *Wirbelwind* self-propelled flak unit was rushed into production on Hitler's orders. Above all, the German high command trusted the training and discipline of their men – particularly their night-fighting ability – to smash the invasion before the Allies could bring their superior numbers to bear.

It bears repeating that the bulk of the German army remained on the Eastern Front, where the Red Army was poised to launch five operations, each of which was larger than Operation Overlord, the Allied invasion of Normandy. Of the 285 divisions available to Hitler, 164 were in the East compared to 60 in the West. And half of the latter were poor-quality infantry divisions, filled out with wounded, semi-invalids, older men (a quarter of the German army was aged over 34 by 1944) and foreign troops of doubted loyalty. Many divisions included a battalion of former Soviet troops, 'volunteers' for the anti-Communist army RONA, whose reliability was increasingly suspect as the Red Army's westward advance gained momentum.

The infantry divisions had an impossibly long coastline to defend. In northeast France, divisional sectors averaged 80km (50 miles); along the Normandy coast, 193km (120 miles); and 322km (200 miles) along the shores of the Atlantic and Mediterranean.

Mobile defence

German hopes in France rested on 11 armoured and four airborne divisions, the paratroops functioning as elite ground troops rather than in their intended role. Across the Channel were the equivalent of 50 divisions, including 21 American, 15 British, three Canadian and one each from Poland and France.

As commander of Army Group B, Field Marshal Rommel worked hard to make the 'Atlantic Wall' of Goebbels' propaganda an effective shield. Slave labour combined 17 million cubic yards of concrete with 1.5 million tons of iron to build a network of bunkers, pillboxes, observation towers and machine gun nests. Anti-tank ditches were dug inland; steel girders were fixed at low water to impale incoming landing craft.

But his disagreement with von Rundstedt over how to fight the battle was never resolved. Hitler assigned some panzer divisions to Rommel, others to Rundstedt's reserve, but decreed that none could move without his personal authorization.

In the months before D-Day, the Allied air forces systematically bombed the French railway system. Bridges, marshalling yards, and key junctions were attacked in a campaign that cost the lives of 10,000 French civilians. As a result, German reinforcements

GÜNTHER VON KLUGE (1882–1944)

Born in Posen (now Poznan) to a Prussian military family, von Kluge was an artilleryman who served as a staff officer during World War I.

• He commanded the Fourth Army in Poland in 1939 and in the offensive against France in May 1940. He was promoted to Field Marshal in 1940. Never comfortable with panzers, he had a strained relationship with Heinz Guderian in France and later in the invasion of the Soviet Union in 1941.

• In late 1941, he replaced von Bock as commander of Army Group Centre, until suffering serious injury in a car crash in October 1943.

• He replaced von Rundstedt as commander of OB West in July 1944. Peripherally implicated in the bomb plot of 20 July against Hitler, he committed suicide in August 1944.

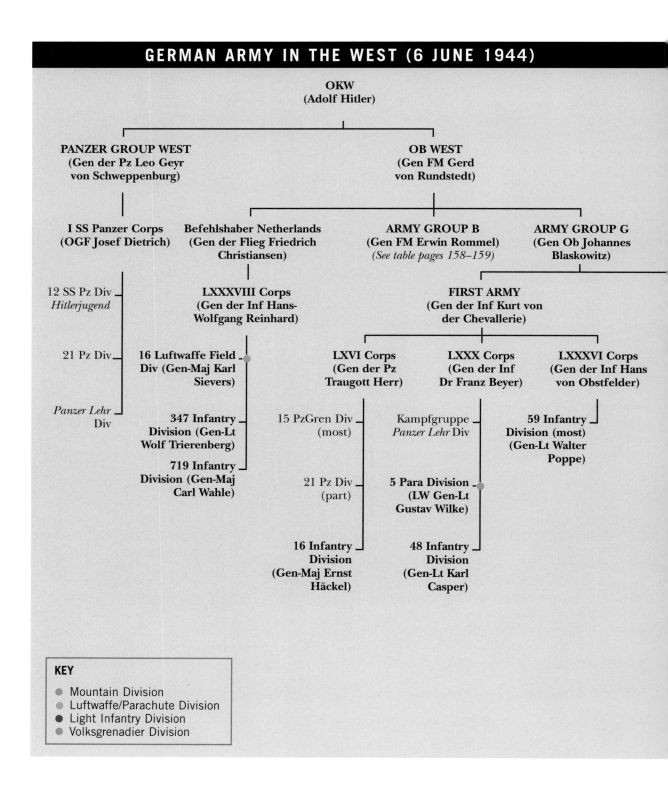

GERMAN ARMY IN THE WEST (6 JUNE 1944)

OKW
(Adolf Hitler)

PANZER GROUP WEST
(Gen der Pz Leo Geyr
von Schweppenburg)

OB WEST
(Gen FM Gerd
von Rundstedt)

I SS Panzer Corps
(OGF Josef Dietrich)

Befehlshaber Netherlands
(Gen der Flieg Friedrich
Christiansen)

ARMY GROUP B
(Gen FM Erwin Rommel)
(See table pages 158–159)

ARMY GROUP G
(Gen Ob Johannes
Blaskowitz)

12 SS Pz Div
Hitlerjugend

LXXXVIII Corps
(Gen der Inf Hans-
Wolfgang Reinhard)

FIRST ARMY
(Gen der Inf Kurt von
der Chevallerie)

21 Pz Div

16 Luftwaffe Field
Div (Gen-Maj Karl
Sievers)

LXVI Corps
(Gen der Pz
Traugott Herr)

LXXX Corps
(Gen der Inf
Dr Franz Beyer)

LXXXVI Corps
(Gen der Inf Hans
von Obstfelder)

Panzer Lehr
Div

347 Infantry
Division (Gen-Lt
Wolf Trierenberg)

15 PzGren Div
(most)

Kampfgruppe
Panzer Lehr Div

59 Infantry
Division (most)
(Gen-Lt Walter
Poppe)

719 Infantry
Division (Gen-Maj
Carl Wahle)

21 Pz Div
(part)

5 Para Division
(LW Gen-Lt
Gustav Wilke)

16 Infantry
Division
(Gen-Maj Ernst
Häckel)

48 Infantry
Division
(Gen-Lt Karl
Casper)

KEY

- Mountain Division
- Luftwaffe/Parachute Division
- Light Infantry Division
- Volksgrenadier Division

Crucially, the German command in Normandy at the time of the Allied invasion was split between Rommel and von Rundstedt. Although nominally under von Runstedt's command, Rommel had independent plans to beat the Allied landings on the beaches. But when the landings began, Rommel was in Germany (visiting his wife), many junior officers were away (ironically on an anti-invasion staff exercise) and Hitler was asleep. Hitler was still asleep by the middle of the morning, by which time Rommel's staff had badgered Rundstedt to request the *Führer's* permission to commit the panzers. No-one dared wake him. It was not until the late afternoon of 6 June that the nearest armoured unit was given permission to move – which meant that Rommel's defensive strategy had collapsed before the battle had really begun.

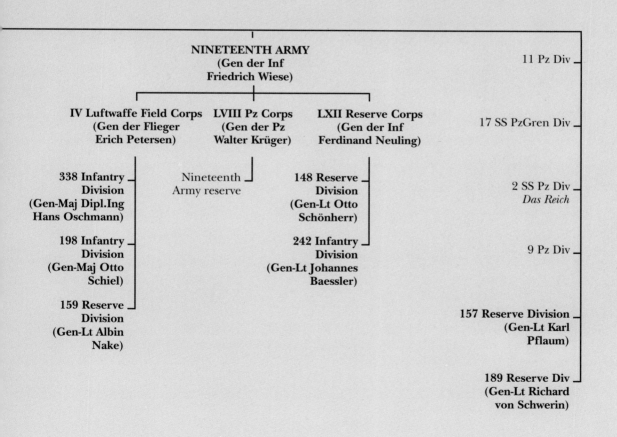

NINETEENTH ARMY
(Gen der Inf
Friedrich Wiese)

11 Pz Div

IV Luftwaffe Field Corps
(Gen der Flieger
Erich Petersen)

LVIII Pz Corps
(Gen der Pz
Walter Krüger)

LXII Reserve Corps
(Gen der Inf
Ferdinand Neuling)

17 SS PzGren Div

338 Infantry
Division
(Gen-Maj Dipl.Ing
Hans Oschmann)

Nineteenth
Army reserve

148 Reserve
Division
(Gen-Lt Otto
Schönherr)

2 SS Pz Div
Das Reich

198 Infantry
Division
(Gen-Maj Otto
Schiel)

242 Infantry
Division
(Gen-Lt Johannes
Baessler)

9 Pz Div

159 Reserve
Division
(Gen-Lt Albin
Nake)

157 Reserve Division
(Gen-Lt Karl
Pflaum)

189 Reserve Div
(Gen-Lt Richard
von Schwerin)

D-DAY LANDINGS: 6 JUNE 1944

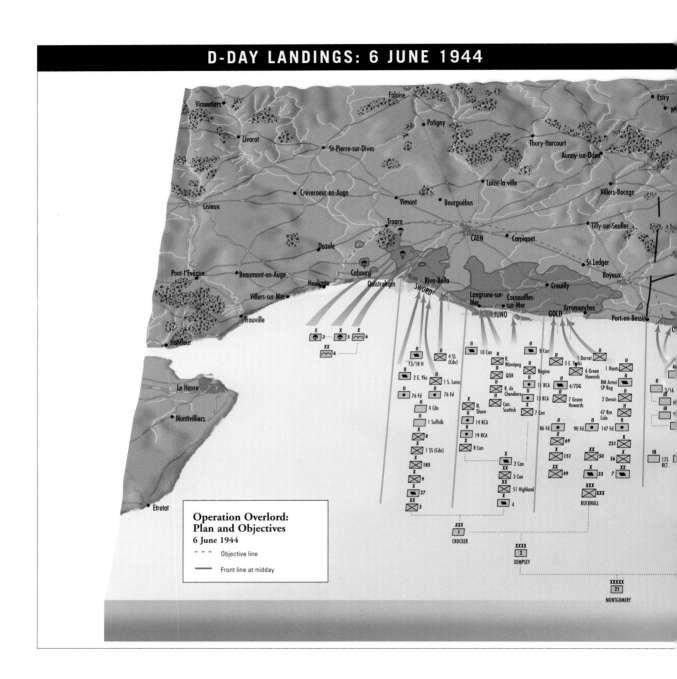

Operation Overlord:
Plan and Objectives
6 June 1944

- - - Objective line

——— Front line at midday

found it slow going to reach the front: the 9th and 10th SS Panzergrenadier divisions took as long to cross France as they did travelling from Russia to the Franco-German border. On the morning of 6 June, German commanders received reports of landings from Calais and Normandy, while RAF bombers dropped dummy paratroopers to further confuse the issue. The real attack, the Germans assumed, would come at Calais, even after they knew that the Allies were ashore in strength. Normandy was only a feint.

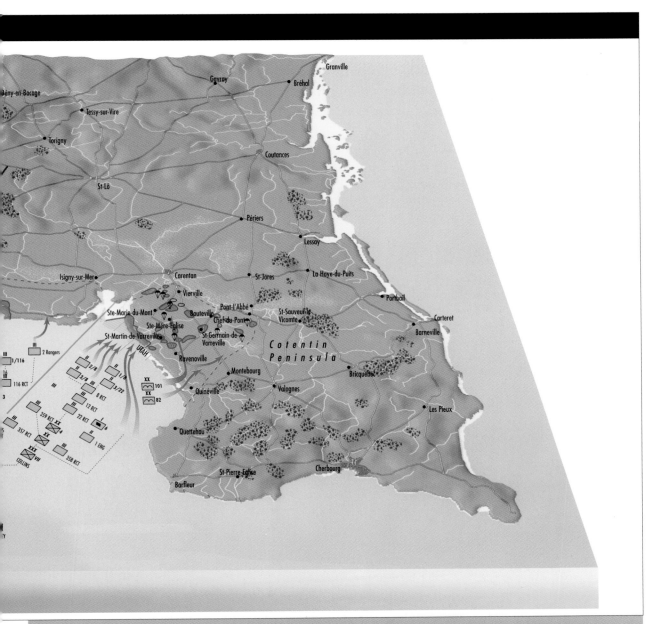

6 June 1944

The Allied landings took place on a 96.5km (60-mile) front, with five divisions assaulting from the sea and three by air. The airborne forces were the first into action. Two US airborne divisions were dropped at the foot of the Cotentin peninsula. At the Eastern end of the landing area, the British 6th Airborne Division was tasked with seizing a bridgehead between the River Orne and the Caen Canal, halfway between Caen and the coast. This would secure the eastern flank of the invasion force. British and Canadian forces landed on the three eastern beaches, codenamed Gold, Juno and Sword. The US Army divisions landed on Utah and Omaha beaches.

Normandy breakout

For the first six weeks of the Allied invasion of Normandy, the German troops defending 'Fortress Europe' had slowed any British and American advances to a crawl. But that was about to change, as the Americans prepared to break out.

As early as 11 June 1944, Montgomery stated that his objective was to draw the greatest possible weight of enemy strength on to the eastern end of the bridgehead, towards Dempsey's forces aimed at Caen. This would weaken the Germans opposing Bradley, thus facilitating a break-out in the west.

Montgomery's assessment was accurate. On 24 July, four days after Operation Cobra was launched, the stalemate was over. Bradley's tanks were in open country. Initially, to their amazement, the Americans met resistance, but it was only a thin grey line. By 28 July, the US VII and VIII Corps had pushed the Germans back over 20km (12 miles). The *Fallschirmjäger* of General Meindl's II Parachute Corps counterattacked the left flank of the salient, but were brushed aside by the Americans. Crossing the river Sienne near Coutances, troops from the two corps linked up to trap German troops at Roncey. By 30 July, the Americans had reached Avranches and were across the Sélun River a day later.

Counterattack

Despite this rupture of their left flank, the German forces in Normandy held on – though in the west Montgomery was hammering away at Caen and had outflanked the bomb-ravaged town.

Von Kluge, who had replaced von Runstedt in command in Normandy, was finally given leave by Hitler to release the armoured divisions from the Pas de Calais area for a counterattack. The Mortain counterattack was launched on 6 August and made some progress against the First Army and those corps of Patton's Third Army not fighting in Brittany. The attacks were finally stopped and broken up by artillery fire and devastating fighter-bomber strikes.

As the Allies ranged into France, they threatened to trap the bulk of the German forces in a huge pocket at Falaise. By 10 August, the US XX Corps had reached

Nantes and, a day later, Angers. Patton's Third Army liberated Le Mans on 8 August and then swung north to Argentan on 13 August. The Canadians drove through to Falaise on 16 August.

Falaise Pocket

US and Anglo-Canadian forces pressed forward from Normandy. The Fifth Panzer Army and the composite force *Panzergruppe Eberbach*, were caught in a trap with a narrow exit to the east.

Some Germans did manage to slip through the Allied lines at night, but up to 50,000 were taken prisoner. Between 5000 and 10,000 died men in the Falaise pocket. In total, the Normandy campaign had cost the Germans 200,000 men (including 91,000 POWs), 1500 tanks, 3500 guns and 20,000 vehicles. With them went any hope of stemming the Allied advance.

Field Marshal Model replaced von Kluge, who had committed suicide. By the time he had gathered up the

14–25 August 1944

Once the American armies had broken out from the western end of the Normandy beachhead, there was little the Germans could do but flee. Divisions had been whittled down to battalion size, with little or no transport or heavy equipment. The troops who broke out from Falaise could do little but retreat to the Seine.

Initially, Paris was to be bypassed, the destruction of the German Army in the field being considered more strategically important. However, for political reasons, it was decided that Leclerc's 2nd French Armoured Division should be released to free the city at the head of General Gerow's V US Corps. Leclerc's tanks entered the city on the afternoon of 24 August, five days after a Free French uprising in the city, and the German garrison surrendered on 25 August.

wreckage, he had only 24 infantry divisions and 11 panzer divisions, all of which had been reduced to a fraction of their authorized strength. The German forces would have had ample time to pull back to the Seine River and to form a strong defensive barrier line there had it not been for Hitler's by now characteristic orders that there should be no withdrawal.

Paris liberated

The Allied armies had reached the Seine 11 days before they had expected to do so, and had freed Paris 55 days ahead of schedule. The American Seventh Army, which landed on the French Riviera on 15 August, had broken German opposition in the South and linked up with Patton's forces by mid-September.

There was some disagreement within the Allied high command. Montgomery wanted to concentrate on a single thrust northeastward through Belgium into the heavily industrialized Ruhr Valley (an area vital to Germany's war effort); the U.S. generals argued for continuing to advance eastward through France on a broad front, in accordance with the pre-invasion plan.

Montgomery's Second Army began its advance on August 29, entered Brussels on September 3, took

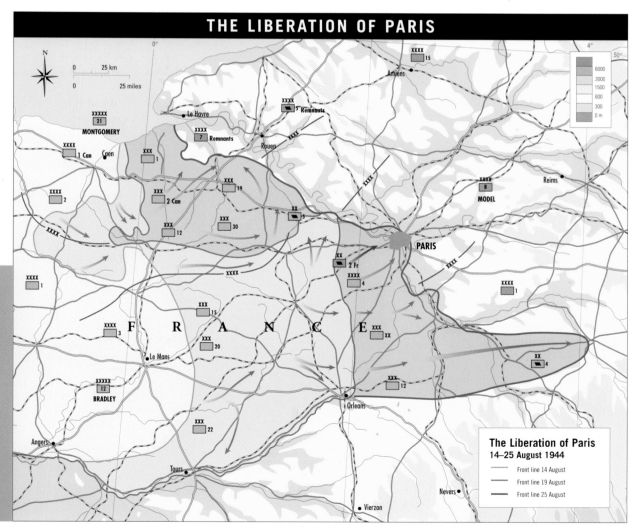

THE LIBERATION OF PARIS

The Liberation of Paris
14–25 August 1944

Front line 14 August
Front line 19 August
Front line 25 August

Antwerp, with its docks intact, on September 4, and went on, three days later, to force its way across the Albert Canal. The US First Army took Namur on the day of the capture of Antwerp and was nearing Aachen.

Far to the south, however, Patton's US Third Army, having raced forward to take Verdun on 31 August, was already beginning to cross the Moselle River near Metz on 5 September. This meant that there was an obvious possibility of achieving a breakthrough into Germany's economically important Saarland and pushing on up the Rhine from the south.

Everywhere, British and American troops were embraced as liberators. Even the most pessimistic allowed themselves to think again of peace.

Retreat in confusion

The German infantrymen, many of them on foot with minimal weaponry, retreated along congested roads,

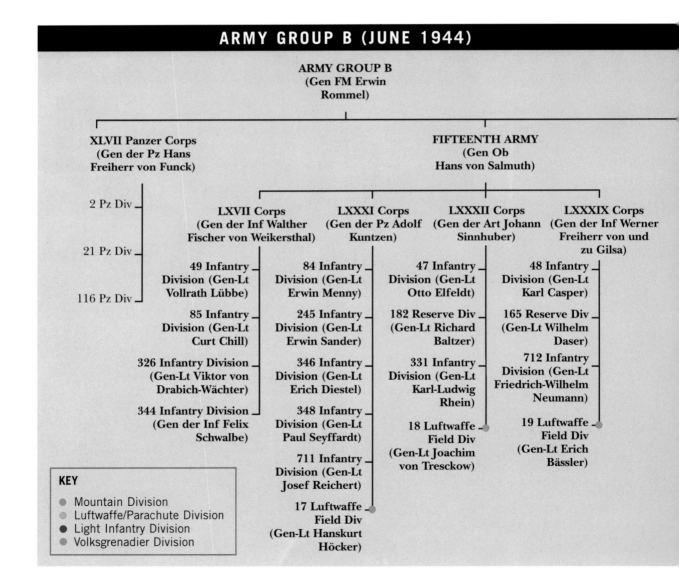

ARMY GROUP B (JUNE 1944)

ARMY GROUP B
(Gen FM Erwin Rommel)

XLVII Panzer Corps
(Gen der Pz Hans Freiherr von Funck)

- 2 Pz Div
- 21 Pz Div
- 116 Pz Div

FIFTEENTH ARMY
(Gen Ob Hans von Salmuth)

LXVII Corps
(Gen der Inf Walther Fischer von Weikersthal)

49 Infantry Division (Gen-Lt Vollrath Lübbe)

85 Infantry Division (Gen-Lt Curt Chill)

326 Infantry Division (Gen-Lt Viktor von Drabich-Wächter)

344 Infantry Division (Gen der Inf Felix Schwalbe)

LXXXI Corps
(Gen der Pz Adolf Kuntzen)

84 Infantry Division (Gen-Lt Erwin Menny)

245 Infantry Division (Gen-Lt Erwin Sander)

346 Infantry Division (Gen-Lt Erich Diestel)

348 Infantry Division (Gen-Lt Paul Seyffardt)

711 Infantry Division (Gen-Lt Josef Reichert)

17 Luftwaffe Field Div (Gen-Lt Hanskurt Höcker)

LXXXII Corps
(Gen der Art Johann Sinnhuber)

47 Infantry Division (Gen-Lt Otto Elfeldt)

182 Reserve Div (Gen-Lt Richard Baltzer)

331 Infantry Division (Gen-Lt Karl-Ludwig Rhein)

18 Luftwaffe Field Div (Gen-Lt Joachim von Tresckow)

LXXXIX Corps
(Gen der Inf Werner Freiherr von und zu Gilsa)

48 Infantry Division (Gen-Lt Karl Casper)

165 Reserve Div (Gen-Lt Wilhelm Daser)

712 Infantry Division (Gen-Lt Friedrich-Wilhelm Neumann)

19 Luftwaffe Field Div (Gen-Lt Erich Bässler)

KEY
- Mountain Division
- Luftwaffe/Parachute Division
- Light Infantry Division
- Volksgrenadier Division

which were continually strafed. Directives to build defensive lines were immediately overtaken by the Allied advance. But gradually, the headlong retreat slowed and order began to emerge from the chaos.

The pace of the Allied advance had by now passed its peak. Tenacious resistance by German garrisons in French ports was restricting Allied supplies. The armies of liberation were short of frontline infantry replacements. Men were exhausted, vehicles in

desperate need of overhaul. The advance slowed – and then stopped.

The Germans had lost nearly 300,000 men during the retreat – either killed, wounded, missing, or taken prisoner – but an Allied victory was not necessarily assured. By the beginning of September, German forces had turned round and were once more standing firm, this time along the 650km (404 miles) between Switzerland and the North Sea.

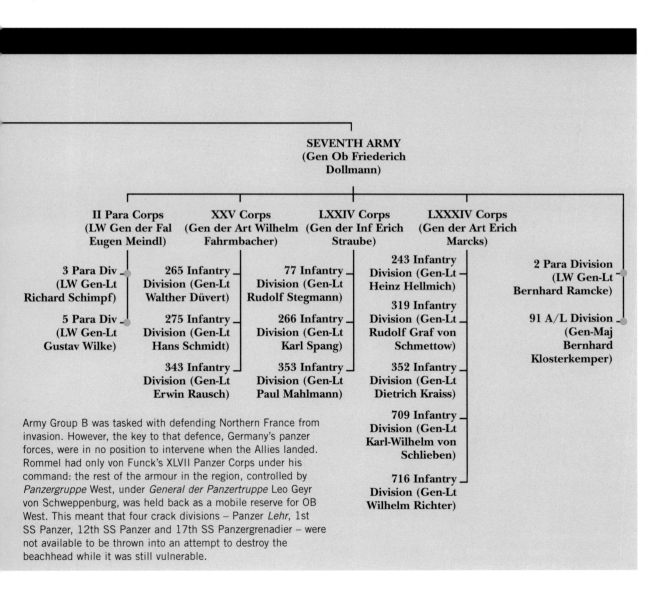

SEVENTH ARMY
(Gen Ob Friederich Dollmann)

II Para Corps (LW Gen der Fal Eugen Meindl)	XXV Corps (Gen der Art Wilhelm Fahrmbacher)	LXXIV Corps (Gen der Inf Erich Straube)	LXXXIV Corps (Gen der Art Erich Marcks)	
3 Para Div (LW Gen-Lt Richard Schimpf)	265 Infantry Division (Gen-Lt Walther Düvert)	77 Infantry Division (Gen-Lt Rudolf Stegmann)	243 Infantry Division (Gen-Lt Heinz Hellmich)	2 Para Division (LW Gen-Lt Bernhard Ramcke)
5 Para Div (LW Gen-Lt Gustav Wilke)	275 Infantry Division (Gen-Lt Hans Schmidt)	266 Infantry Division (Gen-Lt Karl Spang)	319 Infantry Division (Gen-Lt Rudolf Graf von Schmettow)	91 A/L Division (Gen-Maj Bernhard Klosterkemper)
	343 Infantry Division (Gen-Lt Erwin Rausch)	353 Infantry Division (Gen-Lt Paul Mahlmann)	352 Infantry Division (Gen-Lt Dietrich Kraiss)	
			709 Infantry Division (Gen-Lt Karl-Wilhelm von Schlieben)	
			716 Infantry Division (Gen-Lt Wilhelm Richter)	

Army Group B was tasked with defending Northern France from invasion. However, the key to that defence, Germany's panzer forces, were in no position to intervene when the Allies landed. Rommel had only von Funck's XLVII Panzer Corps under his command: the rest of the armour in the region, controlled by *Panzergruppe* West, under *General der Panzertruppe* Leo Geyr von Schweppenburg, was held back as a mobile reserve for OB West. This meant that four crack divisions – Panzer *Lehr*, 1st SS Panzer, 12th SS Panzer and 17th SS Panzergrenadier – were not available to be thrown into an attempt to destroy the beachhead while it was still vulnerable.

Army Group G

Three days after the Anglo-American landings in North Africa, 8 November 1942, the Germans and Italians occupied Vichy France. By 1944, the occupation troops were preparing for an Allied invasion.

Operation Dragoon – the Allied invasion of southern France – occurred on 15 August 1944. The invasion took place between Toulon and Cannes. The assault troops were formed of three American divisions of the VI Corps, reinforced with a French armoured division.

Army Group G

Opposing them was the German Army Group G. This was originally formed early in 1944, and controlled the German First and Nineteenth Armies. The latter was tasked with defending the South of France and was commanded by *General der Infanterie* Friedrich Wiese. Its main formations were the 148 and 242 Infantry divisions. The IV *Luftwaffe* Field Corps, commanded by *General der Flieger* Erich Petersen, had been based around Montpelier early in the year, but by the time of the invasion it had been transferred to the northern area of the Corps' responsibility, in Alsace.

Headquartered at Marseilles, the divisions were spread out over a wide front, and so could not concentrate to meet the Allied landings. Nor could the German First Army, with four infantry divisions and the 11th Panzer Division, be called to fight; it had been diverted to fight the Allied forces in Northern France after Operation Overlord. As a result, more than 94,000 Allied troops and 11,000 vehicles were able to land on the first day.

A major attack by French resistance fighters, coordinated by Captain Aaron Bank of the OSS, also helped to drive the remaining German forces back from the beachhead in advance of the landing. As a result, the Allied troops encountered little resistance as they moved inland.

German forces broken

The American advance stretched out the deployment of the 148th and 242th German infantry divisions,

resulting in their rupture near Draguignan. The German commander, *General der Infanterie* Ferdinand Neuling of the LXII Corps, hastily deployed his reserves, but was unable to avoid exploitation by the Americans, who now manoeuvred in two directions. While the 45th Division oriented itself to the confluence of the Durance and Verdon rivers, a motorized and armoured group under General Butler forced its way north.

On the coast to the east of the bridgehead, which up to that point had remained quiet, the 36th Division steadily drove back the German defences towards Cannes and Grasse, which forced *Generalfeldmarschall* Albert Kesselring in Italy to shift some troops to protect his flank in the Alps.

On the western flank, the French were nearest to the Americans at the Blue Line, positioned to relieve them and then to attack Toulon. The exploitation to the north had already commenced with violent fighting near Brignolles. The tanks of General Sudre thrust from this position to the west.

Nineteenth Army retreats

The rapid retreat of the German Nineteenth Army resulted in swift gains for the Allied forces. The plans had envisaged greater resistance near the landing areas and under-estimated transport needs. The consequent need for vehicle fuel outstripped supply and this shortage proved to be a greater impediment to the advance than German resistance. As a result, several German formations escaped north up the Rhône valley into the Vosges and Germany.

The Allied forces pursued the retreating Germans up the east bank of the Rhône River, but the push lacked strength. The French I Corps secured the Lomont hills, a range running for 130km (80 miles) from the Doubs River to the Swiss border. German resistance at the end of August and early September was minimal, but as the

German high command regained control of its forces, the Army set up an effective defensive line in front of the Belfort Gap, a corridor of relatively flat terrain that lies between the Vosges Mountains and the Swiss frontier and which is a gateway to the upper reaches of the Rhine.

Holding the Belfort Gap

The same logistics problems that dogged other Allied units in Europe meant that the advance of the troops moving up from the south of France was slowed in front of the Belfort Gap by the German 11 Panzer Division, which had been transferred from First Army to Nineteenth Army. However, the Germans reduced their forces in the gap, and a November offensive by the French First Army and the US Seventh Army collapsed the German presence in Alsace to a roughly circular pocket around the town of Colmar on the Alsatian Plain.

August 1944

Many of the German divisions in the south of France were static units. The 242nd Infantry Division, for example, lacked a reconnaissance unit, but its equipment allocation was near complete, and its troops were reasonably well trained. It was reinforced with two Armenian battalions and one Azerbaijani unit. Although OB West ordered all units of Army Group G to remain in place and defend the coast at any price, they were alarmed at the prospect of fighting against the expected formidable invasion force.

Operation Dragoon was launched on 15 August 1944. The landing took place between Toulon and Cannes, with the initial assault force consisting of three American divisions and one Free French armoured division. American, British and French commando and airborne formations participated in the assault. The invasion forced was supported by French, British and American battleships, seven Allied escort carriers, and more than 50 cruisers and destroyers.

OPERATION DRAGOON: INVASION OF SOUTHERN FRANCE

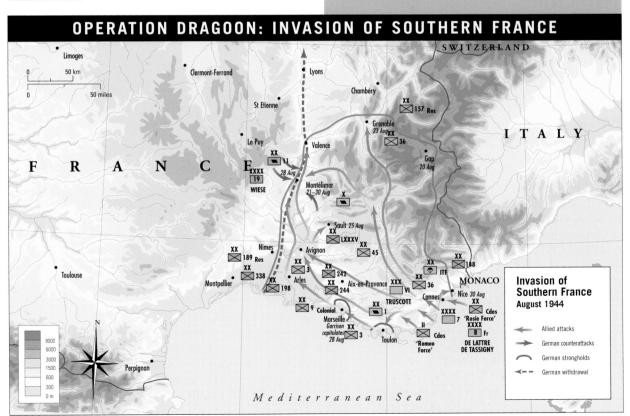

Northwest Europe: 1944

The Allied advance into occupied Europe had begun to run out of fuel and supplies by September 1944, and German resistance was stiffening. The German ability to form *ad hoc* battle groups came as a severe shock to the Allies, nowhere more than at Arnhem.

To retain the initiative, the British commander, Field Marshal Sir Bernard Montgomery, planned to break open the German defences in the north before they had the chance to solidify.

The strategy of Operation Market Garden was simple. Three-and-a-half airborne divisions would land along a 100km (60 mile) corridor and the ground forces would charge along it to link up with them within three days. If all went to plan, British tanks could be through Holland and into Germany's industrial heartland before winter. Given the collapse of German forces on the eastern front, the operation held out the prospect of an end to the war in 1944.

Rhine defences

German defence rested on a succession of rivers running parallel to the frontline. The first obstacles faced by the Allies were the Meuse-Escaut and Zuid-Willems canals. Some 25km (15 miles) northeast lay the river Maas, with a bridge at Grave.

Some 15km (9 miles) northeast of Grave, there was a major bridge over the river Waal at Nijmegen. A further 15km (9 miles) north of Nijmegen was the biggest obstacle of all: the lower Rhine. There was a modern road bridge at Arnhem plus a railway bridge and a ferry crossing just upstream.

Misjudged opposition

The British were confident of success. Military intelligence convinced them that the opposition to their elite paratroop formations would come only from second-rate German units consisting of old men, teenage conscripts and Dutch SS-men who could not wait to change sides. Unfortunately, these had received timely reinforcements.

The 9th and 10th SS Panzer Divisions were being sent to the Arnhem area to refit and re-organize. Curiously,

British intelligence lost track of both divisions, and their presence so near to the airborne landing zones upset the Allied plan from the very beginning.

On Sunday 17 September, the peoples of Britain and Holland looked skyward to an airborne armada heading south. A total of 1545 transports and 478 gliders were in the air, escorted by 1131 fighters: the formation was 16km (10 miles) across and 150km (93 miles) deep. Fewer than 50 *Luftwaffe* interceptors were available to attack, and they made little impression. Flak caught some as they neared the landing zones, but within 80 minutes there were 20,000 paratroopers on the ground.

Landings begin

Field Marshall Model himself fled his headquarters at Oosterbeek as British paratroops landed on top of his headquarters. At the same time, the British XXX Corps attacked along the road to Eindhoven. The advance of the tanks was preceded by a rolling artillery barrage that knocked out many of the German anti-tank guns that lay in wait in nearby woods.

The US 101st Airborne division captured the bridge over the canal at Veghel. The US 82nd Airborne took the bridge at Grave. But the bridge at Nijmegen was held by the SS. Although 2 Para, commanded by 34-year-old Major John Frost, seized one end of the bridge at Arnhem, his battalion was then isolated.

General Bittrich's SS corps may have been in urgent need of rest and replenishment, but it reacted with blistering speed. The Allies could not have known that their entire battle plan had been captured by the Germans. The Germans knew every detail of Operation Market Garden before it happened.

By the afternoon of 18 September, tanks from the British Guards Division had linked up with the Americans at Eindhoven. A day later, the ground troops were in Nijmegen: an advance of 80km (50 miles) in 48 hours. Nijmegen was finally taken by a desperate effort. On the afternoon of the 20th, American infantry began to cross the Waal downstream where the German defenders were thinly stretched.

'Hell's Highway'

But XXX Corps was far behind schedule. The British in Arnhem had been expected to hold the bridge for just two days. So far, they had resisted for four. The route to them, the road from Eindhoven to Arnhem, was christened 'Hell's Highway' by the Americans, who had to hold it against repeated German counterattacks.

The road was elevated on a bank for much of the way, and armour moving along it was an irresistible target for German gunners. There was no way around knocked-out vehicles; the surrounding terrain was waterlogged and could not support armoured vehicles.

2 Para's last stand ended in surrender on 21 September. A final effort to save the British position in Arnhem came on the same day. The British landed the Polish Parachute Brigade south of the Rhine, the other side of the river from the 1st Airborne Division.

The next day, two *Kampfgruppen* counterattacked at Veghel. The advancing XXX Corps was compelled to pull back one of its armoured brigades to keep the road open.

On 25 September, the British survivors were withdrawn over the Rhine. It was a difficult and dangerous operation. The British Paras had to extricate themselves from a small perimeter that was surrounded by a vigilant enemy who threatened to overrun the positions at any time. Just over 2000 men finally escaped. Following the surrender, the Germans captured 6000 men from the 1st Airborne Division.

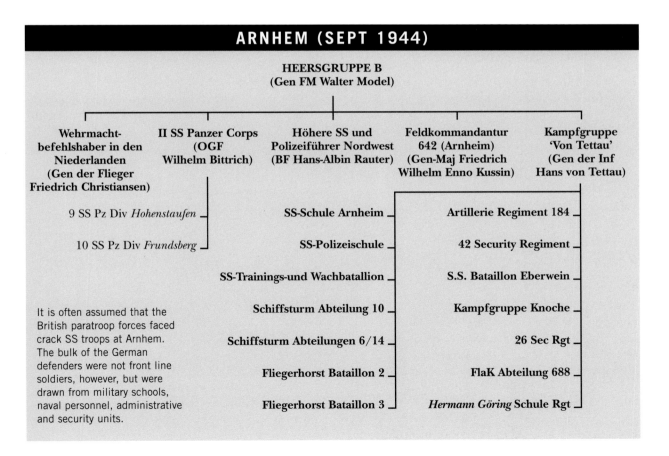

ARNHEM (SEPT 1944)

HEERSGRUPPE B
(Gen FM Walter Model)

Wehrmacht-befehlshaber in den Niederlanden (Gen der Flieger Friedrich Christiansen)	II SS Panzer Corps (OGF Wilhelm Bittrich)	Höhere SS und Polizeiführer Nordwest (BF Hans-Albin Rauter)	Feldkommandantur 642 (Arnheim) (Gen-Maj Friedrich Wilhelm Enno Kussin)	Kampfgruppe 'Von Tettau' (Gen der Inf Hans von Tettau)
9 SS Pz Div *Hohenstaufen*		SS-Schule Arnheim	Artillerie Regiment 184	
10 SS Pz Div *Frundsberg*		SS-Polizeischule	42 Security Regiment	
		SS-Trainings-und Wachbatallion	S.S. Bataillon Eberwein	
		Schiffsturm Abteilung 10	Kampfgruppe Knoche	
		Schiffsturm Abteilungen 6/14	26 Sec Rgt	
		Fliegerhorst Bataillon 2	FlaK Abteilung 688	
		Fliegerhorst Bataillon 3	*Hermann Göring* Schule Rgt	

It is often assumed that the British paratroop forces faced crack SS troops at Arnhem. The bulk of the German defenders were not front line soldiers, however, but were drawn from military schools, naval personnel, administrative and security units.

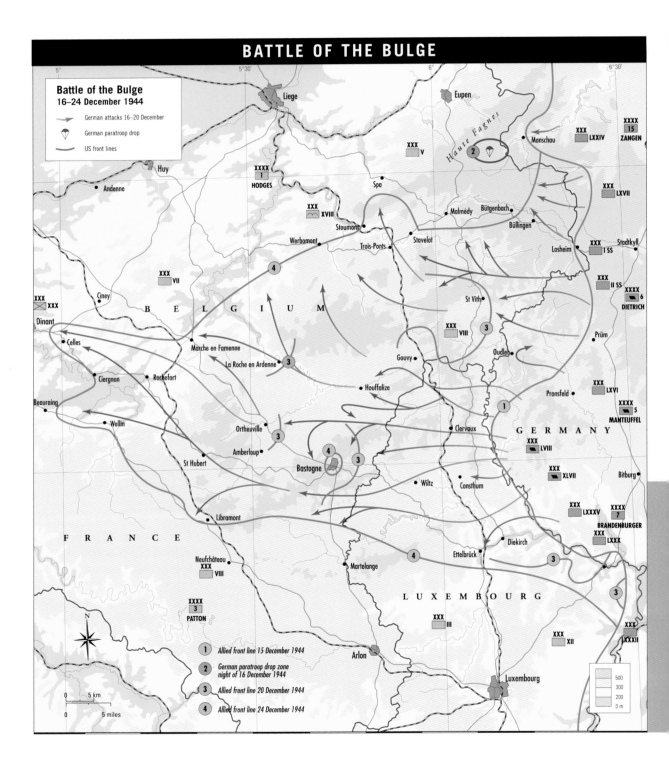

BATTLE OF THE BULGE

Battle of the Bulge
16–24 December 1944

→ German attacks 16–20 December

🪂 German paratroop drop

⌣ US front lines

Liege
Eupen
Huy
Andenne
Monschau
XXX LXXIV
XXXX 15 ZANGEN
XXX V
Haute Fagnes
②
XXXX 1 HODGES
Spa
XXX LXVII
XXX XVIII
Malmédy · Bütgenbach
Stoumont
Büllingen
Werbomont
Trois-Ponts · Stavelot
XXX I SS · Stadtkyll
XXX VII
Ciney
B E L G I U M
St Vith
XXX II SS
XXXX 6 DIETRICH
XXX XXX
Dinant
Marche en Famenne
XXX VIII
③
Prüm
Celles
La Roche en Ardenne
③
Gouvy
Oudleb
Ciergnon · Rochefort
Houffalize
XXX LXVI
Beauraing
Pronsfeld
XXXX 5 MANTEUFFEL
Wellin
Ortheuville
③
Clervaux
G E R M A N Y
Amberloup
④
③
XXX LVIII
St Hubert
Bastogne
Wiltz · Consthum
XXX XLVII · Bitburg
Libramont
XXX LXXXV
XXXX 7 BRANDENBURGER
F R A N C E
Diekirch
XXX LXXX
Neufchâteau
④ Ettelbrück
③
XXX VIII
Martelange
L U X E M B O U R G
XXX XII
XXXX 3 PATTON
N
XXX III
XXX LXXXII
① Allied front line 15 December 1944
② German paratroop drop zone night of 16 December 1944
③ Allied front line 20 December 1944
④ Allied front line 24 December 1944
Arlon
Luxembourg

0 ___ 5 km
0 ___ 5 miles

500
300
200
0 m

The Ardennes Offensive

At 5.30 a.m. on the misty morning of 16 December 1944, in the snow-covered hills of the Belgian Ardennes, 200,000 men of German Army Group B launched an attack against the VIII Corps of the US First Army.

From north to south, the German armies committed to the offensive were the Sixth SS Panzer Army under *Generaloberst der Waffen-SS* Josef 'Sepp' Dietrich, the Fifth Panzer Army under the energetic General Hasso-Eccard von Manteuffel and the Seventh Army under General Erich Brandenburger. The three armies were designated as Army Group 'B' under the overall command of the hard-driving Field Marshal Walther Model.

Early success

Bad weather had grounded the Allied air forces, and the German assault initially enjoyed considerable success against the six US divisions in the area. Three of these were new to Europe, and three were resting in what was regarded as a quiet area that had therefore been nicknamed the 'Ghost Front'. Under the shock of the attack, some 9000 men from the 106th Division were captured on the Schnee Eifel on 19 December.

Considerable gains were made following attacks by elements of the Fifth Panzer Army. This formation had only two panzer divisions, and included a high proportion of poor-quality Volksgrenadier divisions. The timetable of the Fifth Panzer Army was delayed by the determined defence at St Vith, where the 7th Armoured Division, a combat command of the 9th Armoured and a surviving regiment of the 106th Division formed a horseshoe-shaped defence around the town. The town should have fallen by the second day, according to German plans. General von Manteuffel finally seized it on December 21.

The thrust by the 2nd Panzer and Panzer *Lehr* divisions took them to a point less than 10km (6 miles) from the Meuse at Dinant. Here, on 24 and 25 December, they encountered the British 29th Armoured Brigade, part of the British XXX Corps that had been moved south to provide defence in depth.

German fuel reserves at the beginning of the campaign were critically low. Continued success of the operation was dependent upon the capture of enemy fuel dumps. Although it was a close-run thing, Sixth SS *Panzerarmee* failed to capture the huge fuel depot at Stavelot, and two further stockpiles were denied the Germans by furious local defence.

Decisive air power

On 23 December, the weather cleared and the Allied air forces came out in strength. Fighter bombers attacked German vehicles and artillery positions, while medium bombers hit the crowded road and rail network in Germany. The good visibility also allowed supplies to be air-dropped by C-47s to the 101st Airborne Division in Bastogne.

By Christmas Eve, the OKW realized that *Wacht am Rhein* had run its course. It would not be until 8 January that Hitler finally authorized a withdrawal. The offensive delayed the end of the war by about six weeks and destroyed the bulk of the German armoured reserve.

16–24 December 1944

On 16 December 1944 the Germans launched a massive armoured offensive through the Ardennes, later to be known as the Battle of the Bulge. Hitler's plan was to use two panzer armies to drive for Antwerp, splitting in half the Allied armies threatening the Reich. Four thinly stretched American divisions were battered by the 16 divisions of the Fifth Panzer Army and the Sixth SS Panzer Army.

However, news that SS men had massacred prisoners of war stiffened American resistance, and German progress slowed. By 20 December, German forces had carved out a wide, bulge-shaped bridgehead but were still 32km (20 miles) short of the Meuse River. Over the Christmas period, the skies cleared, and Allied air forces were free to harrass the panzer forces. Within weeks, the Allies had fought the Germans to a standstill.

ARDENNES OFFENSIVE (DECEMBER 1944)

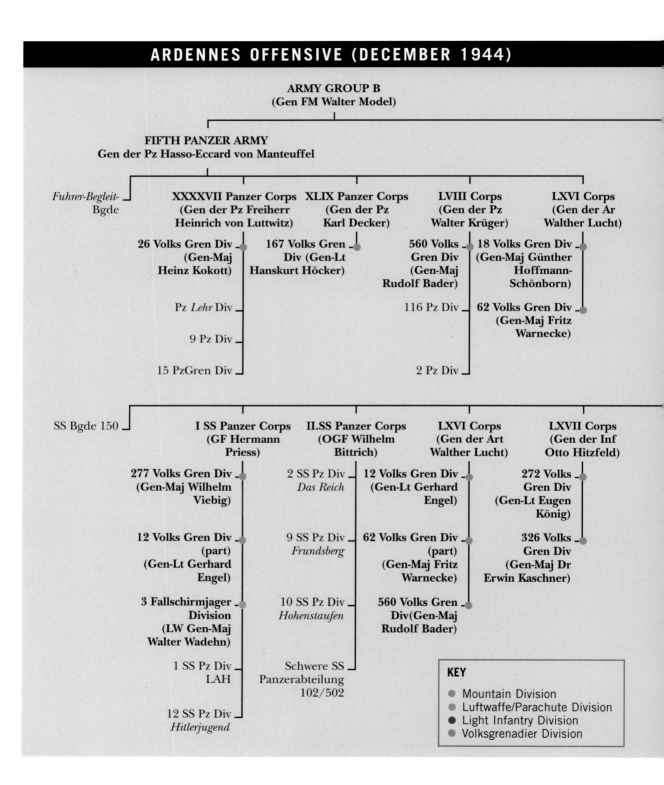

ARMY GROUP B
(Gen FM Walter Model)

FIFTH PANZER ARMY
Gen der Pz Hasso-Eccard von Manteuffel

Fuhrer-Begleit- Bgde

XXXXVII Panzer Corps (Gen der Pz Freiherr Heinrich von Luttwitz)	**XLIX Panzer Corps** (Gen der Pz Karl Decker)	**LVIII Corps** (Gen der Pz Walter Krüger)	**LXVI Corps** (Gen der Ar Walther Lucht)
26 Volks Gren Div (Gen-Maj Heinz Kokott)	167 Volks Gren Div (Gen-Lt Hanskurt Höcker)	560 Volks Gren Div (Gen-Maj Rudolf Bader)	18 Volks Gren Div (Gen-Maj Günther Hoffmann-Schönborn)
Pz *Lehr* Div		116 Pz Div	62 Volks Gren Div (Gen-Maj Fritz Warnecke)
9 Pz Div			
15 PzGren Div		2 Pz Div	

SS Bgde 150

I SS Panzer Corps (GF Hermann Priess)	**II.SS Panzer Corps** (OGF Wilhelm Bittrich)	**LXVI Corps** (Gen der Art Walther Lucht)	**LXVII Corps** (Gen der Inf Otto Hitzfeld)
277 Volks Gren Div (Gen-Maj Wilhelm Viebig)	2 SS Pz Div *Das Reich*	12 Volks Gren Div (Gen-Lt Gerhard Engel)	272 Volks Gren Div (Gen-Lt Eugen König)
12 Volks Gren Div (part) (Gen-Lt Gerhard Engel)	9 SS Pz Div *Frundsberg*	62 Volks Gren Div (part) (Gen-Maj Fritz Warnecke)	326 Volks Gren Div (Gen-Maj Dr Erwin Kaschner)
3 Fallschirmjager Division (LW Gen-Maj Walter Wadehn)	10 SS Pz Div *Hohenstaufen*	560 Volks Gren Div (Gen-Maj Rudolf Bader)	
1 SS Pz Div LAH	Schwere SS Panzerabteilung 102/502		
12 SS Pz Div *Hitlerjugend*			

KEY
- Mountain Division
- Luftwaffe/Parachute Division
- Light Infantry Division
- Volksgrenadier Division

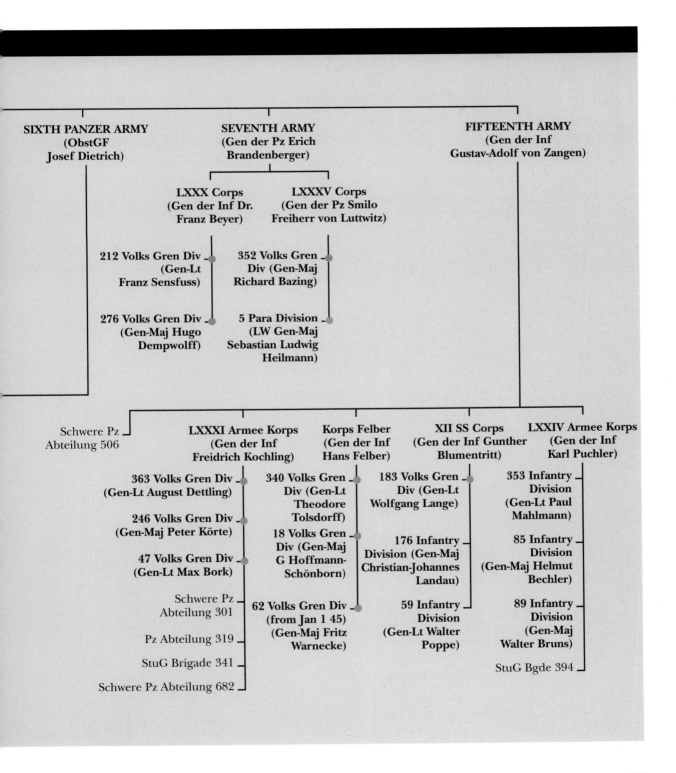

SIXTH PANZER ARMY
(ObstGF
Josef Dietrich)

SEVENTH ARMY
(Gen der Pz Erich
Brandenberger)

FIFTEENTH ARMY
(Gen der Inf
Gustav-Adolf von Zangen)

LXXX Corps
(Gen der Inf Dr.
Franz Beyer)

LXXXV Corps
(Gen der Pz Smilo
Freiherr von Luttwitz)

212 Volks Gren Div
(Gen-Lt
Franz Sensfuss)

352 Volks Gren
Div (Gen-Maj
Richard Bazing)

276 Volks Gren Div
(Gen-Maj Hugo
Dempwolff)

5 Para Division
(LW Gen-Maj
Sebastian Ludwig
Heilmann)

Schwere Pz
Abteilung 506

LXXXI Armee Korps
(Gen der Inf
Friedrich Kochling)

Korps Felber
(Gen der Inf
Hans Felber)

XII SS Corps
(Gen der Inf Gunther
Blumentritt)

LXXIV Armee Korps
(Gen der Inf
Karl Puchler)

363 Volks Gren Div
(Gen-Lt August Dettling)

340 Volks Gren
Div (Gen-Lt
Theodore
Tolsdorff)

183 Volks Gren
Div (Gen-Lt
Wolfgang Lange)

353 Infantry
Division
(Gen-Lt Paul
Mahlmann)

246 Volks Gren Div
(Gen-Maj Peter Körte)

18 Volks Gren
Div (Gen-Maj
G Hoffmann-
Schönborn)

176 Infantry
Division (Gen-Maj
Christian-Johannes
Landau)

85 Infantry
Division
(Gen-Maj Helmut
Bechler)

47 Volks Gren Div
(Gen-Lt Max Bork)

Schwere Pz
Abteilung 301

62 Volks Gren Div
(from Jan 1 45)
(Gen-Maj Fritz
Warnecke)

59 Infantry
Division
(Gen-Lt Walter
Poppe)

89 Infantry
Division
(Gen-Maj
Walter Bruns)

Pz Abteilung 319

StuG Brigade 341

StuG Bgde 394

Schwere Pz Abteilung 682

Defence of the Reich: 1945

By the end of 1944, Germany was doomed. Allied forces were driving into the German heartland from the east, the west and the south, and it would be only a matter of time before the 'Thousand Year Reich' collapsed. But the German Army kept on fighting.

Although few of the *Luftwaffe's fallschirmjäger* divisions were para qualified, they played a major part in the defence of the Reich.

In January 1945, Germany was poised to reap the whirlwind, as Allied forces to both the west and east prepared to tear into the heartland of the *Reich*. The German army was on the defensive, having lost the Battle of the Bulge, and Allied armies stood on the borders of Germany itself.

They had yet to penetrate the home territory of the Reich, but senior commanders, notably Heinz Guderian, knew that this was the calm before the storm. He knew that when the Allies decided to attack, there would be no way that Germany could be saved.

Germany still fighting

The Allies were still extremely wary of the Nazis. In the Ardennes, the massive German attack had recently succeeded in wiping out one-tenth of all American and British armour. The American newsreels were warning their forces in propaganda films that the Nazi beast had not yet been destroyed.

To the east, the Soviets were struggling to wrest control of Budapest in one of the most bitter of all the struggles of World War II. A huge push by an SS panzer army was attempting to break the siege of Hungary's capital. Further north, the Red Army's offensive of the previous year had been halted on the east bank of the Vistula, before Warsaw.

Hitler's last mistake

Incredibly, Hitler weakened the defences on the Warsaw–Berlin axis in order to reinforce German forces in Hungary. General Guderian told Hitler that the Red Army massing against Germany's eastern defences enjoyed overwhelming materiel superiority – of 20:1 in artillery; 11:1 in infantry; and 7:1 in armour.

Hitler refused to listen and told Guderian to sack his intelligence chief – to which Guderian retorted that he might as well fire his chief-of-staff too.

On the very day predicted by Guderian, the Russian offensive was launched. Marshal Konev's First Ukrainian Front broke out of the Sandomierz bridgehead to tear a 35km (22 mile) hole in the German defences in southern Poland; at the same time, the Third Ukrainian Front attacked East Prussia.

Two days later, Zhukov's First Byelorussian Front attacked from its bridgeheads over the Vistula and surrounded Warsaw. On 17 January 1945, the city – razed to the ground after the abortive rising the previous autumn – was taken by the First Polish army.

Krakow was liberated the next day. German units assembling for a counterattack at Lodz were caught deploying, and swept back to the river Oder.

East Prussia was cut off. The Third Panzer Army fell back into Königsberg and the Samland peninsula. The beleaguered Germans were joined by the former garrison of Memel, evacuated on 29 January under the protective fire of the surviving units of the German Navy, including the heavy cruiser *Prinz Eugen*.

Desperate defences

From the Baltic to southern Poland, improvised *Kampfgruppen* fought desperately, firstly to win time for German forces to make good their escape, and then to break free themselves. Although unit cohesion had been lost, the German soldiers, fighting as small groups, took

DIVISIONAL STRENGTH BY THEATRE: 1945					
	Jan	Feb	March	April	May
Germany	3	3	3	0	0
East	146	173	173	163	78
West	79	68	72	67	4
Norway	15	13	13	11	0
Italy	28	27	26	23	2
Southeast	15	13	13	12	11

DIVISIONAL STRENGTH BY TYPE: 1945					
	Jan	Feb	March	April	May
Panzer	35	38	38	35	21
PzGrenadier	18	20	20	20	7
Cavalry	4	5	5	5	4
Infantry	197	201	203	183	48
Mountain	14	14	13	13	8
Security	5	4	4	4	0
Luftwaffe	4	4	4	4	1
Parachute	8	9	10	8	3

a huge toll on the advancing Soviet forces. The Germans fought as all soldiers do, for their unit rather than any notion of National Socialism.

The gunners counted for wave after wave of Soviet armour. Counterattack followed attack; the *Ostheer* was going to go down fighting. But the Red Army advance was remorseless, progressing 400km (249 miles) in a fortnight to seize footholds on the west bank of the Oder. From there to Berlin was but an hour's drive on the autobahn.

Hitler made his final broadcast to the German people on 30 January 1945, the 12th anniversary of his appointment as Chancellor of Germany. He exhorted his people to fight on.

Into the heart of Germany

The hot rake of war swept from the ancient Prussian heartland of East Prussia to Berlin itself. The Red Army smashed its way to the Nazi capital in what its historians termed the Vistula-Oder operation – an object lesson in *blitzkrieg* that became a model for future Soviet war plans. Like the original German *blitzkrieg* into Russia in 1941, military expertise was combined with biblical savagery.

Western Front: 1945

While the bulk of the German Army was fighting for its existence on the Eastern Front, German troops in the west were offering patchy but occasionally very stiff resistance to the advancing British, American, Canadian and French armies.

In March, the Anglo-Americans prepared themselves for the final assault on Germany. Eight armies were aligned along the west bank of the Rhine. On 23 March, the British Second and American Ninth Armies operations – codenamed, respectively, Plunder and Grenade – were launched.

Allies across the Rhine

These were spectacular affairs involving large numbers of amphibious craft, massive air and artillery preparations and the dropping of two airborne divisions behind the German defences on the east bank of the river. They were lightly opposed.

Once through the initial lines of German defence, the Allied armour was free to sweep across the North German Plain. The Allied army now contained 85 divisions and numbered four million men, while the real strength of the German Army in the west was only 26 divisions. The evolution of Eisenhower's plan in the west had already been changed by the fortuitous capture of the bridge at Remagen on 7 March. A catalogue of human error had led to its seizure. Hitler was furious

and several unfortunate officers were summarily shot *pour encourager les autres*. The position could not be immediately exploited, but on 22 March, Patton's Third Army established another bridgehead after a surprise assault at Oppenheim.

Stand fast order

The German defences of the Rhine were therefore compromised at two widely separated places, in the Ruhr and at its confluence with the river Rhine at Mainz. This meant that the whole *Wehrmacht* position in the west was now threatened with envelopment on a large scale. This design was assisted by Hitler who issued another of his disastrous stand-fast orders, when German forces would have been better served by a withdrawal from the Ruhr.

Ruhr Pocket

The British and Canadian armies advanced into northern Germany, aiming for Hamburg. Meanwhile, by 4 April, the US Ninth and First Armies had surrounded the Ruhr, Germany's industrial heartland. This huge

8 February – 21 March 1945

In February 1945, the task for the Allied armies was to cross the Rivers Rör, Our and Saar and to reach the Rhine. By 21 February, Goch, Cleve and Calcar were in British and Canadian hands, and the Americans took Mönchen Gladbach on 1 March and Cologne five days later. On 7 March, the Ludendorff Bridge at Remagen was taken intact by the US First Army. On 23 March, Montgomery's Twenty-First Army Group stormed the Rhine at Wesel, preceded by two divisions of paratroopers. By nightfall, the ground troops had joined up with the paratroopers, and the Rhine bridgeheads were secure. Further south, the Americans launched their own crossings, mostly mounted by fewer men with limited resources. Patton, eager to beat Montgomery across the river, had sent an assault regiment of the US 5th Division, part of his Third Army, to cross the Rhine, in rubber boats, between Nierstein and Oppenheim. Securing the far bank, they were joined by the rest of the Division. By the end of March, Darmstadt and Wiesbaden were in American hands, and US armoured columns were driving for Frankfurt-am-Main. Further south, the French had pushed an Algerian division across the river at Gemersheim. Most German troops knew that the war was lost and were ready to surrender, though a few young volunteers along with diehard SS men continued to fight to the last.

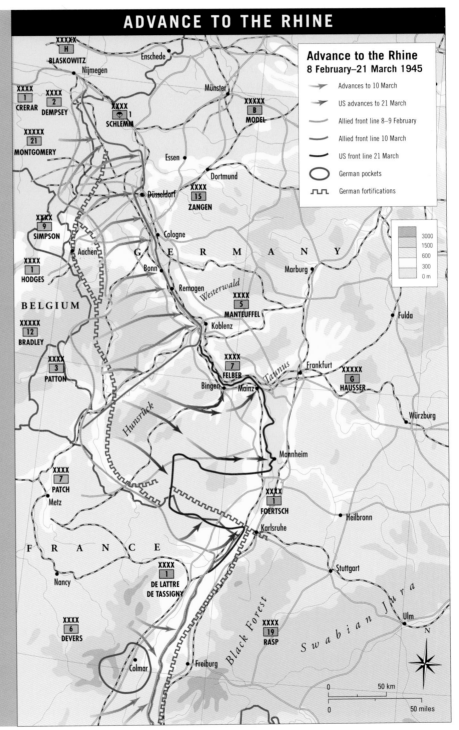

ADVANCE TO THE RHINE

Advance to the Rhine
8 February–21 March 1945

→ Advances to 10 March
→ US advances to 21 March
⌐ Allied front line 8–9 February
⌐ Allied front line 10 March
⌐ US front line 21 March
◯ German pockets
⊓⊔ German fortifications

3000
1500
600
300
0 m

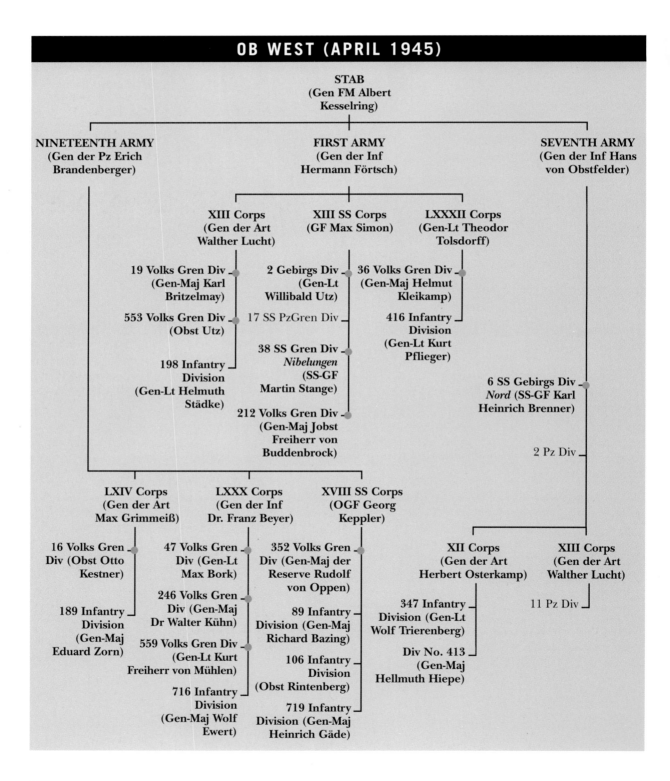

OB WEST (APRIL 1945)

STAB
(Gen FM Albert Kesselring)

NINETEENTH ARMY
(Gen der Pz Erich Brandenberger)

FIRST ARMY
(Gen der Inf Hermann Förtsch)

SEVENTH ARMY
(Gen der Inf Hans von Obstfelder)

XIII Corps
(Gen der Art Walther Lucht)

XIII SS Corps
(GF Max Simon)

LXXXII Corps
(Gen-Lt Theodor Tolsdorff)

19 Volks Gren Div (Gen-Maj Karl Britzelmay)

553 Volks Gren Div (Obst Utz)

198 Infantry Division (Gen-Lt Helmuth Städke)

2 Gebirgs Div (Gen-Lt Willibald Utz)

17 SS PzGren Div

38 SS Gren Div *Nibelungen* (SS-GF Martin Stange)

212 Volks Gren Div (Gen-Maj Jobst Freiherr von Buddenbrock)

36 Volks Gren Div (Gen-Maj Helmut Kleikamp)

416 Infantry Division (Gen-Lt Kurt Pflieger)

6 SS Gebirgs Div *Nord* (SS-GF Karl Heinrich Brenner)

2 Pz Div

LXIV Corps
(Gen der Art Max Grimmeiß)

LXXX Corps
(Gen der Inf Dr. Franz Beyer)

XVIII SS Corps
(OGF Georg Keppler)

16 Volks Gren Div (Obst Otto Kestner)

189 Infantry Division (Gen-Maj Eduard Zorn)

47 Volks Gren Div (Gen-Lt Max Bork)

246 Volks Gren Div (Gen-Maj Dr Walter Kühn)

559 Volks Gren Div (Gen-Lt Kurt Freiherr von Mühlen)

716 Infantry Division (Gen-Maj Wolf Ewert)

352 Volks Gren Div (Gen-Maj der Reserve Rudolf von Oppen)

89 Infantry Division (Gen-Maj Richard Bazing)

106 Infantry Division (Obst Rintenberg)

719 Infantry Division (Gen-Maj Heinrich Gäde)

XII Corps
(Gen der Art Herbert Osterkamp)

XIII Corps
(Gen der Art Walther Lucht)

347 Infantry Division (Gen-Lt Wolf Trierenberg)

Div No. 413 (Gen-Maj Hellmuth Hiepe)

11 Pz Div

pocket contained the remnants of German Army Group B together with elements of Army Group A's Parachute units. It fell on 18 April, yielding 325,000 prisoners. The last few German units surrendered on 21 April. Model, the 'Führer's Fireman', committed suicide.

On 13 April, Vienna fell to the Red Army and the Allies liberated Belsen and Buchenwald concentration camps. Nuremberg, the spiritual home of the Nazis, fell to the US Seventh Army on 20 April, while Dachau was liberated by the US Army on the 25th.

Crossing the Elbe

On the evening of 11 April, the US Ninth Army reached the river Elbe – designated the previous year as the demarcation line between the Soviet and Western occupation zones in Germany. At Magdeburg, the 2nd

LATE WAR GERMAN ARMIES: DEPLOYMENT				
Army	Jan 1945 Army Group	Jan 1945 Location	May 1945 Army Group	May 1945 Location
First Army	G	Rhine	G	Danube
Second Army	Centre	Vistula	Weichsel	Prussia
Fourth Army	Centre	E.Prussia	Reserve	Königsberg
Sixth Army	South	Hungary	Ostmark	Austria
Eighth Army	South	Hungary	Ostmark	Moravia
Ninth Army	A	Vistula	Weichsel	S of Berlin
Tenth Army	C	Northern Apennines	C	Po Valley and Alps
Eleventh Army	Weichsel	Vistula River	OB West	Western Germany
Twelfth Army	Not operational		Weichsel	Elbe and Berlin
Fourteenth Army	C	Bologna	C	Po Valley and Alps
Fifteenth Army	B	Ruhr	B	Ruhr
Sixteenth Army	North	Courland	Courland	Courland
Seventeenth Army	A	Upper Silesia	Centre	Central Silesia
Eighteenth Army	North	Courland	Courland	Courland
Nineteenth Army	OB Oberrhein	Colmar	G	Stuttgart
Twentieth Mtn Army		Norway		Norway
Twenty-First Army	Not operational		Weichsel	
Twenty-Fourth Army		Swiss border		Swiss border
Twenty-Fifth Army	H	Netherlands	OB Nordwest	Netherlands
First Pz Army	A	Poland	Centre	Slovakia
Second Pz Army	South	Yugoslavia	Southeast	Austria
Third Pz Army	Centre	Memel	Weichsel	Pomerania
Fourth Pz Army	A	Vistula	Centre	Oder
Fifth Pz Army	B	Ardennes	B	Ruhr
Sixth Pz Army	B	Ardennes	Ostmark	Austria
Ligurian Army	C	North Italy	Not operational	
East Prussian Army	Not operational			East Prussia

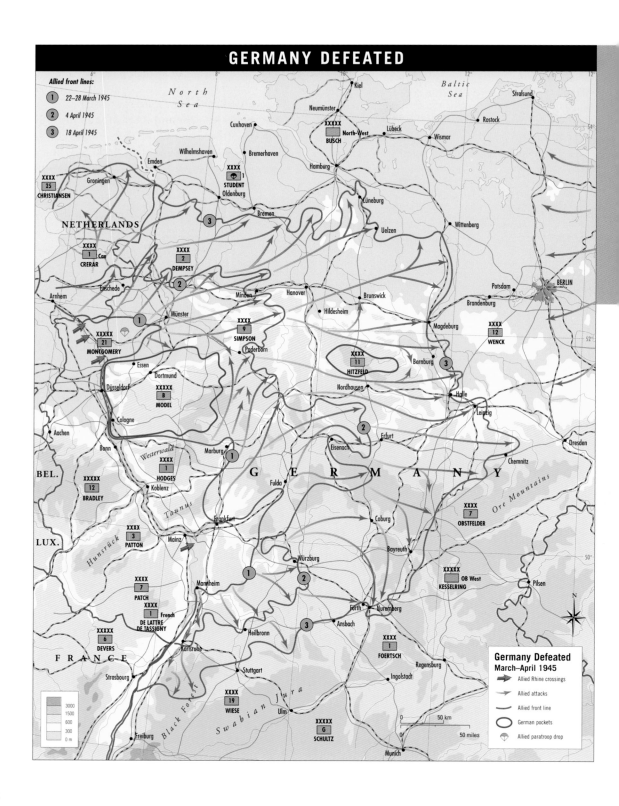

GERMANY DEFEATED

Allied front lines:

1. 22–28 March 1945
2. 4 April 1945
3. 18 April 1945

Germany Defeated
March–April 1945

→ Allied Rhine crossings

→ Allied attacks

— Allied front line

⬭ German pockets

⏚ Allied paratroop drop

March–April 1945

Launching out of the huge bridgehead stretching up the east bank Rhine from Bonn, Allied troops drove deep into Germany. Elements of the US Ninth Army crossed the Weser on 4 April. By 11 April, they were approaching the Elbe. On 24 April, the US First Army reached its stop line on the Mulde, and the next day made to first link up with Soviet forces at Torgau. Germany had been divided in two. Soon afterwards, on 3 May, troops from the Second British Army of Montgomery's Twenty-First Army Group met the spearheads of Rokossovsky's Second Byelorussian Front at Wismar on the Baltic. The third act in the dismemberment of the Third Reich came with the Vienna Offensive, which ended on 13 April 1945 with the Soviet capture of the city. The US Seventh Army occupied the Tyrol early in May, linking up with the US Fifth Army, which had advanced from Northern Italy.

Armoured Division seized a bridgehead across the river. The next day, the 83rd Division established another at Barby. Its soldiers thought they were going to Berlin. They were only 80km (50 miles) away on 14 April.

Orders quickly came down the line that they were not to press for the German capital, though had they moved then, Berlin would have fallen to the Americans and not the Soviets. Eisenhower was, however, bound by the inter-Allied Agreement reinforced at Yalta. American forces in the central sector would stay where they were, while the British and Americans continued to clear Northern Germany and the southernmost US units and French armies overran Bavaria.

The Germans could not hit back. Although Speer had dispersed arms manufacture, the Allied pounding of the marshalling yards and the destruction of *Reichsbahn* rolling stock created difficulties in deploying military hardware from the factories to the frontline.

In the west, a siege mentality set in. German mobility was undermined. Her armour could not be moved because of Allied fighters and diminishing stocks of fuel. The *Luftwaffe* was now irrelevant. American and British fighter bombers roamed the skies, hovering over German airfields, preventing the deployment of aircraft.

But at this time of emergency, Hitler retreated from the public view. From 16 January 1945, he vowed never to leave Berlin. He incarcerated himself in the spartan underworld of a bunker, beneath the Chancellery in the heart of Berlin. Here, he moved the pawns of his diminishing divisions around the ever-retreating front lines.

Eastern Front: 1945

Hitler's grip on reality was slipping, but his belief in his command genius was not. He gave a series of orders that now served to shorten the life of the *Reich*. His favoured method of defence, in east and west, was to create a series of *Festungs*, or fortresses.

The fate of these towns is best illustrated by the example of Breslau. In September of 1944, Hitler declared it to be a fortress, which was to be part of the so-called Eastern Wall on the river Oder. Initial work on fortifications for the city started as early as June 1944, but it was not until September that serious work began. The plan was to defend the city by creating two defensive rings and stockpiling supplies against a long-term siege. Fortifications were built around the city in addition to two major walls. The defences ran as far as 20km (12 miles) from the centre of the city. The work was done by forced labourers, volunteers, women, children and old men.

The 80,000-strong garrison under *Gauleiter* Karl Hanke and City Commandant General Krause (later fired by Hanke because he wanted to evacuate the civilian population) was composed of a variety of units. They included the newly formed 609th Infantry Division, elements of 269th Infantry Division, school and reserve units, improvised SS, 38 *Volkssturm* battalions (each 400-men strong), *Hitlerjugend*, police, *Luftwaffe* ground units and remnants of destroyed combat formations.

The garrison was supplied by air with supplies by the German Army and Red Cross and was even reinforced with two specialist parachute battalions. Soviet attacks began on 8 February and encountered heavy resistance from LVII Panzer Korps as well as counterattacks from 19th and 20th Panzer Divisions.

The high point of the battle came on 13 February when 19th Panzer Division desperately defended an autobahn, the only link between the encircled city and the remainder of the German forces. At the same time, the 17th and 269th Infantry Divisions were ordered to breakout in order to join other formations in the area.

In late March, the fate of Breslau was sealed as the last strong German formations south-east of Opeln were destroyed. Fighting in the city continued as Soviets pushed German defenders deeper into the city, who in turn destroyed every house and block behind them to slow the Red Army's advance.

On 6 May 1945, the City Commandant signed an act of conditional surrender, but none of the conditions were kept by the Soviets. Some 6000 German soldiers and 170,000 civilians were killed, while 45,000 were taken prisoner.

Battles in Hungary

Meanwhile, the siege of Budapest continued. The last German attempt to relieve the city failed on 1 January 1945. Soviet troops fought their way into the eastern half of the city house-by-house, grinding their way to the Danube at incredible cost.

The defenders were split into several pockets, which finally surrendered on 18 January. The same horrific process then began on the opposite bank as Buda was conquered with the same combination of flame-throwers, explosive charges and point-blank fire from self-propelled guns. More than 16,000 German and Hungarian troops tried to break out on 16 February, once the end was near. They were wiped out in a series of running battles and only a handful of individuals escaped to German lines.

Spring Awakening

Hitler's last military offensive – Spring Awakening – began on 6 March at Lake Balaton, Hungary. A total of 31 divisions, including 11 panzer and panzer-grenadier divisions took part, although all were substantially below authorized strength. The strike force included some 800 tanks, most in the Sixth SS Panzer Army, commanded by SS *Oberstgruppenführer* 'Sepp' Dietrich. Dietrich soon realized the assault was futile. An early thaw left the Hungarian plain waterlogged. The operating conditions were impossible for his super-heavy King Tiger tanks.

The last strength of the *Reich's* battered armies had been squandered. It defies belief that Hitler could have ordered an attack in Hungary, rather than defend his own people who were in such desperate straits further to the north.

Fleeing from the Red Army

Five million German civilians fled to escape the Red Army. Two million were evacuated by sea from German-held ports along the Baltic, noted for the worst maritime disaster in history – the sinking of the 25,000-ton liner *Wilhelm Gustloff* by a Soviet submarine. She had over 8000 people aboard, of whom only 650 survived.

Some 1.39 million German civilians remained unaccounted for. If some people reached safety but never advertised it, many more died at the hands of the Red Army. Most Soviet officers condoned the killings; some even exhorted their men to do their worst as a repayment for the Nazi crimes inflicted over the previous four years in Russia.

January–February 1945

Since Hitler had deployed the cream of the German armed forces in the Ardennes, the *Wehrmacht* had little to counter the new Soviet offensive launched on 12 January 1945. Guderian had proposed to evacuate the divisions of Army Group North stuck in the Courland to the *Reich* via the Baltic Sea, in order to get the necessary manpower for the defence, but Hitler forbade it. In addition, Hitler commanded that several crack SS divisions be moved from the Ardennes front to Hungary, where they would be used in operation *Frühlingserwachen* (Spring Awakening) to relieve Budapest and secure the Hungarian oilfields.

Attacking from the Vistula, the Red Army drove onto German soil for the first time. Silesia fell quickly, and by the end of January, Zhukhov's First Byelorussian Front was on the Oder River. There, Stalin called a halt, to allow time to prepare for the final assault on Berlin.

ADVANCE TO THE ODER

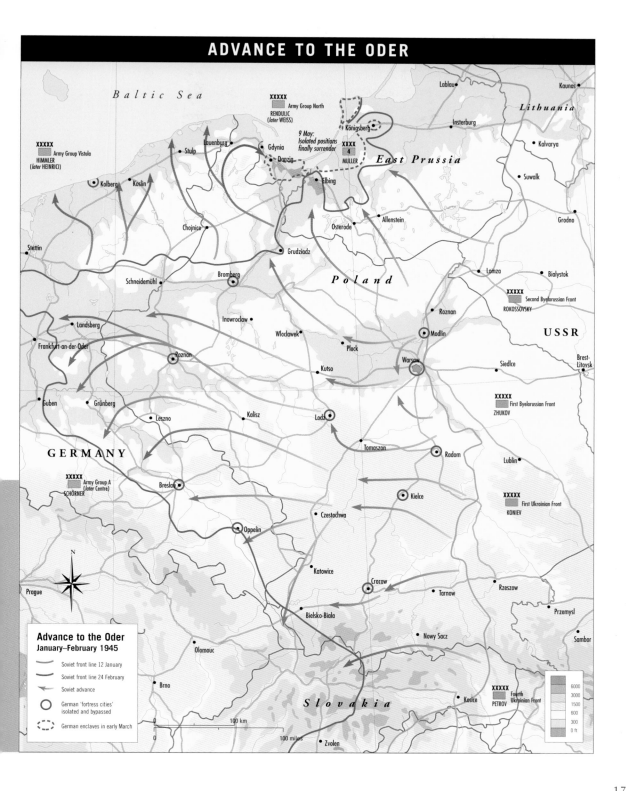

Advance to the Oder
January–February 1945

— Soviet front line 12 January

— Soviet front line 24 February

← Soviet advance

○ German 'fortress cities'
isolated and bypassed

⊙ German enclaves in early March

0   100 km

0   100 miles

Map labels:

Baltic Sea

Lithuania

XXXXX Army Group North
RENDULIC
(later WEISS)

XXXXX Army Group Vistula
HIMMLER
(later HEINRICI)

9 May:
Isolated positions
finally surrender

XXXX 4 MÜLLER

East Prussia

Lablau

Insterburg

Kaunas

Kalvarya

Suwalk

Grodno

Königsberg

Lauenburg

Gdynia

Danzig

Elbing

Stulp

Kolberg

Koslin

Stettin

Chojnice

Osterode

Allenstein

Grudziadz

Schneidemühl

Bromberg

Poland

Lomza

Bialystok

Inowroclaw

Roznan

USSR

Second Byelorussian Front
ROKOSSOVSKY **XXXXX**

Landsberg

Wloclawek

Plock

Modlin

Siedlce

Brest-Litovsk

Frankfurt-an-der-Oder

Roznan

Kutso

Warsaw

Guben

Grünberg

Leszno

Kalisz

Lodz

First Byelorussian Front
ZHUKOV **XXXXX**

Lublin

GERMANY

Tomaszon

Radom

XXXXX Army Group A
SCHÖRNER
(later Centre)

Breslau

Kielce

First Ukrainian Front
KONIEV **XXXXX**

Oppelin

Czestochwa

Katowice

Cracow

Tarnow

Rzeszow

Bielsko-Biala

Przemysl

Nowy Sacz

Sambor

Olomouc

Prague

Brno

Slovakia

Kosice

PETROV **XXXXX** Foerth
Ukrainian Front

Zvolen

6000
3000
1500
600
300
0 ft

ARMY GROUP CENTRE (MARCH 1945)

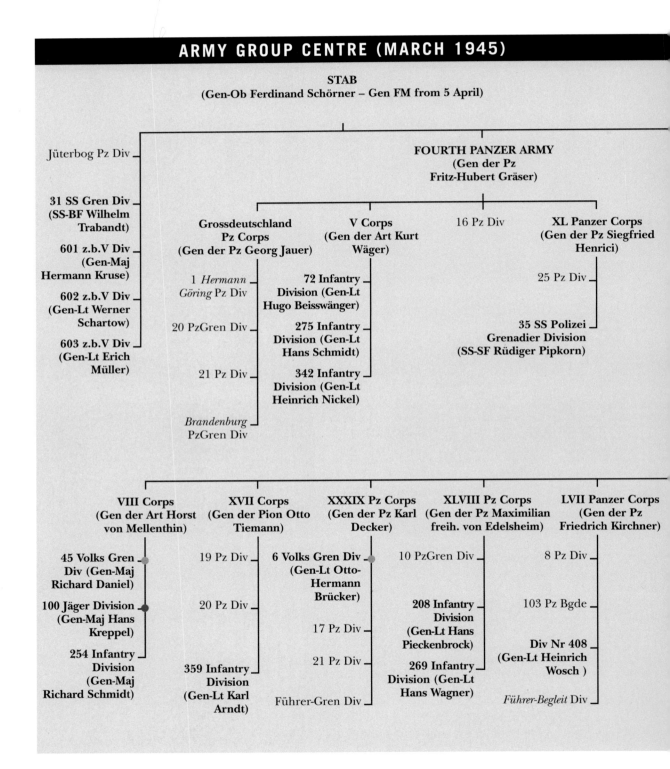

STAB
(Gen-Ob Ferdinand Schörner – Gen FM from 5 April)

Jüterbog Pz Div

31 SS Gren Div
(SS-BF Wilhelm Trabandt)

601 z.b.V Div
(Gen-Maj Hermann Kruse)

602 z.b.V Div
(Gen-Lt Werner Schartow)

603 z.b.V Div
(Gen-Lt Erich Müller)

FOURTH PANZER ARMY
(Gen der Pz Fritz-Hubert Gräser)

Grossdeutschland Pz Corps
(Gen der Pz Georg Jauer)

1 *Hermann Göring* Pz Div

20 PzGren Div

21 Pz Div

Brandenburg PzGren Div

V Corps
(Gen der Art Kurt Wäger)

72 Infantry Division (Gen-Lt Hugo Beisswänger)

275 Infantry Division (Gen-Lt Hans Schmidt)

342 Infantry Division (Gen-Lt Heinrich Nickel)

16 Pz Div

XL Panzer Corps
(Gen der Pz Siegfried Henrici)

25 Pz Div

35 SS Polizei Grenadier Division
(SS-SF Rüdiger Pipkorn)

VIII Corps
(Gen der Art Horst von Mellenthin)

45 Volks Gren Div (Gen-Maj Richard Daniel)

100 Jäger Division (Gen-Maj Hans Kreppel)

254 Infantry Division (Gen-Maj Richard Schmidt)

XVII Corps
(Gen der Pion Otto Tiemann)

19 Pz Div

20 Pz Div

359 Infantry Division (Gen-Lt Karl Arndt)

XXXIX Pz Corps
(Gen der Pz Karl Decker)

6 Volks Gren Div (Gen-Lt Otto-Hermann Brücker)

17 Pz Div

21 Pz Div

Führer-Gren Div

XLVIII Pz Corps
(Gen der Pz Maximilian freih. von Edelsheim)

10 PzGren Div

208 Infantry Division (Gen-Lt Hans Pieckenbrock)

269 Infantry Division (Gen-Lt Hans Wagner)

LVII Panzer Corps
(Gen der Pz Friedrich Kirchner)

8 Pz Div

103 Pz Bgde

Div Nr 408
(Gen-Lt Heinrich Wosch)

Führer-Begleit Div

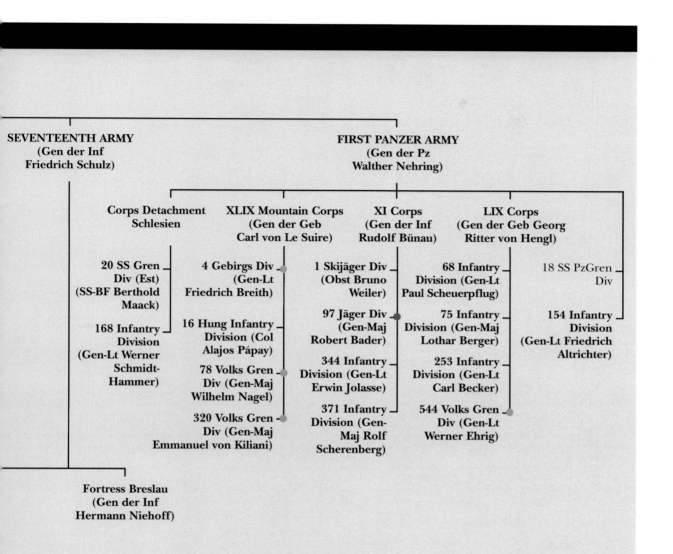

SEVENTEENTH ARMY
(Gen der Inf
Friedrich Schulz)

FIRST PANZER ARMY
(Gen der Pz
Walther Nehring)

Corps Detachment
Schlesien

XLIX Mountain Corps
(Gen der Geb
Carl von Le Suire)

XI Corps
(Gen der Inf
Rudolf Bünau)

LIX Corps
(Gen der Geb Georg
Ritter von Hengl)

20 SS Gren
Div (Est)
(SS-BF Berthold
Maack)

168 Infantry
Division
(Gen-Lt Werner
Schmidt-
Hammer)

4 Gebirgs Div
(Gen-Lt
Friedrich Breith)

16 Hung Infantry
Division (Col
Alajos Pápay)

78 Volks Gren
Div (Gen-Maj
Wilhelm Nagel)

320 Volks Gren
Div (Gen-Maj
Emmanuel von Kiliani)

1 Skijäger Div
(Obst Bruno
Weiler)

97 Jäger Div
(Gen-Maj
Robert Bader)

344 Infantry
Division (Gen-Lt
Erwin Jolasse)

371 Infantry
Division (Gen-
Maj Rolf
Scherenberg)

68 Infantry
Division (Gen-Lt
Paul Scheuerpflug)

75 Infantry
Division (Gen-Maj
Lothar Berger)

253 Infantry
Division (Gen-Lt
Carl Becker)

544 Volks Gren
Div (Gen-Lt
Werner Ehrig)

18 SS PzGren
Div

154 Infantry
Division
(Gen-Lt Friedrich
Altrichter)

Fortress Breslau
(Gen der Inf
Hermann Niehoff)

A new Army Group Centre was created on 25 January 1945
by the renaming of Army Group B (formerly Army Group
North Ukraine), which had retreated to southern Poland in the
autumn of 1944. Army Group Centre's primary role was to
oppose the Soviet forces attacking across the Vistula River
towards Berlin.

KEY
- Mountain Division
- Luftwaffe/Parachute Division
- Light Infantry Division
- Volksgrenadier Division

Army Group North

The Soviet Baltic offensives in the latter half of 1944 had driven the German Army Group North back from the siege of Leningrad to the borders of the Reich in Prussia. However, the Army Group was still a considerable fighting force.

On 10 October 1944, the Red Army reached the Baltic north of the city of Memel, cutting off the 26 divisions of Army Group North. The Germans managed to hold a line at the Neman River, defending the main part of East Prussia.

On 13 January 1945, General Ivan Chernyakhovsky's Third Byelorussian Front launched an offensive into East Prussia. In spite of stiff resistance from the German Third Panzer Army, the Soviet attack ended any hope of overland relief for Memel.

The Soviet advance meant that Army Group North was permanently cut off from its land-based connections with the rest of the Eastern Front. The German armies were trapped in a pocket on the Courland Peninsula in Latvia.

Recognizing that there was very little likelihood of the trapped troops being able to make a breakout or of Army Group Centre being able to smash a relief corridor through East Prussia, Hitler renamed the formation Army Group Courland on 25 January 1945.

Courland battles

Colonel-General Heinz Guderian, the Chief of the German General Staff, demanded that the troops in the Courland Pocket be evacuated by sea and used for the defence of the Third Reich. As had become usual, however, Hitler refused to allow any withdrawal and ordered the German forces in Courland to hold out. He believed them necessary to protect German submarine bases along the Baltic coast.

The Red Army knew that the poorly supplied forces penned in the pocket were not a serious threat. Nevertheless, offensive action by the Red Army against the Courland Pocket continued: there were six major battles between 15 October 1944, and 4 April 1945. The Army Group surrendered on 9 May 1945, when 200,000 Germans went into Soviet captivity.

FERDINAND SCHÖRNER (1892–1973)

Born in Munich, Schörner (pictured above left) joined the Bavarian Army and was decorated for gallantry in the battle of Caporetto in 1917.

• A mountain specialist, he commanded the 6th *Gebirgsjäger* Division in the Balkans (1941) and Northern Russia (1941–42). By 1943, he was in command of the XL Panzer Corps. In 1944, as *Generaloberst,* he commanded Army Group North.

• In January 1945, Schörner was given command of the newly created Army Group Centre, which conducted a fighting retreat westwards, enabling more than 1.5 million people from Eastern Germany to escape the Red Army.

• On 4 April 1945, Schörner was promoted to Field Marshal and was named as the last Commander-in-Chief of the German Army following Hitler's suicide.

ARMY GROUP NORTH (MARCH 1945)

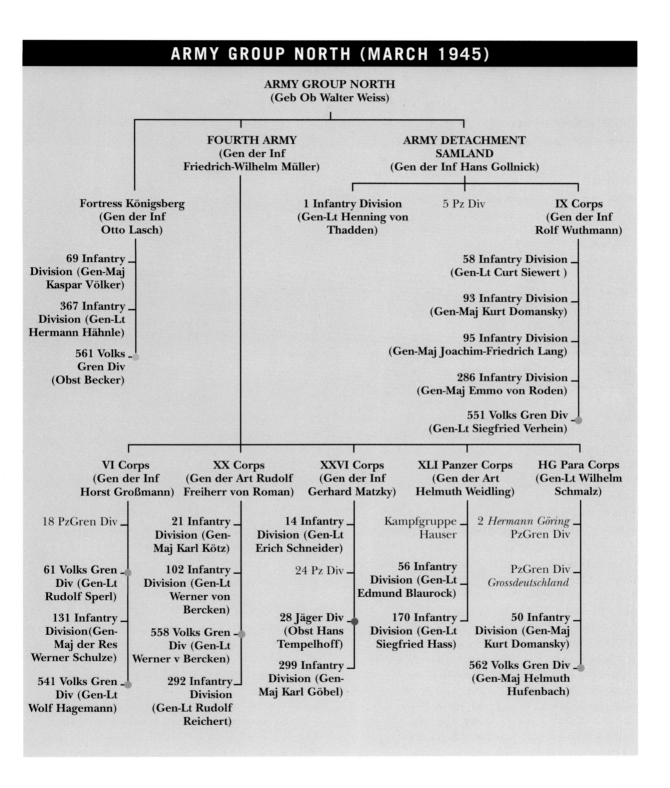

ARMY GROUP NORTH
(Geb Ob Walter Weiss)

FOURTH ARMY
(Gen der Inf
Friedrich-Wilhelm Müller)

**ARMY DETACHMENT
SAMLAND**
(Gen der Inf Hans Gollnick)

Fortress Königsberg
(Gen der Inf
Otto Lasch)

1 Infantry Division
(Gen-Lt Henning von
Thadden)

5 Pz Div

IX Corps
(Gen der Inf
Rolf Wuthmann)

69 Infantry
Division (Gen-Maj
Kaspar Völker)

367 Infantry
Division (Gen-Lt
Hermann Hähnle)

561 Volks
Gren Div
(Obst Becker)

58 Infantry Division
(Gen-Lt Curt Siewert)

93 Infantry Division
(Gen-Maj Kurt Domansky)

95 Infantry Division
(Gen-Maj Joachim-Friedrich Lang)

286 Infantry Division
(Gen-Maj Emmo von Roden)

551 Volks Gren Div
(Gen-Lt Siegfried Verhein)

VI Corps
(Gen der Inf
Horst Großmann)

XX Corps
(Gen der Art Rudolf
Freiherr von Roman)

XXVI Corps
(Gen der Inf
Gerhard Matzky)

XLI Panzer Corps
(Gen der Art
Helmuth Weidling)

HG Para Corps
(Gen-Lt Wilhelm
Schmalz)

18 PzGren Div

61 Volks Gren
Div (Gen-Lt
Rudolf Sperl)

131 Infantry
Division(Gen-
Maj der Res
Werner Schulze)

541 Volks Gren
Div (Gen-Lt
Wolf Hagemann)

21 Infantry
Division (Gen-
Maj Karl Kötz)

102 Infantry
Division (Gen-Lt
Werner von
Bercken)

558 Volks Gren
Div (Gen-Lt
Werner v Bercken)

292 Infantry
Division
(Gen-Lt Rudolf
Reichert)

14 Infantry
Division (Gen-Lt
Erich Schneider)

24 Pz Div

28 Jäger Div
(Obst Hans
Tempelhoff)

299 Infantry
Division (Gen-
Maj Karl Göbel)

Kampfgruppe
Hauser

56 Infantry
Division (Gen-Lt
Edmund Blaurock)

170 Infantry
Division (Gen-Lt
Siegfried Hass)

2 *Hermann Göring*
PzGren Div

PzGren Div
Grossdeutschland

50 Infantry
Division (Gen-Maj
Kurt Domansky)

562 Volks Gren Div
(Gen-Maj Helmuth
Hufenbach)

Army Group *Weichsel*

The capture of Berlin represented psychological completion. Had Eisenhower not ceded the German capital to the Soviets, and with it most of Eastern Germany, he might have provoked a Third World War.

The Red Army deserved the prize of Berlin. They needed to redeem the countless atrocities committed on their own people by the invaders. However, among the western armies there were many hot-blooded Generals who disagreed. They thought that whilst they were in Europe to get rid of one dictator, they might as well take the opportunity to rid the world of the Communist dictator Stalin as well.

Race for Berlin

Alarmed at the progress of the Anglo-American forces, Stalin ordered his top commanders to race each other to Berlin – the 'lair of the Fascist Beast'. He deliberately refused to agree unit boundaries between Konev and Zhukov. The Soviets made intensive preparations for the final attack. They still believed that the Germans had the ability to counterattack in strength and wanted to leave nothing to chance. The two rival commanders had between them 1,640,000 men, with 41,600 guns and mortars, 6300 tanks and the support of three air armies totalling 8400 aircraft.

Facing them were seven panzer divisions and 65 infantry divisions in some sort of order. There were also 100 independent battalions, formed for the most part from remnants of obliterated divisions. The German force was given the grandiloquent name of Army Group *Weichsel* (Vistula) and was entrusted to the command of General Heinrici.

Oder offensive

At dawn on 16 April, a tremendous artillery and air bombardment opened all along the Oder and Neisse rivers. Out of the Soviet bridgeheads stormed the first waves of shock troops. There was no finesse in these massed attacks. The Soviet artillery was arranged wheel to wheel in a row, and thundered away for hours in a massive preliminary barrage.

When the shelling halted, the tanks moved forward. The T34s lumbered from their hides. They carried with them the descent infantry squads riding on their hulls.

Storm over Berlin

Konev's troops stormed the river Neisse under the cover of 2000 Soviet aircraft; 60-ton bridges were in position that afternoon and his tanks were ready to exploit the territory all the way to the Spree. Zhukov's attack faltered, the intensity of his artillery barrage notwithstanding. Zhukov allowed impatience to overcome his military judgement, and ordered both his tank armies to attack without waiting for the infantry to break into the defences.

Zhukov could override both his battle plan and his infantry commanders, but even the indomitable Marshal could not command the Germans to give in. Even though many of the defenders were *Volkssturm* units composed of boys and old men, their anti-tank guns commenced a frightful slaughter of Soviet armour as the vehicles struggled across the swampy plain below. When the tanks fought their way on to the German position, they found themselves among minefields and were attacked by infantry teams with *Panzerfausts*.

Berlin in sight

Zhukov's men stormed the Seelow heights – the last major barrier before Berlin – after 800 aircraft bombed the defences and the gunners unleashed another formidable concentration of fire. However, Konev's tanks had not only reached the Spree River – his T-34s drove straight into the river where an old map marked a ford. Under fire all the way, they roared across and quickly established a bridgehead on the opposite bank. Berlin lay waiting. Konev's tanks raced north, where Rybalko's Third Guards Tank Army joined Katukov's First Guards Tank Army, part of Zhukov's Front.

By 19 April, Zhukov had advanced 32km (20 miles) on a 64-km (40-mile) wide front. As they moved irresistibly forward, they annihilated the bulk of the German Ninth Army, among the last complete formations of *General der Infanterie* Theodor Busse's Army Group *Weichsel* (Vistula), which lay immobilized in their path by a lack of fuel.

Hitler still had a chance to escape from Berlin by air or road, but on April 23 he declared that he would stay in Berlin to the end. He also confided in his staff that he would commit suicide rather than fall into Soviet hands.

26 April–2 May 1945

Although Berlin was doomed, it was not going to be a easy victory for the Red Army. The canals, *U-Bahn* (subway) and vast stone-built apartments and public buildings with cellars were ideal for street fighting. The outermost belt of the concentric defences was about 32km (20 miles) from the city centre; the next about 16km (10 miles), where the S-Bahn suburban railway provided a line of defence. Finally in the centre was the 'Z', or the *Zitadelle*. Within the *Zitadelle* were the main government offices and the *Führerbunker* – the two-story concrete bunker by the Reich Chancellery where Hitler was now living a troglodyte life.

BATTLE FOR BERLIN

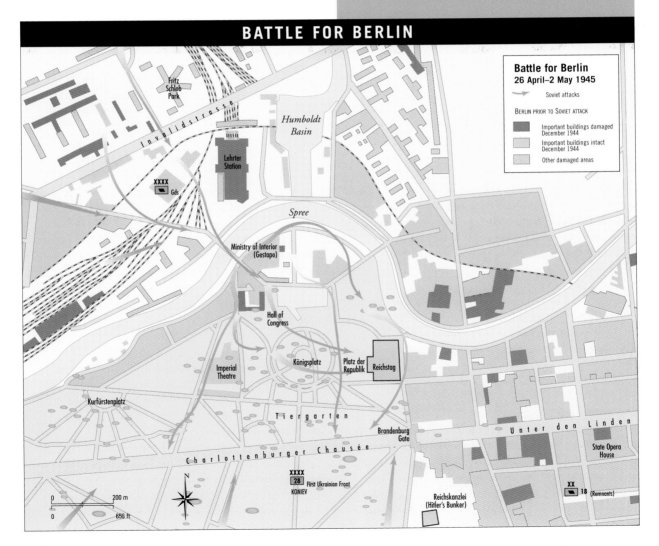

Battle for Berlin
26 April–2 May 1945

→ Soviet attacks

BERLIN PRIOR TO SOVIET ATTACK

Important buildings damaged December 1944

Important buildings intact December 1944

Other damaged areas

ARMY GROUP WEICHSEL (MARCH 1945)

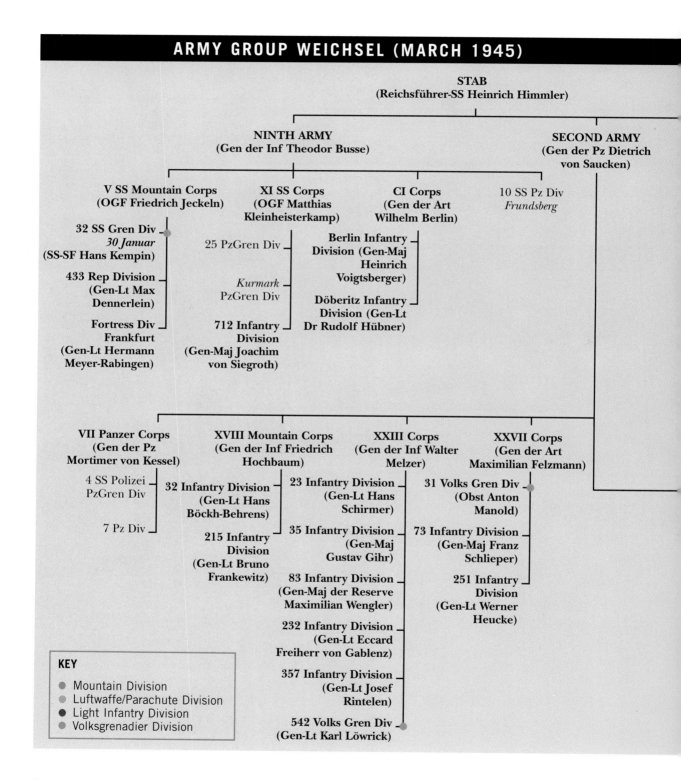

STAB
(Reichsführer-SS Heinrich Himmler)

NINTH ARMY
(Gen der Inf Theodor Busse)

SECOND ARMY
(Gen der Pz Dietrich
von Saucken)

V SS Mountain Corps
(OGF Friedrich Jeckeln)

XI SS Corps
(OGF Matthias
Kleinheisterkamp)

CI Corps
(Gen der Art
Wilhelm Berlin)

10 SS Pz Div
Frundsberg

32 SS Gren Div
30 Januar
(SS-SF Hans Kempin)

25 PzGren Div

Berlin Infantry
Division (Gen-Maj
Heinrich
Voigtsberger)

433 Rep Division
**(Gen-Lt Max
Dennerlein)**

Kurmark
PzGren Div

Döberitz Infantry
Division (Gen-Lt
Dr Rudolf Hübner)

**Fortress Div
Frankfurt
(Gen-Lt Hermann
Meyer-Rabingen)**

712 Infantry
Division
(Gen-Maj Joachim
von Siegroth)

VII Panzer Corps
(Gen der Pz
Mortimer von Kessel)

XVIII Mountain Corps
(Gen der Inf Friedrich
Hochbaum)

XXIII Corps
(Gen der Inf Walter
Melzer)

XXVII Corps
(Gen der Art
Maximilian Felzmann)

4 SS Polizei
PzGren Div

32 Infantry Division
(Gen-Lt Hans
Böckh-Behrens)

23 Infantry Division
(Gen-Lt Hans
Schirmer)

31 Volks Gren Div
(Obst Anton
Manold)

7 Pz Div

215 Infantry
Division
(Gen-Lt Bruno
Frankewitz)

35 Infantry Division
(Gen-Maj
Gustav Gihr)

73 Infantry Division
(Gen-Maj Franz
Schlieper)

83 Infantry Division
(Gen-Maj der Reserve
Maximilian Wengler)

251 Infantry
Division
(Gen-Lt Werner
Heucke)

232 Infantry Division
(Gen-Lt Eccard
Freiherr von Gablenz)

357 Infantry Division
(Gen-Lt Josef
Rintelen)

542 Volks Gren Div
(Gen-Lt Karl Löwrick)

KEY
- Mountain Division
- Luftwaffe/Parachute Division
- Light Infantry Division
- Volksgrenadier Division

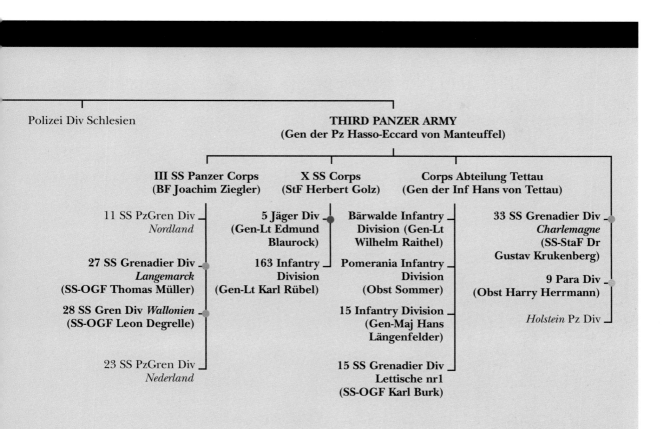

Polizei Div Schlesien

THIRD PANZER ARMY
(Gen der Pz Hasso-Eccard von Manteuffel)

III SS Panzer Corps
(BF Joachim Ziegler)

X SS Corps
(StF Herbert Golz)

Corps Abteilung Tettau
(Gen der Inf Hans von Tettau)

11 SS PzGren Div
Nordland

5 Jäger Div
(Gen-Lt Edmund
Blaurock)

Bärwalde Infantry
Division (Gen-Lt
Wilhelm Raithel)

33 SS Grenadier Div
Charlemagne
(SS-StaF Dr
Gustav Krukenberg)

27 SS Grenadier Div
Langemarck
(SS-OGF Thomas Müller)

163 Infantry
Division
(Gen-Lt Karl Rübel)

Pomerania Infantry
Division
(Obst Sommer)

9 Para Div
(Obst Harry Herrmann)

28 SS Gren Div *Wallonien*
(SS-OGF Leon Degrelle)

15 Infantry Division
(Gen-Maj Hans
Längenfelder)

Holstein Pz Div

23 SS PzGren Div
Nederland

15 SS Grenadier Div
Lettische nr1
(SS-OGF Karl Burk)

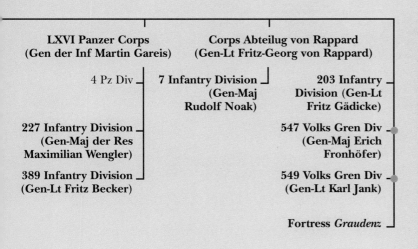

LXVI Panzer Corps
(Gen der Inf Martin Gareis)

Corps Abteilug von Rappard
(Gen-Lt Fritz-Georg von Rappard)

4 Pz Div

7 Infantry Division
(Gen-Maj
Rudolf Noak)

203 Infantry
Division (Gen-Lt
Fritz Gädicke)

227 Infantry Division
(Gen-Maj der Res
Maximilian Wengler)

547 Volks Gren Div
(Gen-Maj Erich
Fronhöfer)

389 Infantry Division
(Gen-Lt Fritz Becker)

549 Volks Gren Div
(Gen-Lt Karl Jank)

Fortress *Graudenz*

Heeresgruppe Weichsel (Army Group Vistula) was formed in 1945, mainly from elements of Army Group Centre. It was tasked with protecting Berlin from the advancing Soviet armies pushing towards the Vistula River. Heinrich Himmler had always had ambitions to command in the field, and persuaded Hitler to make him the first commander of Army Group Vistula on 24th January 1945. General Gotthard Heinrici replaced Himmler as commander of Army Group Vistula on 20 March. Under the command of Heinrici, the army group fought through the Battle of Berlin, with some of its elements not surrendering until the end of the war in Europe on 8 May 1945. Army Group Vistula's strength was about 500,000 troops, but at this stage in the war few units were fully equipped or trained.

Last battles

On 20 April 1945, the *Führer* celebrated his 56th birthday. The last pictures showing Hitler alive were taken at the *Führerbunker* and show him congratulating a line of youthful *Hitlerjugend* 'soldiers', awarding each with an Iron Cross.

A day later, the Soviet Third Guards Tank Army stormed the *Wehrmacht's* headquarters at Zossen, 24km (15 miles) south of Berlin.

On 21 April, Zhukov's tanks entered the northern suburbs, and the units behind them regrouped for siege warfare. Assault groups were formed from a company of infantry, supported by half a dozen anti-tank guns, a troop of tank or assault guns, a couple of engineer platoons and a flame-thrower platoon. Overhead, the artillery and rocket launchers fired salvoes to prepare the way for the next stage – house-to-house fighting.

Berlin surrounded

On 25 April, the Fronts of Zhukov and Konev linked up east of Ketzin, near Potsdam and west of Berlin; the city was now surrounded. Trapped inside it was the garrison of 200,000 and a pocket with about the same number from the Ninth Army and Fourth *Panzerarmee* to the south and east of the city. Berlin, already badly damaged by Allied air raids, would be fought for street by street, from the outer suburbs to the Reichstag in the centre.

Still Hitler issued orders. He urged on a relief attack by Twelfth Army under General Walter Wenck on the Elbe Front. The Army consisted of 12 divisions formed from veterans, disbanded units and new conscripts. The attack began on 26 April and reached to within 30km (19 miles) of Berlin, but was stalled after two days of hard fighting. For the Ninth Army, the attack offered the only escape route from capture by the Soviets, and it continued to fight westwards until April 29.

Final assault

On 26 April, some 464,000 Soviet troops, supported by 12,700 guns, 21,000 rocket launchers and 1500 tanks, surrounded the inner city of Berlin. The Soviets massed artillery at a density of 650 guns per kilometre, virtually wheel to wheel.

By the 29 April, the fighting was less than a 0.4km (0.25 mile) from the *Reich* Chancellery, which had also been smashed by heavy Soviet shells.

Deep beneath the surface, Hitler still exercised his authority. He appointed Grand Admiral Karl Dönitz his successor as *Führer*, and dismissed Albert Speer for refusing his orders to turn Germany into a wasteland.

Hitler committed suicide at 3 p.m. on 30 April. But the German garrison fought on. Above him, the fight for the *Reichstag* was reaching its climax.

Berlin surrenders

The battle for the *Reichstag* raged late into the evening, when two Red Army men of the 1st Battalion of the 756th Regiment hoisted the Soviet flag over the *Reichstag's* dome. At 3 p.m. on May 2, General Karl Weidling, the Commandant of the Berlin garrison, instructed all units to surrender and about 136,000 men marched into captivity. They left behind the bodies of 125,000 Berliners who had died in the siege – many, desparate, by suicide.

The cost to the Red Army had also been terrible. In three weeks, Zhukov, Konev and Rokossovsky's fronts had lost 304,887 men killed, wounded and missing – 10 per cent of their total strength and the heaviest casualty list suffered by the Red Army in any battle of the war.

GERMAN CASUALTIES: 1944–45		
	1944	**1945**
Germany	–	1,230,045
East	1,232,946	–
West	244,891	–
Other	278,419	57,495

ARMY GROUP COURLAND (MARCH 1945)

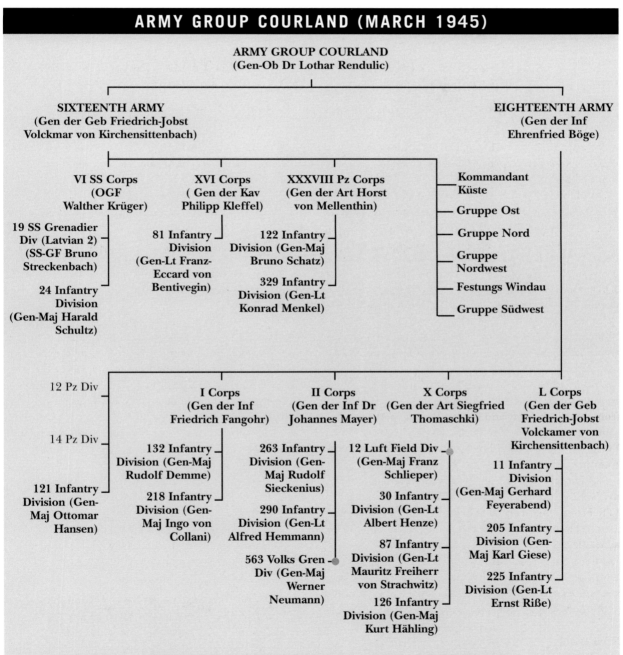

ARMY GROUP COURLAND
(Gen-Ob Dr Lothar Rendulic)

SIXTEENTH ARMY
(Gen der Geb Friedrich-Jobst
Volckmar von Kirchensittenbach)

EIGHTEENTH ARMY
(Gen der Inf
Ehrenfried Böge)

VI SS Corps
(OGF
Walther Krüger)

XVI Corps
(Gen der Kav
Philipp Kleffel)

XXXVIII Pz Corps
(Gen der Art Horst
von Mellenthin)

Kommandant
Küste

19 SS Grenadier
Div (Latvian 2)
(SS-GF Bruno
Streckenbach)

81 Infantry
Division
(Gen-Lt Franz-
Eccard von
Bentivegin)

122 Infantry
Division (Gen-Maj
Bruno Schatz)

Gruppe Ost

Gruppe Nord

24 Infantry
Division
(Gen-Maj Harald
Schultz)

329 Infantry
Division (Gen-Lt
Konrad Menkel)

Gruppe
Nordwest

Festungs Windau

Gruppe Südwest

12 Pz Div

I Corps
(Gen der Inf
Friedrich Fangohr)

II Corps
(Gen der Inf Dr
Johannes Mayer)

X Corps
(Gen der Art Siegfried
Thomaschki)

L Corps
(Gen der Geb
Friedrich-Jobst
Volckamer von
Kirchensittenbach)

14 Pz Div

132 Infantry
Division (Gen-Maj
Rudolf Demme)

263 Infantry
Division (Gen-
Maj Rudolf
Sieckenius)

12 Luft Field Div
(Gen-Maj Franz
Schlieper)

11 Infantry
Division
(Gen-Maj Gerhard
Feyerabend)

121 Infantry
Division (Gen-
Maj Ottomar
Hansen)

218 Infantry
Division (Gen-
Maj Ingo von
Collani)

290 Infantry
Division (Gen-Lt
Alfred Hemmann)

30 Infantry
Division (Gen-Lt
Albert Henze)

205 Infantry
Division (Gen-
Maj Karl Giese)

563 Volks Gren
Div (Gen-Maj
Werner
Neumann)

87 Infantry
Division (Gen-Lt
Mauritz Freiherr
von Strachwitz)

225 Infantry
Division (Gen-Lt
Ernst Riße)

126 Infantry
Division (Gen-Maj
Kurt Hähling)

Army Group Courland was created when the Red Army reached the Baltic Sea near the Neman River on 10 October 1944. As a result, what was then known as Army Group North was cut off in Latvia from the rest of the German Army, and was to stay cut off for the remainder of the war. Approximately 200,000 German troops across 26 divisions were trapped in what was to become known as the Courland Pocket. Army Group North was renamed Army Group Courland on 25 January 1945.

List of Abbreviations

RANKS

Gen FM	General Field Marshal
Gen-Ob	Colonel-General
Gen der Pz	General of Panzers
Gen der Inf	General of Infantry
Gen der Art	General of Artillery
Gen der Geb	General of Mountain Troops
Gen der Pion	General of Engineers
Gen der Flieg	General of Luftwaffe
Gen-Lt	Lieutenant-General
Gen-Maj	Major-General
Brig-Gen	Brigadier-General
Obst	Oberst (Colonel)
SS-ObstGF	SS Oberstgrüppenführer
SS-OGF	SS Obergrüppenführer
StaF	SS Standartenführer (Lt Colonel)
ObF	SS Oberführer (Colonel)

UNITS

Gebirgs Div	Mountain Division	zbV Div	Special Duties Division
Jäger Div	Light Infantry Division	Res	Reserve
Grenadier Div	Grenadier Division	Abteilung	Battalion/detachment
Luftwaffe Field Div	Luftwaffe Field Division	Vf SS	Verfügungs SS (Armed SS)
Volks Gren Div	Volksgrenadier Division	LAH	*Leibstandarte* Adolf Hitler
Skijäger Div	Ski Division	HG	Hermann Göring
A/L Div	Air Landing Division	Rgt	Regiment
Para Div	Parachute Division	Bgde	Brigade
Inf Div (mot)	Motorized Infantry Division	(mot)	Motorized
Sec Div	Security Division	Gruppe	Group (varying sizes)
Cav Div	Cavalry Division	Kampfgruppe	Battle group
Pz Div	Panzer Division	It	Italian
Arm Div	Armoured Division	Rom	Romanian
Lt Div	Light Division	Hung	Hungarian
PzGren Div	Panzergrenadier Division	(Kroat)	Croatian
Rep Div	Replacement Division		

Commander Index

Page numbers in *italics* refer to tables and illustrations

General Index

Index

Picture Credits

AKG Images: 180
Art-Tech/Aerospace: 16, 70, 98, 168
Cody Images: 6, 19, 28, 34, 49, 50, 62, 64, 76, 134, 151
Süddeutscher Verlag: 124
U.S. Department of Defense: 148

All maps © Amber Books
All colour artwork © Art-Tech

Map Symbol Guide

XXXXX ☐ Army Group	II ⌐⌐ Engineer	II ◫ Antitank
XXXX ☐ Army	XX ⊠ Army Division	II ⬢ Communication
XXX ⊠ Corps	XXX ◠ Airborne	III ☐ Regiment
II ◆ Artillery	▰ Armoured Division	II ☐ Company
I ☐ Platoon	III ⊠ Mechanized Infantry	⚓ Naval